"Soak It!!!"… and Other Railroad Stories

Charles H. Geletzke Jr.

Charles H. Geletzke, Jr.

Copyright © 2023

Charles H. Geletzke, Jr.

P. O. Box 172

Mount Joy, PA 17552-0172

No portion of this book may be reproduced by any process or means without the written permission of the publisher.

All rights reserved.

ISBN: 9798852326324

Front cover: GTW streamlined U-4-b Northern is seen heading westbound passenger Train 17 at Port Huron, Michigan on July 23, 1952. (John Endlar photo; GTWHS collection)

Title Page: GTW 5918 later renamed the "Voodoo Engine" was the lead unit on Train 420 and is seen at Pontiac, Michigan on September 7, 1971 following a devastating head-on wreck in which it was struck by GTW Train 421 with engines 9024 & 4436. The engineer, fireman, and head brakeman were all fatalities! It was later sadly determined that the crew on the headend of Train 421 were all asleep! (Max Houghtaling photo; Geletzke collection)

Rear cover: CN (GTW) Locomotive Engineer at East Yard in Hamtramck, Michigan on March 17, 2011
All photos are by the author unless otherwise stated.

DEDICATION

This volume, my 9th book, is dedicated to my late friend, Robert K. Nairns of Shamokin, Pennsylvania who passed away at the age of 82 on January 11, 2023. Bob was a U. S. Air Force veteran who served from 1960-1964, worked for the *Ceco Steel Mill* and was a virtual expert on coal mining and railroading in the Hard Coal Region of Pennsylvania. Bob and I talked and corresponded for over thirty-five years and he contributed a number of stories to my previous editions. Bob was active in the *Reading Railroad Technical & Historical Society* and the *Shamokin Model Railroad Club*. He will be dearly missed by his family and all who knew him.

Interestingly my wife and I moved from Michigan to Pennsylvania in January 2023. I had planned to drive up and visit Bob Nairns once we got settled. Sadly, Airman Nairns passed away only one week before our move!

Charles H. Geletzke, Jr.

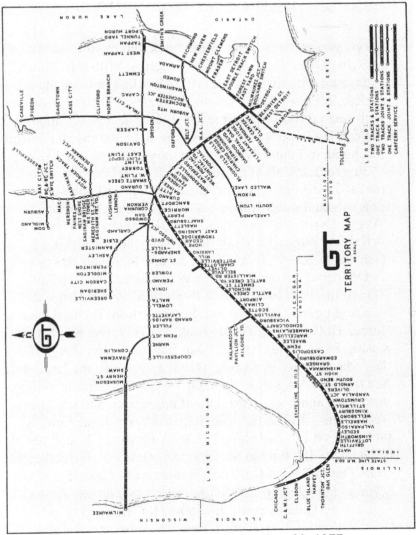

GTW Corporate Map dated October 30, 1977.

Charles H. Geletzke, Jr.

Acknowledgements

I hope you enjoy this, my ninth book and eighth volume of my *"and Other Railroad Stories"* series. With this edition I have now published over 640 individual railroad short stories...all true! If my health continues, I hope to continue with several more similar texts. Please accept my apology for the delay in publishing due to my wife and my move from Michigan to Pennsylvania in January. At this time I would like to thank all of those railroaders and railfans who provided their personal stories and photos and allowed me to include and publish their work. They are...Lawrence D. Akers; Byron Babbish, Esq.; L. E. Batanian; Lawrence R. Bolton; Richard J. Burg; Bob Cerri; the late Orville P. Convis; Bob Dell; David Dell; Joseph DeMike; George A. Dondero II; Tom Dorin; David Dykstra; the late Paul Gosselin; the *Grand Trunk Western Railroad Historical Society*; Eugene Gray; the late E. M. Gulash; Richard Haave; James H. Harlow; Mike Hnatiuk; Chris Howe; Stephen A. Kaslik, Esq.; James Krikau; Dan Lawecki; Douglas Leffler; Jeff Mast; Roger L. Meade; David J. Mrozek; the late John N. Ozanich; Art Single; Jack G. Tyson; and Charlie Whipp. And once again a special note of appreciation to my family members...Leslie E. Geletzke; Brian A. Close; Abby K. Geletzke, M.D.; Josephine F. Close; Finn A. Close; Charles H. Geletzke III; Rachel M. Geletzke; Henry C. Geletzke; the late David Bryant Geletzke; Benjamin L. Geletzke; Maj. Travis P. Geletzke USMC; Jennifer L. Geletzke; Julie C. Geletzke; and Jonathan H. Geletzke.
Your continued interest, help and support is greatly appreciated!

We'll show this book COMPLETE at 8:34 A.M. on July 22, 2023.

CHG

Contents

Book is chronological and chapters were not deemed necessary.

GTW Train 588 approaches the Royal Oak, MI depot with the
GTW 9023 (F3)-4434 (GP9)-7969 (NW2) (Dead in Tow) on
November 16, 1963.

"SOAK-IT!!!"

Written by: C. H. Geletzke, Jr., as told by: GTW Switchman
and Brakeman, George A. Dondero II

I'll never forget my good friend and fellow Grand
Trunk Western Railroad employee, George Dondero telling
about one of his first trips as a Road Brakeman on Train
587/588 one Saturday in the Summer of 1968.

Train 587/588 was a local on the Holly Subdivision
working out of Milwaukee Jct. our terminal in Detroit,
Michigan. Now this job, normally referred to as "The Royal
Oak Switch Run" usually operated from Milwaukee Jct.
westward to Birmingham, Michigan where the train "turned"
and returned to the Motor City. But Saturday's were
frequently a little different and the train would often run
through, 26 miles to the automotive city of Pontiac. On those
days the train performed minimal local switching and

"Soak It!!!"… and Other Railroad Stories

basically served as a short-distance through freight between the two automotive hubs.

George caught the job off the Brakemen's Spare Board and made a relatively quick trip to Pontiac where they yarded their train, turned the power, and picked-up their eastbound train, which included about forty loads of gravel marshaled on the headend, for Detroit.

Now because the line is virtually downhill most of the way from Pontiac all the way down to the Detroit River, their train of about 70 cars was rolling pretty good. Like me, George was raised in Royal Oak and was quite familiar with the locale. Heading east, the engineer was blowing the horn on the lead unit almost continuously from the time they approached Washington Avenue, the first of ten grade crossings extending from a point just east of the Royal Oak depot for one full mile to Ten Mile Road and the location of the Pleasant Ridge commuter station.

As the Switch Run crossed Harrison Street (Milepost 12.3) the crew on the headend could see an automobile, which had just stopped ahead at Ten Mile Road (Milepost 12.0) and was straddling the Eastward Main. Instantly the Fireman yelled "SOAK IT!" and the Engineer put the train into EMERGENCY! Naturally, with forty loads of gravel mined the day previous at Oxford, Michigan on the headend, that train was not about to stop any time soon! As they neared the auto, they quickly determined that it was a *Corvette*…a shiny brand new bright yellow 1968 *Chevrolet Corvette*…and it was not moving! Upon closer instantaneous observation they noticed a man standing off to the side waving his arms violently, and no doubt pleading for them to halt! Sorry sir…it was out of their control. In only seconds they hit that car at probably 40 mph and George said that he could not believe what happened! The fiberglass body of the *Vette* was instantly pulverized and the residue looked and felt like corn flakes pelting the locomotives as they passed the point of impact.

Once the train stopped, George walked back and met the Conductor who arrived at the crossing just before him. By now the Pleasant Ridge Police Department was on site too and he was already speaking with the man who obviously turned out to be the vehicle's driver. At the site of the crash unlike the point of most train-auto accidents, the only obvious debris was a massive 8-cylinder engine block and a good size pile of toasted yellow corn flakes!

It turned out that the driver had just purchased the brand new vehicle at *Matthews Hargreaves Chevrolet*, located only three blocks to the west, on the corner of Woodward Avenue (and only three blocks from the my grandmother's home). The man had just picked the car up; but admitted to the officer that he "had never driven a stick before," and stalled it out on the tracks! Fortunately he had the good sense to vacate the vehicle and other than financially, was not injured.

I do have to say though…all of these years later, I still wonder what he told his insurance agent!?!

AT&SF crane 9976 at Amarillo, TX March 18, 1987. (J. G. Tyson photo)

My Early Days

By: retired AT&SF, NYC, PC, GTW, CN Trainman and Trainmaster, L. D. Akers

I was hired out as a Yardman at Barstow, California, on the Atchison, Topeka & Santa Fe Railway (AT&SF) in the summer of 1960. I was assigned to the Extra Board, which meant 24/7…no guarantee or unemployment. Have to mention that there were no younger employees. Everybody was either a survivor of the Great Depression or WWII, or a Korean War veteran.

One day, I approached the General Yardmaster and asked if I could take next Friday off?"

His immediate answer was, "No!"

I then requested if I could be off the following Friday…the same answer, "No!" Before I could say anything, the GYM said, "Take tomorrow off!"

I said, "But tomorrow is Tuesday!"

He then looked at me and said, "Call it Friday!"

…**Welcome to Railroading!"**

(I have to agree with Mr. Akers! Editor Geletzke)

Next…

Back then, the "old heads" were not friendly…I even worked with a Switchman, who was laid-off from 1928 until 1941…only to be called back because of WWII!!!

The youngest fireman on the Michigan Central (MC) at Jackson, Michigan hired out in 1917…in order to work during the Great Depression, he had to go over to Kalamazoo and work a yard assignment! Those were Hard Times!

Charles H. Geletzke, Jr.

A westbound GTW freight with SD40's 5927 & 5921 crosses 4th Street in Royal Oak, Michigan on August 25, 1984. (Charlie Whipp photo)

GTW's Streamlined Northern's

By: C. H. Geletzke, Jr.

When I was a young boy growing-up in Royal Oak, Michigan in the early 1950's I witnessed a great deal of Grand Trunk Western Railroad steam logging their final miles during the last ten or so years of their lives!

The other day, friend, and former GTW employee, Charlie Whipp posted the attached photo of two GTW SD40's (the 5927 & 5921) pulling a westbound train through my former hometown. I have to state that the location really brought back the memories!

I am going to guess that I was about three or four years old and my father took me "uptown" to get a haircut. If I am correct, the barbershop was located in the little structure just to the left of the train in the first photo (if not, it stood directly across Center Street, a little further to the left). Anyway, owing to my size I was sitting on the padded board placed across the armrests on the barber's chair having my "ears lowered," as my Dad used to say. When all at once we heard the whistle of a westbound train, blowing for the eight street crossings east of the depot. The whistle was one that I had never heard before and we only lived two blocks west of the tracks! I began to panic! You see, the barber had me facing the mirror…away from the tracks! I recall thinking that certainly my Dad will come to my rescue and have the barber spin the chair around. At the last second, I attempted to turn my head; but the experienced old barber held it securely in place…consequently, the only look I got of the train, was its reflection in the huge mirror. Seconds later, my Dad blurted out, "Wow! Did you see that STREAMLINED engine!?! I've never seen one like that before over here!"

I was crushed…devastated actually!

My Dad later described the locomotive as being, "green, black, and red, with gold trim." Years later I would see photos of the engines and I knew immediately that that was the locomotive I had viewed in the mirror.

One Sunday in September of 1961 I talked my Dad into taking our family up to Durand, Michigan to see the GTW steam scrap lines that several of my friends had been talking about. He relented to going right after church; and sadly I did not get to go home and get my camera! To this day, I am still sad about that! Interestingly in Durand, we were permitted to walk all around the locomotives and even climb up in their cabs. In the line was the GTW 6405 a U-4-b streamlined Northern, the only one of six still remaining on the property. I had a great time climbing up into its tongue and grooved maple lined cab interior.

Charles H. Geletzke, Jr.

Only a year or so later, local railfan and President of the *Michigan Railroad Club*, Art Weber, made a 33-1/3 recording available of GTW steam titled: *DETROIT DIVISION**. My parents gave me a copy of it for Christmas and when I heard the recording of the 6405 heading east through Royal Oak on Train 972 not only did I know for sure that that was the class of locomotive that I had seen the day of my haircut; but I recognized its unique whistle as having gone through town during many late evenings while I was supposed to be sleeping.

Thank you for the memories, Charlie Whipp!

- Let me state that an expanded version of the original *DETROIT DIVISION* is available as a cd from the Grand Trunk Western Railroad Historical Society at: http://gtwhs.org

GTW 6405 in scrapline at Durand, Michigan in 1960 or 61. (Al Feldman photo; Geletzke collection)

GTW Alco S-2 8107 and GP9 4933 at the Milwaukee Jct. enginehouse in November 1975. That's Assistant Roundhouse Foreman, Fuller Gamble and Machinist, Ed Richter on the right side of the photo.

Eyebrows

As told to: C. H. Geletzke, Jr.

In my previous book, *Unit Trains and other Railroad Stories*, I included several stories about my friend and late Grand Trunk Western (GTW) Locomotive Engineer, Cager M. Casey, interestingly; I recalled one more story about him that I somehow neglected to include in that volume.

While I do not have a photo of him, I do recall that Engineer Casey did have a very bushy pair of eyebrows. As the story goes, one day in the late 1940's or early 1950;s a GTW switchman down at City Yard, hard by the Detroit River made fun of Cager's eyebrows while standing on the rear platform of an Alco S-2 or S-4 switcher. Apparently this irritated the normally very calm and cordial, Mr. Casey and he stopped the locomotive, got out of his seat, and too went out slowly and deliberately to the rear platform. In a soft voice with his southern drawl he asked the yardman, What's so funny about my eyebrows, Buddy?" Simultaneously, he picked the man up by the front of his shirt, using only one hand, and hung the overall clad man out over the track behind the locomotive! Once again, he inquired, "Now, what's so funny about my eyebrows, Buddy!?!"

As the story goes, from that day forward, NO ONE ever messed with the now legendary GTW Locomotive Engineer, Cager M. Casey!

GTW 6314 at the GTW Elsdon roundhouse in Chicago, Illinois in 1957. (Geletzke collection)

One Day on the Railroad

By: GTW Locomotive Engineer and *Brotherhood of Locomotive Engineers*-General Chairman, Orville P. Convis

My seniority as a Locomotive Engineer and Fireman on the Grand Trunk Western (GTW) started December 10, 1940. I retired March 16, 1981.

On December 22, 1954 I was working as the Fireman on GTW passenger train Number 6 (*Inter-City Limited*), engine 6314 with Engineer, Mike Ross. We left Dearborn Station in Chicago and as we approached the interlocking plant at Blue Island, where we crossed the Indiana Harbor Belt (IHB). I was able to observe from the shadow on the shiny rail that there was something lying on the left side rail. As we came to that location there was a bright shower of sparks. I yelled to the Engineer, "Soak her!"

He put the train into Emergency immediately and shouted back to me, "What's the matter?"

Charles H. Geletzke, Jr.

About that time the engine was on the ground. We derailed to the left and ahead of us, I knew in my mind, that there was a "take out" for track motor cars plus two sidewalks and Broadway Street that the engine would be hitting. Then we would be hitting a (facing point) crossover from the Eastbound to Westbound Main Line and then going under the bridge for the Rock Island over the Grand Trunk. Our speed at derailment was recorded at 55 miles an hour by personal testimony, because that was the speed of the curve that we just came off of. We traveled roughly the length of six football fields, 12 to 15 hundred feet, before we stopped. We tore up the crossing planks and ran through the crossover and broke a lot of rails loose. When we hit the Westbound Main Line , the ground was frozen hard enough that our engine straightened out and went under the bridge, preventing us from going far enough to the left to strike the abutment of the Rock Island Bridge. As we came east of the bridge, there was a facing point switch to some yard tracks and went far enough to where the engine stopped over the first switch inside the yard with the engine leaning to the left and the wheels of the engine down into the gravel.

There were two newspaper articles regarding the derailment and the delay involved.

After we came to a stop, I went with the Grand Trunk Policeman back to the location of the derailment and we located what had been a locomotive tire. There was, as I remember, about two feet of it in about three different pieces! The Grand Trunk realized that there had been a number of other railroad's trains across the diamond, and using the piece of locomotive tire as evidence, they got a restraining order on a junk yard to keep it from being purchased and a foundry to keep it from being destroyed, until it could be gathered up as evidence.

There had been three cars, I think from the Indiana Harbor Belt Transfer from the Kapalen Junk Yard to the foundry and two of them had been unloaded; but the third one had locomotive scrap and pieces of locomotive tire that were the same circumference as what we had found.

18

"Soak It!!!"… and Other Railroad Stories

The Grand Trunk sued the *Kapalen Junk Yard* for using the car, because it had a hole in the floor…a low side gon. They sued the Indiana Harbor Belt for handling it and I think, the Chicago & Northwestern (C&NW) that provided the car that had the hole in it.

By the time this case reached the courts, Engineer Ross had passed on. I was the only witness the entire day. Each of the defendants had their own lawyer and other "experts" to get some conflicted testimony; but I was told by the Grand Trunk attorney that my testimony was presented very well. The trial continued into the second day, I learned later that the jury, I don't remember how many people…it wasn't a full normal jury, something like three to five men, if I remember right. But anyway, the Grand Trunk got the money back for the estimated cost…and once again, this was the cost of the engine in 1942! It was something like $6,000 they wanted to cover their costs.

Charles H. Geletzke, Jr.

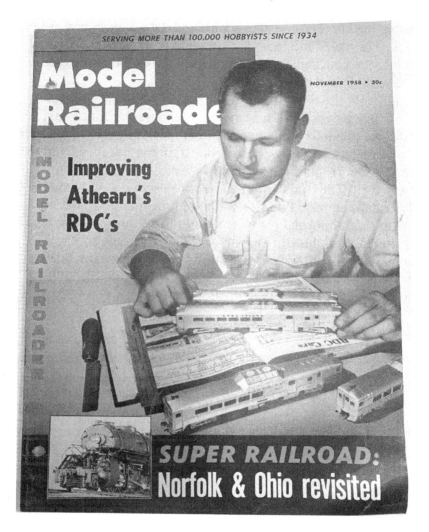

My First Issue of *MR*

By: C. H. Geletzke, Jr.

I would guess that many of you who were becoming railfans and modelers at an early age experienced something similar to this…

"Soak It!!!"… and Other Railroad Stories

As a young boy I can recall visiting *Dunn's Hobby Arcade* in Royal Oak, Michigan and *Models Hobby Shop* in Ferndale with my Dad and was always overwhelmed to see their inventory of model trains and collection of antique toy trains as well. Additionally, I also remember seeing the latest issues of the various model and railroad magazines on the shelves devoted to railroads and always asked my Dad if he would buy one for me…his answer was always the same…"You are too young for those!"

Well, I will never forget, it was a snowy November day in 1958 and one evening this 4th grader happened to be shopping with my Mom in our local corner pharmacy, *Sherman's Drug Store*, in Royal Oak. While she was finding her needed items I happened to be looking at the magazines on the magazine rack and fantastically spotted the November 1958 issue of *Model Railroader*! Let me state that this was the first time that I had ever seen a railroad magazine in that store. I perused the issue quickly from cover to cover! Shortly, my Mom appeared and announced that she was ready to go. I immediately asked if she would buy the magazine for me. Naturally, she asked the price and I immediately responded, "50-cents."

Mom replied, "You have money at home. You can buy it yourself."

That's how both of my parent's were. Like most of their peers of that era, they had come through the Great Depression and they taught us from an early age, if you want something, you'd better earn and save your money and pay for it yourself!

When we arrived home a few minutes later, I immediately checked my bank and found that I did not have near enough money to make that purchase.

Over the next several weeks, I made trips to *Sherman's* and thumbed through that same single issue several times over. Sadly, I still could not find a way to earn the money that I needed. I was worried that any day someone would purchase that one and only copy; or, on December 1st, the magazine might just be removed from the shelf as being "out of date!"

Charles H. Geletzke, Jr.

November was quickly coming to an end and on Thanksgiving our entire family gathered at my Aunt Helen's home in Detroit for a fantastic day. At some point during the festivities, Aunt Helen asked me, "do me a favor and carry out all of the 'returnable' bottles that have been accumulating in the basement closet." She said. "If you take them to the store, you may keep all of the money."

I did some quick calculating and determined that at 2-cents per bottle, I would probably earn enough money to buy the next two issues of *Model Railroader*! I immediately began carrying the bottles out to my parent's car!

The next morning I awoke early and could not wait to have my Mom or Dad drive me to our local store and redeem the bottles. As I stated, I was worried that that magazine was going to disappear!

Well, since Dad had the day off too, we finally drove to our local *National Food Store* and I turned in my stash of bottles plus a few more that Mom and Dad too donated to the cause. As I recall, I earned well over a dollar!

Later that day, I walked through the snow via the shortest and most direct route to *Sherman's*. The path took me through the playground of my former grade school, *Oakridge Elementary* where I previously attended Kindergarten through the 3rd Grade, and I followed the ditch along the service road. The ditch had a thin layer of ice on top of the water and even though I was in a hurry, I could not resist trying to walk on top of the ice and broke through most of it, which would send the cold water gushing into my boots as my feet plunged through! Us kids always called that a "SOAKER!" Finally, I crossed Rochester Road and 13 Mile Road and entered the drugstore lobby. With less than two and a half days remaining in the month, I rushed over to the newsstand, and immediately spied the magazine, which I had carefully hidden behind the other periodicals on my last visit. I picked-up the magazine, hurried to the cashier and paid for the coveted first issue of a railroad magazine that I would ever acquire.

Over the next several weeks I read through that magazine many times over…eventually I had most of it

"Soak It!!!"… and Other Railroad Stories memorized and in time practically wore the cover off. I loved that issue and still have it today. Sadly, I never acquired the December issue; but I was able to purchase all of the twelve for 1959. My parents as a Christmas present gave me a subscription to *MR*, which began in January 1960. I have maintained that subscription ever since. Sadly, I am now reaching the time of my life where I have to decide what I am going to do with all of the issues of all of the railroad periodicals and books that I have purchased since. I am truly thrilled that *Kalmbach Publishing* has chosen to scan and put all of their wonderful publications on cd's making them available to younger generations! I only wish that their competitors would do the same!

To all of you modelers and railfans out there living and deceased, thank you for taking the time to share your work with the rest of us over the decades…here it is over sixty years later and I still look forward to each and every issue!

D&TSL depot, yard office, and Dispatcher's Office at Dearoad in River Rouge, Michigan on April 11, 1925. (Geletzke collection)

Charles H. Geletzke, Jr.

TANGERINE

As told by the late D&TSL-GTW-CN Conductor, Paul Gosselin

When I was about eight years old, in the early 1960's, I would often go to work with my dad (Fern Gosselin) when he worked the Friday third trick Detroit & Toledo Shore Line Railroad (D&TSL) dispatching job at Dearoad in River Rouge, Michigan. Usually, I would take some of my toys and play in the back of the second floor Dispatcher's Office. Eventually, I would fall asleep and dad would take me home in the morning. Believe it or not, I learned a great deal about railroading during those visits.

On the big oak desk, which sat in the bay window at the front of the office, was an old fashioned microphone with a large horn shaped opening. I'll bet it was almost as old as Alexander Graham Bell!

I'll never know what possessed me to do it; but one night while my dad was out of the office, I stuck a tangerine in that horn. When my dad returned, he couldn't believe what I had done. Fortunately, he did not get mad; instead he tried to reach in the horn with his fingers and pull the fruit out. Wouldn't you know, his fingers were too big and there was no way to get a grip on it; so he inserted his pocket knife and cut the round orange object into sections. Of course, juice ran all over the inside of the microphone and over the desk too.

For the next two weeks, old Charlie Hargis, who was the Chief Dispatcher, had a fit over the smell of orange juice whenever he talked to the operators down the line!

This story originally appeared in the book, *The Detroit & Toledo Shore Line Railroad-Expressway For Industry* written by: Charles H. Geletzke, Jr. and Wilbur E. Hague published in 2011.

GTW Pontiac, MI coal dock, roundhouse and water tank on
August 16, 1962.

Why Four Decimal Points?

By: C. H. Geletzke, Jr.

I've told you before that since I was two years old all
I wanted to do was work for the railroad! I tried to hire out
when I was seventeen; but Mr. Tucker in the Grand Trunk
Western Railroad's (GTW) Personnel Department located in
Detroit's Brush Street Depot told me that I was "too young!"
He did allow me to take all of the tests and then told me to
return "when you are eighteen."

As instructed, I paid him another visit over "Easter
Break" during my senior year of high school in 1967. Mr.
Tucker recalled my previous visit and instructed me to return
for "Student Trips" as a Switchman in Detroit on June
10th…there was only one problem…the 10th was during our
week of final exams and Graduation was scheduled for the
16th! Once I was aware of the exact dates, I immediately
contacted Mr. Tucker and tried to arrange a later date. He

25

Charles H. Geletzke, Jr.

was very apologetic; but stated that was "the ONLY scheduled class!" Naturally, I was devastated!

As I explained in my earlier book, *So, You Think You'd Like to Railroad and Other Railroad Stories* I began contacting every railroad in or near the City of Detroit...without success! Being an honest person, they were all ready to hire me until I truthfully and affirmatively answered the question, "Are you going to go on to college in the fall?" Yes, each time I shot myself in the foot!

By this time, I was beginning to get worried and knew that I had to find some kind of a job...any kind...to help pay for college; so I started calling on other various firms...but I must say, I lacked the enthusiasm that I had for any kind of a railroad job.

The very next day I paid a visit to the *Jones Motor Freight*'s terminal in Troy, Michigan. The Dock Foreman looked at me, asked for my phone number, and said "I can call you periodically as "Casual Help," which meant that I would work occasionally as needed to load and unload semi-trailers. He actually called that same evening and said to "report as soon as possible," which turned out to be 6:00 P.M. I worked until 2:30 A.M. and I must say that that was probably the most physically challenging job that I ever worked...(except perhaps on the few days that I helped the GTW's section gang in Kalamazoo and during the Blizzard of 1978)! But, let me also state that this job did have one true benefit! It paid $3.66/hour, which in 1967 was BIG money! And, I received a paycheck nightly at the end of the shift.

Even though they called me to work almost every evening, I did not relinquish my search or hope of finding a railroad position.

One day it occurred to me that perhaps the GTW hired separately in each individual terminal. I then drove north from my parent's home in Royal Oak, Michigan to the GTW's Johnson Avenue yard office in Pontiac. As it turned out they were not doing any hiring in the Transportation Department; but Linda Karwoski, the Trainmaster's Secretary suggested that I drive up to the roundhouse and talk with Bob Slaght, the Roundhouse Foreman.

"Soak It!!!"... and Other Railroad Stories

I immediately followed Linda's suggestion and met with Mr. Slaght. Once again he asked the usual question, and once again I answered truthfully. Miraculously, he then immediately sent me to the Doctor's Office for a pre-employment physical exam! I passed without any problems, returned to the roundhouse with the paperwork, and was immediately hired. My date of hire was, July 6, 1967. My position was that of Fire Builder...which was actually now just a Laborer. I've told you before that I was thrilled! I had finally become a professional railroader!

Now here was the interesting part and actually the point of this story. On this job my rate of pay was **$2.5788 per hour**...$1.0812 per hour less than I would be earning in the truck terminal, working for the competition! Yes, this would be a huge reduction in earnings; but I was seeking an education in railroading in addition to funds for college. Let me state emphatically, throughout my entire 45-year railroad career, this was the ONLY time that my wages were stated with four decimal places! Why I have never been able to find out. The craft was a part of and represented by the *Laborers' International Union of North America*. I would have thought that the hourly pay would have been rounded up to $2.58 per hour; but no, contractually the carrier was apparently saving $.0012 per hour...which equated to $.0096 per day...or $.0480 per week, or a grand total of $2.4960 per year! Apparently several individuals did some hard bargaining!?!

Interestingly, during this span of time the *Laborers'* working agreement on the railroad had expired and they were essentially working "without a contract."

After completing my regular second shift position on Saturday, September 16, 1967 at 11:30 P.M. I resigned my position to be driven the next day by my parents' to *Central Michigan University* to begin my Freshman Year. I began glasses on Monday the 18th.

Just prior to Christmas I was totally surprised when I received a GTW pay check in the mail! Apparently the *Laborers'* contract was settled and I received a check for back-pay covering all of the hours that I worked "without a contract." I was thrilled!

Charles H. Geletzke, Jr.

Throughout my railroad career, because the railroad industry was considered essential to the National Defense, my union brothers and I continued to work without a contract following the expiration of most contracts; but at the end, following contract negotiations, we ALWAYS received a check for Back-Pay…every time except ONCE!!! And that too will be a future story!

It's any wonder my hearing is IMPAIRED!?!

By: C. H. Geletzke, Jr.

All of you who began working in train and engine service prior to the mid-1980's no doubt recall that when the engineer set the brakes on the train using the Automatic Brake Valve, all of the air in the trainline would be exhausted into the locomotive cab and the amount of noise associated with that could be almost debilitating! Multiply that by thousands of brake applications over an entire career and it is any wonder that most railroaders from the Operating Department sounded as if they were screaming when they talked with others.

But on Monday, July 15, 1968 I was a participant in an event which seriously topped all of those brake applications! Now by this time I had been railroading for just over a year and on this day I was ordered to deadhead from my home terminal, Milwaukee Jct. in Detroit, 26-miles to the GTW's Johnson Avenue yard office in Pontiac, Michigan. I was called to work Trains 544 and 545, the "Richmond Local" for the first time, and was to go on duty at Pontiac at 12:00 Noon…allowing for the deadhead, I actually went on duty at Milwaukee Jct. at 11 o'clock A.M.

On this particular day, the crew was made-up of Engineer, Leo Martell, an old steam man who hired-out in the 1920's and a man that I highly respected! The Fireman, was a new man, David Reed. Danny Wilkins was the Conductor, Nick Mazick was the Flagman, and I was the Head Brakeman. For power, we had a passenger GP9, the

"Soak It!!!"… and Other Railroad Stories
GTW 4930. The train itself worked from Pontiac across the Pontiac Belt Line and Romeo Subdivision approximately 50-miles to Richmond, turned on the wye there, and returned to Pontiac. As I just stated, this was my first time to be called for this job; however in 1966 I did ride a Michigan Railroad Club fantrip over the line pulled by the CN 6218 a 4-8-4 Northern.

We departed Pontiac at around 1 o'clock and worked at the towns of Auburn Heights, Rochester, Rochester Jct. (where we interchanged with the Penn Central-former NYC), Washington, and on into Romeo…a town widely recognized for the peaches that were grown there!

At Romeo we switched the *Wickes Lumber Co., Interpace* (*International Pipe & Ceramics Corp.*), and the new *Ford Motor Co.-Tractor Division*. Additionally, downtown there was a West Side Team Track and a House Track that basically served as public team tracks. I will never forget, we were in the process of spotting several 40-foot boxcars loaded with lumber in the West Side Team Track and I was riding the leading stirrup and ladder on the "point car," down to make a "joint" (coupling) at the far east end of the track, guiding Engineer Martell with hand signals (It would still be several more years before this assignment would receive radios.). As I neared the car at the far end, I gave Leo a signal for "One more car length," and he slowed down nicely. I then gave him an "Easy" signal and he slowed to a crawl. Lastly, I gave him one more "Easy" signal and then dropped my right arm to my side indicating a nice gentle "STOP." But, as the two couplers came together and as the knuckles closed, there came an EXPLOSION, which almost jarred me off the car!!!

It was at that point that I looked toward the far end of the car we were now coupled to and there stood Brakeman Mazic laughing his head off! It would be at least five minutes before I would be able to hear anything again! I was furious!

It turned-out that Nick had inserted a torpedo into the knuckle of the car we were coupling to and for a man in his late 50's, this childlike idiot thought it was the funniest thing he'd ever seen! From that day on I lost all respect for him.

Charles H. Geletzke, Jr.

Interestingly, he died later that summer from a heart attack. Yes, I'll never forget…I walked into the Pontiac Crew Dispatcher's Office and written on the Call Board were the words, "Mazic Died." I figured he had worked a job and exceeded his 16-hours on duty…I quickly found-out that I was wrong.

One more item for you died in the wool GTW fans. In our Bulletin Book on that July 15th date was a System Bulletin stating, "Effective immediately, switch lamps will begin being removed from switch stands and will be replaced with reflective targets." On the return trip that day on Train 545 we once again had to deliver a carload of tires to the PC at Rochester Jct. Now this automatic diamond and interchange track actually was located within the confines of *Bloomer State Park* and was not easily accessed by road. It was also an extremely dark night and being my first trip working the line, I had to signal Engineer Martell with my lantern to move very cautiously toward the turnouts, without any switch lamps, it was extremely difficult to spot the switchstands!

Oh yes, we returned to Pontiac and tied-up at 10:10 P.M.

View looking south on the GTW toward the NYC diamond and depot at Oxford, MI on February 26, 1966. Track curving off to the right was the Lead to *American Aggregates Corp.*

Inexperience

By: retired GTW and CN Locomotive Engineer and Road Foreman of Engines, Roger L. Meade

When I hired into engine service on the Grand Trunk Western Railroad (GTW) in 1969, I was one of a handful of men actually hired "off the street" as the saying went, rather than transferred from another operating position (brakeman or switchman), or non-op position, as had been the usual practice. This probably was due to a couple of circumstances. One, the war in Vietnam was at its height; so military demands on manpower took precedence. Also, fresh in memory was the GTW's unfortunate treatment of its firemen after the implementation of Award 282, the Federal Law that allowed the railroads to cut the number of jobs available to firemen, and sever from service any with less than 10-years seniority in engine service. This the GTW did with a vengeance, and in addition, forced any men of over 10-years

31

service who could not hold one of the regular fireman jobs that still existed within their home terminal to follow their seniority to wherever they could work, be it Battle Creek, Chicago, or even Milwaukee, Wisconsin! This created a great deal of bitterness among those so forced away from home and family for essentially artificial reasons. One of the engineers that later helped train me, Leo Leach, had a little story he liked to tell new men like me about those days…

The GTW found, not long after implementing Award 282 and firing any man with less than 10-years, that they had a shortage of engineers thanks to a booming economy as a result of the war in Vietnam. Leo liked to say, with a grin, that "the company forgot to get an agreement from the Engineers not to die or retire before they put Award 282 into effect!"

When the company decided they better get some more men trained as engineers, they offered transfers into engine service to employees from other crafts; but not near enough decided to take the chance! They had watched the young firemen lose their jobs, and logically figured the same would happen to them with the first downturn in business. Thus, the GTW turned to completely inexperienced men, like me, to go into engine service. Fresh from four years in the Air Force, I had nothing to lose, and a job I wanted to gain!

Why was experience so important? On the GTW, enginemen had "system seniority," that is, they could work any job in or from any terminal on the entire railroad from Chicago to Port Huron or Muskegon to Detroit, plus several branches serving Kalamazoo, Bay City, Jackson, Richmond, Greenville, Grand Haven, and Caseville, and points in between. The only limiting factor was sufficient seniority to hold a regular job or the extra board at one of those terminals.

Now, all of those lines had their own physical characteristics…grades, curves, yards, industries, crossings at grade, interchanges, operation over other railroads using the other's rules and instructions, condition of the track structure, track speed allowed, permanent slow orders, signal system or train orders used, etc. etc. The only way to really learn

32

"Soak It!!!"… and Other Railroad Stories
everything you needed to know to operate safely and smoothly was "time in the seat," hopefully with good engineer instructors to pass on knowledge and tips. This meant lots of hours in yard service, then freight service, and finally passenger service to become competent to be on your own.

Another variable factor was the other employees you worked with or around. Unless you had a regular job with a regular crew, you worked with a constantly changing bunch of trainmasters, yardmasters, train dispatchers, crew dispatchers, trainmen, switchmen, trackmen, signal maintainers, crossing guards, roundhouse employees, and clerical personnel. Which ones were competent, which ones you could trust without question, which ones were brand new or still learning their job or the territory, which ones needed to be watched, which ones might want to put you in a bind out of malice or spite, and which ones might withhold information to make you look stupid or to see if you got yourself into trouble. Luckily, there were not a lot of those last types, and it wasn't unusual for someone else to give you a "heads-up" about them, if you didn't already know! Actually, it was always desirable to help your fellow employees do a good job to maintain a smooth, on-time operation; but naturally, there were always a few that did not recognize that fact!

There were also personal characteristics it was smart to be aware of for smooth operation. As an example, one switchman I worked with in Flint was very competent and a pleasure to have on a crew; but he had a quirk that an engineer needed to be aware of. When making a radio controlled joint or coupling between long cuts of cars, where visual communication was not possible, Ron's car lengths got progressively shorter the closer we got to making the joint! So, he might call out "ten cars" and they would be like double-length auto carriers, then "five cars" and they became normal 60-foot cars, then "three cars" and they became 40-foot or less, and finally "one car-that'll do" and that one car was an ore jimmy! Once you had worked with Ron a couple of times you were clued into this quirk and could deal with his routine; but good to keep in mind to avoid rough joints! The point was that Ron was consistent in his inconsistency; so if you knew what to expect there was no problem.

I can provide a prime example in my own case where inexperience was a potential for a problem...or even a disaster! I'll bet any operating person with substantial time in grade can cite their own examples of disaster avoided. It's part of the process of gaining experience.

I was working as fireman on the Caseville Local with Engineer, Lynn Hogg; Conductor, Larry Crawley; and I believe Jerry Black and Ray Wartella as brakemen. The routine was to set-off all revenue cars at Imlay City on the southward leg of the trip and to run "cab light" from there back to Pontiac. This day there was gravel work to do at Oxford. We were to pull and weigh about 40-cars of gravel and bring them with us to Pontiac.

Being a fireman in Pontiac meant that I did not get much chance to work long freight assignments. Pontiac freight was mostly local branch line jobs on the Jackson, Romeo, and Cass City Subdivisions. These were mixed freight, extended switch runs really, short relatively light trains at medium speed.

On the day in question, Engineer Hogg decided I could handle the weighing of the cars at Oxford and he elected to stay at the yard office rather than on the engine with me. I knew that you do not use air brakes while weighing. Without air in the cut, we'd pull the loads out onto the Mainline and south until clear of the scale. The cars were then nudged back one at a time onto the scale and then given a push into the collection track, where the caboose had already been spotted. The flagman would ride the cars to the joint, make the air joint, and walk back to catch the next car. If memory serves, the station agent or operator felt he could get the weights on slowly moving cars passing over the scale; so we pulled the full 40-cars out as one cut from the yard track, upgrade toward the New York Central (NYC) diamond and town of Oxford. This would save us time. Pulling those cars up out of the yard required a heavy throttle with our two GP-9's. I got them moving to about 10 mph or so, and then slacked-off on the power enough to keep them moving like that. Jerry started easing me off; so I shut the throttle and started applying the engine brakes; which, since there was no air on the cut, were the only brakes available! Now 40-cars got us well up the Main to the point where the grade crests. I had not been thinking about that! The engine brakes seemed anemic to say the least. The tail car passed the switch to the scale and Jerry was giving me a strong "washout" (Stop signal); but I was already doing all possible to stop those cars. Also, the track curved slightly as you got closer to the NYC diamond and then started a gentle down grade toward town. I started seeing myself at the head of a runaway train, ending up at the bottom of Muck Creek, just short of the Pontiac Yard Limit sign! That was if I was lucky enough to not run into a conflicting move on the NYC diamond! I began wondering if I should set the Independent Brake full-on, leave the engine, and begin winding on hand brakes on the cars. But the idea of not being able to stop the cut and not being able to run fast enough to catch the engines soon disabused me of that idea!

Well, it turned out there was just enough brake with the two geeps to get me stopped; but I was partway into the curve, so that I could no longer see Jerry. Even going over to the left side of the cab to look back from the inside of the curve did not help. I finally gave him three short toots on the whistle to signal "Backup" and started easing back.

The rest of the day went much smoother; but it was a valuable lesson learned…at least partially…but, that is another story, or three!

Penn Central Train JT-3 derailed at Dearborn, MI on May 19, 1969. (D. J. Mrozek photo)

Skipping After-School Track Practice

By: David J. Mrozek

For anyone who knew me as a middle school student, it was readily apparent that I was a railroad enthusiast. One look at my notebooks and the loose leaf sheets within covered with sketches of trains and locomotives told my story. My after school free time and many of my weekend hours were spent hanging out at the Penn Central (PC) block station and train order office at Town Line in Dearborn, Michigan.

As railroad facilities go, Town Line wasn't much. It was little more than a small, Michigan Central standard plan, wood frame structure, which years ago could be found functioning as block station / train order offices, or even section shanties, at many locations along the MC's main and secondary lines. However, the magical aspect of the place for a young rail enthusiast was what took place inside…being able to witness firsthand the business of operating a railroad, plus of course, the excitement of "train time!"

Railroad management frowned upon the practice of teenage kids hanging out there and issued, on at least one occasion, a notice to all Town Line operators stating that going forward, the practice would not be tolerated! We had to find other pastimes for a while; but eventually we were allowed back. Perhaps the reason why some of the operators continued to allow us inside was because we were dependable "runners" – riding our bikes up to the nearby *Kroger* store or *Civic Drugs* to get them a bag of chips and a cold pop. If we were lucky, sometimes they would give us extra change to treat ourselves to a bag of chips as well.

By 1969, track team practice after school and our weekly track meets were cutting into my "Town Line time," which was now largely limited to weekend sessions, or for a change of pace, I would ride my bike to the N&W, C&O, and PC locomotive servicing facilities to take photos. Such was life for this 14-year-old, 9th grader.

As the school day began on Monday, May 19, 1969, I was immediately greeted by some of my friends with the question, "Did you hear about the big train derailment in west Dearborn last night?" Yes, I had and I wanted to get up there right after school to see what had happened. But oh man, I had track practice after school. What to do? After 3rd hour gym class, I told the track coach I had to miss track practice today. Thankfully, he didn't press me for a reason why, so I was free to take the bus home right after school, grab a snack, hop on my bike, and pedal the three miles to west Dearborn to check out the aftermath of the big derailment. Despite PC wrecking crane X25 and a *J. J. Curran* crane having been on the scene all day, there were still rail cars scattered all over.

As the local Dearborn newspapers reported, 31 cars of an eastbound Penn Central freight had derailed between Mason and Monroe Streets, with one of the errant rail cars crashing through the wall of the nearby *Club Car Wash*. Years later, when sharing the photos I took after school that day with longtime friend, former Penn Central employee, and

Charles H. Geletzke, Jr.

rail historian, Jim Harlow, he provided some additional details about the wreck and what contributed to it.

The eastbound train that derailed was JT-3...a Jackson to Toledo run that typically consisted of large numbers of empty auto parts cars from Lansing and other mid-state locations, gathered together in the yard at Jackson and assembled into trains. Frequently, a crew change on JT-3 took place at Town Line, before the train was routed down the Junction Yard Branch to join the Detroit-Toledo mainline at control point YD in River Rouge for the balance of the trip to Toledo. JT-3's westbound counterpart was TL-2...a Toledo to Lansing train that handled loaded outbound parts cars.

According to the operator on duty at Town Line that night, the operator at Wayne Junction, where the C&O's Toledo-Saginaw line crossed the PC's Detroit-Chicago mainline, had spotted a flaming hotbox as JT-3 sped over the diamond and past the tower at 60 mph. According to Penn Central Northern Region employee timetable No. 3, dated April 27, 1969, freight trains were allowed to travel at 60 mph between Town Line and Jackson, with no speed restriction for the diamonds at Wayne Junction. There were, of course, additional speed restrictions in place at Dearborn, Ypsilanti, Ann Arbor, and Jackson for both freight and passenger traffic.

Sadly, once he saw the problem, the operator at Wayne Junction was unable to get his hands on a fusee, light it, and scamper down the tower stairs in time to alert the conductor riding in the waycar that his train was potentially headed for disaster. Failing in that effort, he did notify the Jackson East dispatcher, the operator at Town Line, and made a desperate attempt to contact the train crew by radio. Both Wayne Junction and Town Line were equipped with limited range, less than reliable, block station-to-train radios; but not all road locomotives had them, nor did all conductors carry portable handset radios with them in the waycar back then. The dispatcher ordered the operator at Town Line to hop in his car and, if possible, flag the train down with a fusee in west Dearborn...about three miles away. As the operator turned left off Michigan Avenue and onto Monroe Street, the head-end was just going by and moments later, JT-3 started derailing right before his very eyes!

According to Penn Central's Rules for Conducting Transportation publication dated April 28, 1968, Rule 626 and 627, concerning operators witnessing a passing train with a condition endangering itself or another train on an adjacent track, were followed as prescribed in the rule book. However, the Northern Region rules examiner also required block operators to be on the ground inspecting passing trains, if their duties permitted, with pen, paper, and fusee at the ready should a defect be observed. An investigation was held and the operator at Wayne Junction was fired for what management viewed as a rules infraction. They felt that he was in a position and would have had time to give the conductor a "washout" (STOP) signal with a fusee; but failed to do so.

Unlike the turmoil facing PC management, Tuesday, May 20th was just another school day for me with track practice afterwards. But, I was also very eager to get my roll of Kodak Plus-X black and white film developed and printed, and be able to add the derailment photos to my growing collection of railroad stuff!

Charles H. Geletzke, Jr.

GTW Train 546 the "Jackson Local" at MAL Crossing in Jackson, MI returning to Pontiac in March 1974. (Doug Leffler photo)

Cottonwood Trees

By: C. H. Geletzke, Jr.

Over Memorial Day weekend my wife and I were walking through our neighborhood when she noticed the first of the season's Eastern Cottonwood seeds flying like little cotton balls through the air. When she brought it to my attention, it instantly brought back memories for me of working the Grand Trunk Western Railroad's (GTW) Trains 547/546, the "Jackson Local" between Pontiac and Jackson, Michigan.

Now I don't pretend to know if you, the reader, are exposed to these fluffy flowery cotton like seeds in your geographical location; but for us in southeastern Michigan their four week flight is an annual event and will clog the air filters on everything!

Working for the GTW we were very fortunate to have cabooses that were not only well maintained; but came equipped with many added accessories compared to most of the other carriers. One of the features of all GTW cabs, both

40

"Soak It!!!"… and Other Railroad Stories

wooden and steel, during warm weather, was the much appreciated inclusion of screens not only on all of the windows; but also on the doors on each end of the car.

Thus I recalled during the early summer of 1970, just before I joined the Marine Corps, I was working as the regular flagman on our Jackson Local. I will never forget how we backed our train east out of Pontiac Yard each morning and shoved down to the tower at M.A.L. Jct., (Milepost 35.3), reversed, and then headed west toward Jackson (M.P. 105.8) and how the bright white cottonwood seed would envelop our train. It was always amazing to me that by the time we reached our first stop at either Orchard Lake (M.P. 40) or Walled Lake (M.P. 47.6) the front end of the caboose would just be covered with the white cottony seeds! Thankfully, because the car was equipped with the front screen door, we could keep the seeds from blowing through the cab's interior and yet still maintain a little air circulation. Usually around the town of South Lyon (M.P. 59) and again at Stockbridge (M.P. 88.6) I would walk out there with the broom and sweep all of the seed off to the side of the car. On the return trip from Jackson this action would be repeated on the opposite end of the car.

For some reason I don't ever recall doing this on any of the other subdivisions…probably just memory loss or old age!

Answer to a Test Question

By: C. H. Geletzke, Jr.

The other day my wife and I were having a discussion regarding the problems that Our Country's Military is having finding young men and women who not only are able to pass the physical fitness requirements of the various branches; but also have the necessary required mental skills.

When I enlisted in the Marine Corps Reserves in 1970 I was sent to MCRD (Marine Corps Recruit Depot) in

Charles H. Geletzke, Jr.

San Diego, California for Bootcamp. Immediately upon graduation I officially became a "Hollywood Marine!"

If I recall correctly, on our third or forth morning there, they marched our entire company across the Parade Deck to a big hall where all of us were seated at tables and for a major portion of the day were given various intelligence and ability tests. Naturally, we were all exhausted from the amount of physical activity we had encountered over the past several days, not to mention the lack of "sufficient" sleep! As I remember, subjects on the test included math, English or grammar, physics, history, science, some chemistry, mechanics, knowledge of various tools, geography, our knowledge of foods, sports questions, traffic laws, questions about hobbies or interests we may have been exposed to, a test to see if we could receive Morse Code…which got progressively faster and faster, and also a section designed to test our writing ability. Now here it is over fifty years later, and would you believe that I still recall one of the questions on that test!?! Yes, I almost fell over when the following multiple choice or "Pick a Winner" test question appeared in the Hobby or perhaps Transportation section of the test…the question was: **"What does HO stand for?"** Now having been an avid reader of both *Model Railroader Magazine* and *Railroad Model Craftsman* for the previous 12-1/2 years, I immediately knew the answer! **"Half O."** Meaning HO Scale model trains were approximately half the size of O scale trains.

Now I have no idea whether this question still appears on the military ability tests that are administered today; but in actuality I have no regrets about giving away the answer to the question if indeed it is! After all, what person of "enlistment age" would ever even see this, unless they were a modeler or a railfan!?!

Oh yes, by now you might be wondering how knowing the correct answer affected my placement in a MOS…Military Occupational Specialty. Well following my thorough Marine Corps training, my MOS became 0351. All 0300-series were Infantry positions…0351 was an Anti-Tank Assault Man. We specialized in the use of the 106mm

"Soak It!!!"… and Other Railroad Stories
Recoilless Rifle, the 3.5-inch Rocket Launcher (Bazooka), and the flame-thrower. I don't believe that any of those heavy "crew-served" weapons and their ammunition are still in use by the military today…but, compared to all of my brother Infantry Marines out there at that time, we were colloquially referred to as "Super Grunts" and our motto was…"Truck it or F**k it!"

Semper Fi!

GTW Port Huron, MI Car Shops October 10, 1995.

No Two Days Alike!

As told by GTW Car Inspector, Bob Dell to his son, David Dell

My dad, Bob Dell, worked 42-years in the Port Huron (Michigan) Shops for the Grand Trunk Western Railroad (GTW), first as a Riveter and Welder, before becoming an Inspector.

As part of the job of inspecting cars for defects, he would have to crawl underneath and on top and inside. Often he would write-up issues along the roof of the car by lying on the roof and hanging over the side! He became quite adept at

43

writing upside down and backwards, so the notes could be read from the ground.

During his interior inspections, checking the wood lining or for holes in the roof or along the seams, he found a myriad of apparently lost items. Some of those were racks of Pontiac 4-cylinder engines that had never made it to the assembly plant, some 64-miles away. Once, after he opened the lid on a tank car he found a bicycle lying inside with all of the paperwork still in the package tied to the handlebars! He headed back to the office for a length of rope to recover it, only to find that someone had come along and beat him to it!

On one trip to the east end to inspect a pair of 50-foot box cars inside the Freight Sheds, he opened the doors only to find them loaded with artillery shells!!! The sheds were adjacent to a residential area and at one time, unclaimed furniture and other freight was sold off to the inhabitants of the neighborhood. He immediately got on the radio, called for a locomotive, and soon enough a switch crew came down and pulled the car out to some other location in the yard.

Probably the funniest incident was when he was walking up to a boxcar with the door ajar. He noticed a light in the dark interior. Walking as quietly as he could on the ballast, he listened so he would have some idea of what was going on. When he determined that whatever was going on wasn't going to kill him, he flung the door back to find three or four guys sitting around a candle and a Ouija board trying to conjure up some spirit. He said they were so intent on their task at hand, that they jumped so high they could have hit their heads on the roof of the car, he scared them so badly!

GTW Port Huron, MI Car Shops June 29, 1992. (J. G. Tyson photo)

Somebody's Watching You!
As told by GTW Car Inspector, Bob Dell, to his son, David Dell

Oxy-Acetylene torches cannot burn through two pieces of steel, layered on each other! The Torch can't heat the back sheet, to allow it to blow the molten steel from the front sheet, through it. One day, my dad, Bob Dell, who drove rivets and welded for more than 20-years in his 42-year career in the Port Huron (Michigan) Car Shops for the Grand Trunk Western Railroad (GTW), was using his stick welder to burn holes through a car that had steel patches welded over the base metal. Very soon after starting the task, a boss with a clipboard, came by and asked what he was doing. My dad told him he was burning holes, and the boss started making notes.

When my dad saw him taking notes on his very official looking clipboard, he changed the welding rod and turned his welder down, so he wouldn't blow any more holes through the steel. The Boss came over and asked what he was doing now, to which he replied, "I'm welding." The boss scratched out the notes and began writing down new data. Again my dad saw him changing his information, so he dropped the rod out of the stinger, put a burning rod in its place, and spun the dial on the welder. He proceeded to start burning holes again, and the boss then asked if he was burning again. My dad answered in the affirmative and the boss scribbled out the welding notes and started writing burning notations. My dad gave him a minute or two for his writing and then turned his heat down, once again. He then quickly changed his rod, once more, and then resumed his welding. At that point the boss walked to the closest garbage can and tossed his clipboard in it!

So endeth the Time Study they tried on my dad!

GTW Port Huron, MI Wheel Shop and Boiler House June 29, 1992 (J. G. Tyson photo)

Dangerous Work

As told by GTW Car Inspector, Bob Dell to his son, David Dell

"Soak It!!!"... and Other Railroad Stories

In 42-years in the Port Huron Car Shops, my dad, Bob Dell, only ever got about one month of overtime from the Grand Trunk Western Railroad (GTW)!

Shortly before Christmas 1972, while the crew of Apollo 17 was making our Nation's last mission to the surface of the moon, my dad was canvassed for overtime work on afternoons, working in the Triple Valve Room in Coach Shop 2. The Shops had bid a rebuild job on several hundred of the brake system valves.

My dad was a welder at the time; but overtime before Christmas was still overtime, and just in time for Christmas! He and a couple of his work buddies all crowded in this small 15 x 20-foot room and spent their time cleaning and tearing down for rebuild of these valves. While he doesn't recall what nasty chemical they actually used for cleaning, none of them had respirators or protective gloves or face shields. The only ventilation was from what little air flow they could get from a standard office door on one side and a standard office type window on the other side of the room. The fledgling OSHA certainly had no idea what was going on in there!

Since that wasn't his normal gig, he only worked there during this special project and for a short time during his apprenticeship. At 91-years old and after 30-years of retirement, he has outlived and collected considerably more Railroad Retirement than any of the regulars that did that job. They almost all died from cancer of the liver and kidney! Most certainly because of the toxic chemicals those guys worked with...

Makes "giving your life for the cause" a whole new meaning!

GTW Port Huron, MI Transfer Table and Car Shop June 29, 1992.
(J. G. Tyson photo)

"GTW 309311 where are you!?!"

As told by retired GTW Car Inspector, Bob Dell, to his son,
David Dell

My dad, Bob Dell, who started his 42-year career in
the Port Huron (Michigan) Car Shops for the Grand Trunk
Western Railroad (GTW) welded and drove rivets for over
22-years. He bid on and finally won an Inspector job that
took him to "the great out of doors!" He would write-up car
discrepancies after walking through the GTW's Tunnel Yard.
Toward the end of his career the Shop Superintendent, Ray
Kelly, up and changed his job responsibilities and title to Car
Locator with two other inspectors. Of course being the Big
Boss, he didn't feel the need to tell my dad's immediate
supervisor, which caused no little amount of consternation!
One of the first things that my dad did, after his
morning coffee, was to walk through the yards adjacent to
the Depot Tracks from 16th Street on the east end all the way
to 32nd Street on the west end. There were eight Shop Tracks

"Soak It!!!"… and Other Railroad Stories

into the Steel Shop and eight RIP Tracks along the south edge of the shop property, in addition to the myriad of crossovers and leads for the Sandblast Track, the Coach Shops, and Machine Shop. He would take his clipboards and pencils and walk back and forth writing down every car number and its location on each track. When he was done with that, and gotten another cup of coffee, he would head upstairs to the Estimator For Repairs (who would call the car owners in the case of rolling stock), and write on a big chalk board all of the information he had gathered. This would lead up to about 10:30 or 11 o'clock every morning.

On more than one occasion the Shop Superintendent called him on his big "handi-talkie," colloquially known as "the Brick" and say, "I need an updated Locator List!"

Apparently a yard crew had gone behind him and made a dozen or more moves, and all of the cars whose locations he had recorded, were no longer where he had said they were!

Out to the yard he would go and start all over.

He always said, "It ain't no way to run a railroad" and it certainly applied in this situation!

My First "Save"

By: retired PC, CR, RI towerman and Block Operator, James H. Harlow

Friction-bearing journals were terrible things (metal against metal with a cotton pad around it, the bottom of which was immersed in oil) before the advent of the much more reliable roller-bearing journal. But as we "old-timers" know, s**t happened when the oil ran out!

I was going to college at the *University of Michigan* in Ann Arbor (or was supposed to be), in late 1970. One cold snowy Sunday morning in November, I got up early in my North Campus dorm room, quietly dressed, snuck out so as not to wake my roommate, and got on a bus that went to downtown Ann Arbor…giving in to the pull to watch trains

Charles H. Geletzke, Jr.

at the Penn Central depot. Getting off at Depot St., I walked the quarter mile or so to what was now PC's small depot. Chuck Muer had bought the large ex-Michigan Central depot to convert it into a restaurant and now PC was using what had been the west baggage room, situated between the large depot and the Broadway St. bridge on the south side of the double-main tracks.

I hadn't been at the depot long when I heard the gurgle and rumble of an eastbound train. At the same time, the operator showed up to start his 7:00 A.M. shift, and just as the train started by slowly, he unlocked the door to the building and went inside. Even though it wasn't snowing hard, I did not follow him in…after all, that's what I came down here for…to immerse myself in the sight and sounds of a train going by! I was thrilled to see that it had three or four smoky Alco's on the point, and then came the train. Through the snow, I could see smoke coming off the VERY FIRST journal box…right behind the engines! I immediately went inside and screamed at the operator about what I had seen!!! He grabbed a fusee and we went outside to watch the rest of the train go by. When he saw the caboose approaching, he cracked off the fusee, swinging down the train as the conductor looked at us from the back platform. After that, we both went inside the warm building and the operator reported the train (which was the division's hottest train, NY4 by the way; a train made up with reefers, hot freight, and sometimes some loaded livestock cars) "bye," to the train dispatcher in Jackson, along with a report of the hotbox, right behind the engines.

Before the train dispatcher responded, a clicking sound (like the "tik-tok" of a clock) started on the train dispatcher's line…he had set-up the "call-in" signal at Geddes siding, east of Ann Arbor, to have the train stop and call him on the wayside telephone there. Remember, not all trains back then were equipped with radios!

We listened to the dispatcher's line as the head brakeman called in and a plan was developed for the train to set-out the first car with its offending hotbox.

50

"Soak It!!!"... and Other Railroad Stories

The next day, I dropped by the depot to watch more trains, in case there were any around. By chance, the car repairman had just arrived there to make his report on the car that NY4 had set-out on the Geddes siding.

The operator told him that it was me that first spotted the "smoker," after which he told me it was a good thing I had spotted it, because it wouldn't have made it to Willow Run Yard (located between Ypsilanti and Wayne)!

Hotboxes didn't happen too often; but just one occurrence was WAY too often...and one had to be in the right place at the right time to catch them!

Delray Connecting Railroad Car Shop on Zug Island in River Rouge, MI on August 31, 1972. Engines are Alco S-1's 66 and 68.

I wonder where they went?

By: C. H. Geletzke, Jr.

In 1971 when I went to work for the Delray Connecting Railroad on Zug Island in River Rouge, Michigan as a switchman it was readily apparent that practically every single turnout on the entire railroad was equipped with a kerosene switch lamp (sadly, to the best of my knowledge they were all unmarked). At that time on their section gang, they even had a Lampman, whose job it was to see that the lamps were all properly filled with fuel, that the wicks were trimmed, and that the lenses were periodically cleaned. Unbeknownst to me, during the last two weeks of the year, ALL of the switch lamps were removed from their switches and replaced by reflectorized targets.

Following my graduation from *Central Michigan University* just prior to Christmas I began working in a managerial position for the DC as Assistant to the General Manager right after the start of the New Year. While in my new job, I was basically a Jack of All Trades; but my major duty was handling all of the railroad's purchasing. I guess it was during the second week on my new job I had occasion to visit a storage room, which was attached to the Employee Garage located immediately behind the railroad's General Office. I was actually inventorying Alco engine parts, which had been given to the DC by the Norfolk & Western Railroad (N&W) in Detroit when they discontinued using Alco locomotives in the Detroit area. I couldn't believe my eyes when I opened the Storage Room door and encountered well over 100 kerosene switch lamps stacked everywhere within the room!

Later while talking with my immediate supervisor, Paul Weissert the General Manager, I mentioned the kerosene lamps. He then asked me "would you like to have one?"

Being a little greedy I countered with, "Would it be possible to have four of them?

Mr. Weissert then said, "Later, go get four good ones!"

I complied with his instruction and later gave one each to two of my Dad's cousins who were semi-railfans, one to Monroe, Michigan railroad artist, Michael S. Delaney, and I kept one for myself, which I still have.

Now, here is the mystery. The next time I had occasion to enter that same Storage Room, all of the lamps were gone! I never arranged for them to be sold and nothing was ever mentioned about them by my bosses; but here it is,

"Soak It!!!"… and Other Railroad Stories
fifty years later and I am still wondering where they all went!?!

Just as a little side note…when I was GTW Assistant Trainmaster/Agent in Kalamazoo, Michigan during the late 1980's I was talking with an Conrail (former NYC-PC) track man and he told me that when the NYC was getting rid of their kerosene lamps in the mid-1960's in that area, they were all dumped in the Kalamazoo River on the south side of Botsford Yard there on the east side of town. Makes me wonder if they are still there and I wonder what kind of condition they would be in all these years later?

PRR X38N 74301 an open-top boxcar was photographed on the DC on Zug Island in River Rouge, MI on June 27, 1972.

Open-Tops for Coke Loading

By: C. H. Geletzke, Jr.

In 1971 and 1972 I was employed by the Delray Connecting Railroad (DC) in Detroit, Michigan. The DC was a terminal switching road located primarily on Zug Island in the Downriver area of Detroit. Their primary function was to handle cars between about eight industries and their interchanging railroads, which were the C&O, DT&I, NYC, PRR, and Wabash. Until November 25, 1925 the D&TSL also had a direct connection via the Wabash and Union Belt of Detroit (UBD) to additionally connect with the DC on "the Island." The DC's two primary customers were the *Allied Chemical Corporation's Semet-Solvay Division* and the *Great Lakes Steel Corporation's* Blast Furnace Division. The "Solvay" as it was commonly called was a major producer of Coke. Vast quantities of coal would arrive by Great Lakes freighters at their facility, which was located at the mouth of the Rouge River. The Delray Connecting would then switch the coal directly from the boats or from stock piles on the ground to Semet-Solvay's coke ovens. The finished coke would then be screened for size and loaded into railroad cars and shipped to the various steel mills and foundries located all around the Midwest.

Without going into a great deal of detail, there were three commonly shipped sizes of coke. Foundry Coke was about the size of very large grapefruits, and as the name implied, was shipped mainly to foundries for metal casting. Second and most common, furnace Coke was made up of lumps about 2-3 inches in diameter and was used in blast furnaces to produce steel. Lastly, was what was known as Coke Breeze, and consisted of the smaller coke particles.

The vast majority of the coke that was shipped out moved in standard railroad hoppers, or by the early 1970's in the larger capacity high side coke hoppers, due to the fact that it is relatively light in weight and yet bulky.

The oddities that I would like to call to your attention were the two "Open-Tops" assigned for loading at the Delray Connecting Railroad. Both were boxcars with their roofs removed. These cars strictly handled Foundry Coke. 2" x 12" wooden slats were nailed across the doorways just like grain doors. There usually was a gap of about one inch between each board. The Chesapeake & Ohio (C&O) car often moved with the doors open and as you can see, the similar Pennsylvania Railroad (PRR) car had no doors at all. When the cars arrived at their destination (one of which was a foundry, *Benton Harbor Malleable Industries* in Benton Harbor, MI), workers would knock the slats loose on one side and shovel the coke out by hand. The cars would always return with the loose slats lying inside of the car.

I am far from an expert on freight cars; but from a photo that I used to have (which I loaned to a former railroad magazine and was never returned), you could have seen that C&O 283402 was a forty foot boxcar. (There was a second car in the series C&O 283062; but I cannot honestly say whether or not it too was assigned for loading at *Semet-Solvay*.) It had a staff brake and four steel channels across the top center of the car to lend support to the car sides. Apparently just the actual corrugated roofing was removed by cutting the rivets. The car was stenciled "When Empty Return to Delray Connecting RR. Detroit, Mich." The A.A.R. mechanical designation for the car was an LP.

The 50' 3" PRR 74301 (the only car in the series) was an X38n. As mentioned earlier, the doors were permanently removed and the sides and ends were strengthened with a type of steel channel. The car appeared to have either a *Universal* or *Miner* Hand Brake. This car too was designated an LP and was stenciled, "When Empty Return to Delray Connecting RR. Detroit, Mich."

Even if you do not have a coke oven or foundry on your model railroad, one of these cars would certainly make an interesting addition in that train on your railroad that handles the "bridge traffic." I'm sure you will get a lot of comments from your friends!

Lastly, similar cars were also used in pulpwood service by both railroads; but that is another story and they certainly were not routed over the Delray Connecting!

Charles H. Geletzke, Jr.

DC SW1 60 was seen at Zug Island in River Rouge, Michigan on August 31, 1972.

Attack of the Moths!

By: C. H. Geletzke, Jr.

I am guessing it was the summer of 1972 and I was working for the Delray Connecting Railroad at which time, I had the BEST working hours of my entire 45-year railroad career! I had only recently gotten to know a number of other railfans located within the Detroit Metropolitan Area (including Windsor, Ontario, Canada!) and together we formed a revolving slide group, which met the first Tuesday of each month in various members' homes. Interestingly, here it is fifty years later and with the exception of the months during Covid, the informal group still periodically gets together.

Well, I will never forget…it was during the month of June, July, or August and the meeting was to be held at the home of Henry W. Burger, in the downriver community of Riverview, Michigan. Now normally our sessions would commence at 8:00 P.M.; but because of Daylight Saving Time and the heat of the year and due to the fact that most of our homes were not air conditioned, we elected to hold this gathering after dark in Henry's driveway, making it actually start around 8:30 P.M. As I recall we had a turnout of around 15 participants including such railfan notables as the late Emery J. Gulash; the late Tom Lendzion; the late owner of *Starr Hobbies*, Bill Maguire and his late son and DT&I employee, Larry; Kenneth D. Borg; the late Ray Sabo; PC Operator, Ken Annett; Earl Minnis; the late PC Dispatcher, Mike McIlwaine; N&W Tugboat Captain, Ted Hanifan; GTW Conductor, Dennis Smolinski; Dr. Norm Herbert D.D.S.; Bob Ballard; streetcar historian Bernie Droulliard; the late John Bjorklund; the late Dick Vartabedian; and a number of others. Let me state that at this time, I really did not know many of these guys very well.

Please permit me to mention that for the previous several months, group member, Dick Vartabedian had called me, ALMOST WEEKLY, begging for me to arrange a visit for him and several his friends to the car shops of the Delray Connecting to enable them to photograph all six of the carrier's units at that time! I promised him, that when it was convenient (for me and the railroad) I would arrange a photo session. Let me also state that he was very demanding in his request…that is, he expected all of the units to be pulled out of the house and had to be "positioned in the proper direction, so that they would experience the full and complete brightness of the sun!" Eventually, I got tired of his incessant calls and finally relented! I quickly became aware that even at our monthly slide shows, Mr. Vartabedian could be equally demanding when it was his turn to set the stage!

So, here we all were in Mr. Berger's backyard and it was finally Mr. V's turn to show his slides. He sat down in the chair next to the "required" *KODAK Carousel* Projector and carefully placed an enormous stack of slides in the stack-loader. Shortly he began his presentation…I am going to guess that we had probably viewed about ten of Dick's slides, when all of a sudden…out of nowhere, a moth flew right inside the projector and could be seen fluttering around behind the lens! Naturally, everyone started laughing, that is,

Charles H. Geletzke, Jr.

with the exception of Dick! He went into a self-induced panic that the winged creature was going "to ruin his slide!"

Let me state that HELP WAS ON THE WAY! Faster than any of us ever expected, Henry Burger leaped out of his seat over on the left side of the audience, pulled a can of insect spray out from under his chair, and practically flew over toward the location of the presenter and the projector. Then, taking no more than a single second, he aimed the nozzle of the can directly down into the top of that expensive *KODAK* machine and fired off a burst of spray killing the winged insect instantly! Simultaneously, Dick Vartabedian went into a rage screaming how Henry had ruined his slide! As for the rest of us we laughed hysterically in total disbelief! Dick screamed and yelled for several minutes until Henry finally took command and asked, "Who's going next?"

After that we never had more than one or two more outdoor shows…While they were a great deal of fun; but because of the late starting time, we had to cut the evening way too short; however in all my years as a railfan I must say that was the only time I ever experienced something like that! And, I am still amazed that the chemical spray did not immediately burst into flames when it contacted that hot projector bulb!?!

Total Exhaustion

By: GTW Operator, RI-BN-SOO Engineer, Richard Haave

Every night in Chicagoland there would be a line of yard engines and transfer jobs in both directions waiting to do their work at Chicago Junction's (CJ) Ashland Avenue yard. We'd pull close enough to couple the air hose on the front of our engine to the standing caboose ahead of us and open the angle cock on our engine. When the guy ahead moved… POW!!!…instant alarm clock!

Confessions of a Quitter or,
"We May Never Pass This Way Again..."*

By: C. H. Geletzke, Jr.

In previous volumes I mentioned how I had been working for the Delray Connecting Railroad in Detroit, Michigan from May 21, 1971 through November 3, 1972 as a Carman Helper, a Switchman, and following graduation from college in December 1971 as Assistant to the General Manager.

After interviewing with the Missouri Pacific Railroad in St. Louis, Missouri in October of 1972, I was offered a position as a Managerial Trainee working out of their St. Louis headquarters in their Management Training Program, which was supposed to last an entire year. To me this was a fantastic opportunity, because not only was it recognized as the best railroad training program in North America at that time; but it was designed so that all of we trainees would spend anywhere from one day up to six full weeks in virtually every department on the railroad! Please allow me to digress a little here to state also, for those trainees who would be going into Freight Sales, they would undergo an 18-month program, as they would be required to additionally spend six full months in one of the railroad's off-line sales offices (These would include points such as Boston, Detroit, New York City, Cleveland, etc.; that is, major cities that were actually not at on-line Missouri Pacific locations.) There were several other major advantages to this training ground. I soon learned that graduates would rise quickly up the ladder following graduation and would immediately move into positions with a great deal of responsibility. Interestingly also, was the fact that there were a number of trainees whose fathers were working in high level positions on other railroads and truck lines and somehow encouraged or possibly "arranged" for their sons to go through and complete the MP's outstanding program! Just off the top of my head, I recall trainees whose fathers worked for the

Charles H. Geletzke, Jr.

Baltimore & Ohio; Chicago & Northwestern; Duluth, Missabe & Iron Range; the Milwaukee Road; and the Missouri Pacific itself; not to mention several major trucking companies. Lastly, upon completion of the program the "former trainee" would receive a 60% pay increase upon moving into his/her new managerial position.

Now since I entered the Training Program and became a MOPAC employee on November 6, 1972; I assumed that I would complete the program on or about November 5, 1973. Well apparently something changed for both me and another trainee, Lawrence Conley, as with only about two weeks notice, each of us was informed on July 17th, that we would be promoted to Assistant Trainmasters and be assigned to managerial positions effective August 1, 1973! Larry, who was married, was told that he would be going to Jefferson City, Missouri and I was instructed to report to Freeport, Texas. Company policy dictated that they would arrange and handle the physical move itself and provide lodging for each of us (and our families) up to 90-days if necessary. In actuality, we were "encouraged" to locate suitable "permanent" housing and secure utilities as quickly as possible!

Now neither Larry nor I ever heard the actual details as to why we were receiving the early step-up...without even completing the program. I always assumed part of the reason was, in my case, because I already had over six year's railroad experience. I cannot recall if Larry had previously worked in the railroad industry before or not; but his father, R. C. Conley, was the Superintendent Transportation on the C&NW, and Larry was certainly a sharp railroader!

With less than two weeks remaining until I would have to leave St. Louis and head for Texas, it occurred to me that I'd better make at least one major preparation! You see at that time I was driving a *1971 Plymouth Duster*, and being from Michigan, at that age, having an air-conditioned vehicle had never been a major priority to me...come to think of it, the vehicle only had an AM radio too! So, I made an appointment with one of the local automotive air-conditioning service dealers and arranged to have an "after-market" unit installed in my car…once completed, that product occupied 1/3 of the leg-room in the front seat! As I've said previously, I always was frugal!

Beginning Wednesday, July 25th, both Larry and I spent three days in Rules and Safety Classes with Mr. T. Turner. On the last day we were given a Rules Exam.

Since I was still in the U. S. Army Reserve's 226th Railway Shop Battalion at that time, I attended my monthly weekend drill on the last weekend of the month.

As far as the move itself, for me, everything was very simple, as I had basically been living out of my suit cases and the trunk of my car since the previous November. On the actual day of the move, I had been subletting the apartment of another trainee, Carl Englund; all I had to do was carry everything down the steps to my car and thoroughly clean his apartment. Following my weekend Reserve drill, I just headed to Texas. On the first evening I drove as far as West Memphis, Arkansas. (I later was told that that little city had a reputation of being one of the toughest towns in the United States! I had no idea; but fortunately did not encounter any trouble.)

Rising early on Monday, July 30th, I ate breakfast and then took off for Freeport, Texas. It was almost dark as I rolled into town and I checked into a room at the *Holiday Inn* in adjacent Lake Jackson.

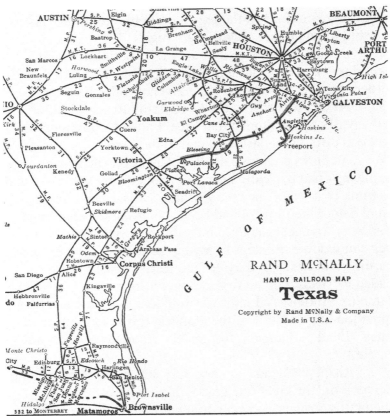

Map of Texas showing the Kingsville Division of the
Missouri Pacific. (Rand McNally *Handy Railroad Atlas of
the U.S.*-1965)

Since I was not scheduled to begin work until August
1st, my plan was to spend the next day exploring the area and
perhaps even do a little railfanning. Well, I immediately
screwed that idea up in a matter of minutes! You see one of
the other fellows, Mike Pipkin, who I had gotten to know
during the training program had also been assigned to
Freeport, only a month or two earlier. Assuming that he
would probably be working evenings I thought that I would
give him a call…**HUGE MISTAKE!** It turned out Mike was
not in the office and instead the telephone was answered by,
Mr. M. G. "Machine Gun" Jackson, the Assistant General

"Soak It!!!"… and Other Railroad Stories

Manager of the Gulf District, headquartered in Houston, who happened to be in the office. He was excited to know that I was "already" in town, and instructed me to report in the morning at 10:00 A.M. and meet the Division Superintendent, Mr. K. M. Holloway. So much for a day of exploration and fun…i.e. railfanning!

On Tuesday, July 31st, while still technically a member of the Management Training Program and still being paid as a trainee, I reported for duty promptly at 10 o'clock and introduced myself to both Mr. Holloway, the Superintendent of the Kingsville Division (headquartered in Corpus Christi) and to Mr. Jackson. Incidentally, following introductions, Mr. Jackson stated to me very matter-of-factly, "Now understand, YOU will be working seven days a week, twelve hours a day, and you WILL have every other weekend off! And oh yes, while you are employed on the Kingsville Division, YOU WILL ALWAYS WEAR HIGH-TOPPED COMBAT BOOTS…so the snakes don't getcha!"

I quickly responded, "I learned that during the Management Training Program"…and that work schedule seemed pretty universal throughout the Operating Department."

MP Freeport, TX Freight Office as seen in Fall 1973.

Together they escorted me through the new freight office and introduced me to Mrs. Brister, the Agent and all of her staff. Interestingly, the east half of the building was still strictly devoted to LTL (Less than Truck Load) Freight, which was trucked in every day except Sunday.

The two corporate officers then explained the workings of the Kingsville Division, and in particular the Brownsville Subdivision, which ran from Brownsville (Milepost 0.7) at the southern tip of Texas up to Settegast Yard (M.P. 377.0) located in Houston. In actuality, at that time the Brownsville Sub. (which was originally the St. Louis, Brownsville & Mexico Railroad or St.LB&M) was divided into three crew districts. The first ran 118 miles south from Kingsville (M.P. 118.4, the division's shop town) to Brownsville. The middle portion of the subdivision ran for a distance of 121.7 miles along the Gulf Coast from Kingsville to Vanderbilt (M.P. 240.1). And the third portion of the Brownsville Subdivision, which I would be responsible for, ran 103.1 miles from Vanderbilt to Algoa (M.P. 343.2) where we actually began operating over Santa Fe (AT&SF) trackage rights on into Settegast Yard. Additionally under my care would be the 15.4 mile long Freeport Subdivision (H&BV or former Houston & Bravos Valley RR) running from the Gulf of Mexico in Freeport (M.P. 15.4) to Angleton, Texas (M.P. 0.0) where the line connected with the Brownsville Sub. at Milepost 320.0.

I quickly learned that the bulk of my time would be spent working between Freeport and Angleton and that on that 15 mile stretch of railroad they operated 12 six –day-a week Traveling Switch Engines and that additionally, there were four more going on and off duty at Angleton. Lastly, I would be responsible for the Sweeny Switcher servicing Phillips Petroleum at Milepost 300.8 in Sweeny, Texas and a seasonal switch engine at Milepost 283.8 in Bay City, Texas. Oh yes, that just accounted for all of the TSE's or Traveling Switchers; additionally over the territory on a normal day there were three through freights operating in both directions between Houston and Vanderbilt and the two HOTEST trains on the entire Missouri Pacific System, Train LFR (Little Rock-Freeport) and AA or "Double-A" (Angleton-Alton & Southern)…more about all of these trains later.

Later in the day, I was introduced to the man in charge of this operation, Trainmaster, V. L. "Vern" Adams; but to me, he was always just Mr. Adams! He was a man in his later 50's (I would guess) and had commenced his railroad career working for his father who was a Section Foreman or Roadmaster on the former New Orleans & Lower Coast Railroad in the bayou country of Louisiana.

Charles H. Geletzke, Jr.

54 BROWNSVILLE SUBDIV.—KINGSVILLE DIVISION

BROWNSVILLE SUBDIV.—SPECIAL INSTRUCTIONS

ABS-CTC (AT&SF-TCS) New South Yard—South Switch Inari and between MP 162.0 Sinton Jct. and Odem MP 154-24.

Operation on AT&SF Ry. between New South Yard and Algoa—be governed by Uniform Code of Operating Rules and Special Instructions Item 7-(a).

Two main tracks between Alvin and Algoa—the track to the right as observed by Southward Train is designated South track. Track to the right as observed by Northward train is designated North Track.

On AT&SF the timetable direction T&NO Jct. to Alvin is eastward, Alvin to Algoa westward.

Southward trains secure clearance Settegast Yd. and AT&SF numbered clearance card at New South Yard.

On AT&SF maximum speed permitted through remote control switches 30 MPH, except 15 MPH through switches at east end of two tracks at Alvin.

AT&SF timetable not required between New South Yard and Algoa.

When using HB&T tracks, Houston, HB&T Timetable and Special Instructions apply.

No. 366 may leave Harlingen without a clearance when train order signal indicates proceed.

No. 366, No. 367 and No. 94 may leave Kingsville without clearance when train order signal indicates proceed.

After No. 366 arrives Kingsville crew designated to handle No. 366 between Kingsville and Odem may assume schedule of No. 366 without train order authority.

After No. 367 arrives Kingsville crew designated to handle No. 367 between Kingsville and Harlingen may assume schedule of No. 367 at Kingsville without train order authority.

Item 13 (1) of Special Instructions will apply between Brownsville and Harlingen.

Maximum Speed:	MPH
Brownsville-Harlingen	35
(Except as below)	
MP 18-0—MP 22-2	20
MP 24-24—MP 25-17	15
Harlingen—MP 118-29	40
MP 118-29—MP 204-10	49
(Except as below)	
MP 154-23—MP 155-03	20
MP 161-17—MP 162-07	15
MP 204-10—Algoa	60
(Except as below)	
MP 215-28—MP 216-01	50
MP 277-07—MP 277-28	50
MP 282-22—MP 285-15	30
MP 305-14—MP 305-17	35
MP 342-28—MP 343-09	25
Algoa—Settegast Yard	45
(Except as below)	
Around two curves on AT&SF MP 0-0 to MP 0.5 west of Alvin	30
Over T&NO crossing MP 19.4	40
T&NO Jct.—Settegast Yard	20

BUSINESS TRACKS:	MP Sta. Nos.
Phillips Petroleum	337.8 B-338
Monsanto Storage (2 tracks)	335.9 B-336
Chocolate Bayou Spur	335.6 B-336
Danbury	327.3 B-327
Brazoria Clemens	308.6 B-309
Pan American Petroleum Spur	298.5 B-299
Abercrombie	297.1 B-297
Celanese Storage (2 tracks)	277.3 B-277
Elmaton	269.6 B-276
Keeran Spur	232.6 B-234
McFaddin	209.4 B-209
Refco Corp.	190.4 B-190
Cranell	173.6 B-174
Calallen	148.1 B-148
Corpus Christi Filtration Plant	147.3 B-147
Lon Hill	146.7 B-147
Driscoll	132.1 B-132
Chemcel	122.8 B-123
Ricardo	112.0 B-112
Riviera	103.1 B-103
Turcotte	82.8 B-83
Yturria	52.4 B-52
Lyford	41.4 B-41
Sebastian	36.9 B-37
Russelltown	14.1 B-14

Yard Limits:

MP 00-0 to MP 28-6 ;
MP 45-12 to MP 48-25;
MP 76-15 to MP 78-15;
MP 116-0 to MP 125-30;
MP 152-20 to MP 154-24.

Max. Wt. Brownsville—Matamoros 240,000 lbs.

Industrial Spurs:

Celanese Industrial Lead—
Breaks out at MP 277
Max. Speed .... 10 MPH.

Phillips Refinery Spur—
Max. Speed .... 10 MPH;

Monsanto Industrial Lead—
Max. Speed .... 15 MPH;

Wye, Algoa—Max. Speed..25 MPH

Monte Alto Industrial Lead
(between Raymondville and Monte Alto 20.9 miles)
Max. Speed .... 15 MPH
Max. Wt. 240,000 lbs.

Business Tracks	Sta. MP No.
LaSara	8.6 BP -8
Hargill	14.8 BW-15
Monte Alto	20.0 BW-5

Rio Hondo Ind. Lead
(San Benito to Rio Hondo—9.0 miles)
Max. speed is 15 MPH except 5 MPH over Highway 77, San Benito.
Max Wt. .... 220,000 lbs.

Business tracks	Sta. M.P. No.
Fresnal	6.6 BS-6
Rio Hondo	9.0 BS-9
Ⓧ MP 5.5 SP Ⓜ	

Brownsville Port Line:
Max. Speed 15 MPH except Highway Crossing MP 6-9..6 MPH

Brownsville Belt Line:
Max. Speed 12 MPH except Street Crossing MP 0-08 to MP 0-16 .... 5 MPH
Ⓧ MP 1-16 SP-G

TIMETABLE NO. 3

Page 54 MP Employee Timetable 3, dated December 1, 1972

"Soak It!!!"… and Other Railroad Stories

BROWNSVILLE SUBDIV.—KINGSVILLE DIVISION 55

SOUTH								NORTH	
SECOND CLASS		All siding switches Algoa to Inari inclusive are No. 15 or 16 turnouts.		Station No.	Sidings			SECOND CLASS	
367	95							366	94
Daily	Daily	Miles	STATIONS			Cars	Feet	Daily	Daily
			W§D ⊙T ⓑ O						
. . . . .	. . . . .	377.0	SETTEGAST YD.	B-379	Yd.	. . .		. . . . .	. . . . .
		368.1 8.9	NEW SOUTH YD. O	B-368	Yd.	. . .			
. . . . .	. . . . .	20.3 0.9	T&NO JCT . . . XSP ᴹ O					. . . . .	. . . . .
		19.4 5.4	T&NO JCT . . . . O						
. . . . .	. . . . .	14.0 4.0	MYKAWA			150	9350	. . . . .	. . . . .
. . . . .	. . . . .	10.0 5.9	PEARLAND . . . . O			108	5400	. . . . .	. . . . .
. . . . .	. . . . .	4.1 4.1	HASTINGS			256	12800	. . . . .	. . . . .
. . . . .	. . . . .	0.0 28.6	ALVIN . . . . TO			Yd.		. . . . .	. . . . .
. . . . .	. . . . .	24.4 343.2	ALGOA 4.2	B-343		. . .		. . . . .	. . . . .
			0.4						
. . . . .	. . . . .	342.8 9.4	BROWNIE . . . . T	B-342		192	9636	. . . . .	. . . . .
. . . . .	. . . . .	333.4 13.4	LIVERPOOL	B-333		110	5494	. . . . .	. . . . .
. . . . .	. . . . .	320.0 14.5	ANGLETON . W ⓑT	B-321		107	5358	. . . . .	. . . . .
. . . . .	. . . . .	305.5 4.7	S. BERNARD R ⓓ ᴹ	B-306		. . .		. . . . .	. . . . .
. . . . .	. . . . .	300.8 9.1	SWEENY . . . . W ⊙ ⓑ	B-301		102	5095	. . . . .	. . . . .
. . . . .	. . . . .	291.7 7.6	ALLENHURST	B-292		108	5394	. . . . .	. . . . .
. . . . .	. . . . .	284.1 0.3	XA.T.& S.F. . . . . ᴹ			. . .		. . . . .	. . . . .
. . . . .	. . . . .	283.8 8.6	BAY CITY . . . . . . T	B-284		102	5121	. . . . .	. . . . .
. . . . .	. . . . .	275.2 10.3	BUCKEYE	B-275		107	5379	. . . . .	. . . . .
. . . . .	. . . . .	264.9 0.3	XS.P . . . . ᴹ			. . .		. . . . .	. . . . .
. . . . .	. . . . .	264.6 14.9	BLESSING	B-265		105	5241	. . . . .	. . . . .
. . . . .	. . . . .	249.7 4.8	LA WARD	B-250		105	5257	. . . . .	. . . . .
. . . . .	. . . . .	244.9 4.8	LOLITA (PCN Conn)	B-245		. . .		. . . . .	. . . . .
			ⓑW						
. . . . .	. . . . .	240.0 10.6	VANDERBILT ⓑ O	B-240	Yd.	. . .		. . . . .	. . . . .
. . . . .	. . . . .	229.5 5.2	CARR	B-230		111	5547	. . . . .	. . . . .
. . . . .	. . . . .	224.3 5.0	PLACEDO XS.P . . ᴹ	B-224		. . .		. . . . .	. . . . .
. . . . .	. . . . .	219.3 3.3	BLOOMINGTON. ⓑ ⊙WT O	B-219		127	6375	. . . . .	. . . . .
. . . . .	. . . . .	216.0 10.3	BARGE CANAL ᴹ ⓓ			. . .		. . . . .	. . . . .
. . . . .	. . . . .	205.7 12.3	INARI	B-205		150	7521	. . . . .	. . . . .
. . . . .	. . . . .	193.4 7.4	GRETA	B-193		145	7252	. . . . .	. . . . .
. . . . .	. . . . .	186.0 6.0	REFUGIO . . . . . ⓑ	B-186		. . .		. . . . .	. . . . .
. . . . .	. . . . .	180.0 17.9	WOODSBORO	B-180		128	6392	. . . . .	. . . . .
. . . . .	. . . . .	162.1 0.1	SINTON	B-162		44	2224	. . . . .	. . . . .
PM	AM	162.0 7.5	SINTON JCT X SP ⒶⓑⓎ			. . .		AM	PM
4 00	3 40	154.5 13.1	ODEM XMP.. ⓖTO	B-155		73	3656	7 25	6 45
4 20	4 05	141.4 16.5	ROBSTOWN XTMⒶ	B-141		115	5773	7 05	6 25
4 45 94	4 30	124.9 6.5	BISHOP . . . . . . Ⓨ ⊙DW ⓑ	B-125		. . .		6 40	6 01 367
5 00 9 00	4 40	118.4 21.0	KINGSVILLE . Ⓨ O	B-119	Yd.	. . .		6 30	5 00
9 30	AM	97.6 20.6	SARITA	B-98		85	4249	5 35	PM
10 05	. . . . .	77.0 9.4	ARMSTRONG . . . Ⓨ	B-77		107	5364	5 01	. . . . .
10 20	. . . . .	67.6 21.2	NORIAS	B-68		82	4098	4 40	. . . . .
10 55	. . . . .	46.4 19.6	RAYMONDVILLE ⓑ ⓎT O	B-46		104	5228	4 05	. . . . .
. . . . .	. . . . .	26.8 1.2	XS.P. . . . Ⓐ ⓑⓎTDW			. . .		. . . . .	. . . . .
11 30	. . . . .	25.6 6.6	HARLINGEN ⓐ§ O	B-25	Yd.	. . .		3 30	. . . . .
PM	. . . . .	19.0 10.0	SAN BENITO	B-19		. . .		AM	. . . . .
. . . . .	. . . . .	9.0 8.3	OLMITO	B-9		. . .		. . . . .	. . . . .
. . . . .	. . . . .	0.7	BROWNSVILLE.§ⓑO	B-0	Yd.	. . .		. . . . .	. . . . .
			377.0						

No. 95 and No. 367 are superior to No. 366.
TIMETABLE NO. 3

Page 55 MP Employee Timetable 3, dated December 1, 1972

FREEPORT SUBDIV.—KINGSVILLE DIVISION 57

Miles	SOUTH ▼ STATIONS NORTH ▲	Station No.	Crews operating between Freeport and Palestine will secure clearance before leaving Angleton.
0.0	ANGLETON . . . . . ⓨ◨WT ⑧	B-321	Yard Limits Entire Subdiv. Maximum Speed .... 30 (Except as Below)
9.5	9.5 CLUTE	BH-8	Freeport-Brazos River Bridge. 10 Hoskins Ind. lead 15
11.4	1.9 HOSKINS JCT . . . . T	BH-6	Except over Bastrop Bayou Bridge MP 8-13 to MP 8-21 10
15.4	4.0 FREEPORT . . . . ◨ⓑWD§	BH-0	Sta.
	15.4		BUSINESS TRACKS: MP No. Ross 7.3 BH-10

Hoskins Ind. Lead:
Max. Wt. 220,000 Lbs.

Freeport & End of Track
220,000 Lbs.

Page 57 MP Employee Timetable 3, dated December 1, 1972.

Now because this will probably be the longest story that I have ever included in any of my books, I am going to summarize the important or relevant information for you.

MP Train 860 ready to depart the east end of 4-track Angleton Yard on October 28, 1973 with units 899-536-1941.

Hours Worked Per Week

Date:	Start Time:	Time Finished:	Total Hours Worked:
Tues. 7-30	1000	2400	14'0"
Wed. 8-1	0001	0230	2'30"
Wed. 8-1	1200	2400	12'0"
Thur. 8-2	0001	0100	1'0"
Thur. 8-2	1230	1930	7'0"
Fri. 8-3	0630	2400	17'30"
Sat. 8-4	0001	0555	5'55"
Sat. 8-4	1330	2400	10'30"
Sun. 8-5	1500	1730	2'30"
Mon. 8-6	1245	2400	11'45"
Tues. 8-7	0001	0530	5'30"
		Week Total:	**88'10"**
Tues. 8-7	1300	2400	11'0"
Wed. 8-8	0001	0500	5'0"
Wed. 8-8	1300	2400	11'0"
Thur. 8-9	0001	0200	2'0"
Thur. 8-9	1300	2400	11'0"
Fri. 8-10	0001	0130	1'30"
Fri. 8-10	1300	2400	11'0"
Sat. 8-11	0001	0230	2'30"
Sat. 8-11	1400	1730	3'30"
Sat. 8-11	2300	2400	1'0"
Sun. 8-12	0001	1530	15'30"
Mon. 8-13	0530	2400	18'30"
Tues. 8-14	0001	0530	5'30"
		Week Total:	**98'30"**
Tues. 8-14	1400	1600	2'0"
Tues. 8-14	1800	1940	1'40"
Wed. 8-15	0001	1201	12'0"
Wed. 8-15	2300	2400	1'0"
Thur. 8-16	0001	1200	12'0"
Thur. 8-16	2300	2400	1'0'
Fri. 8-17	0001	1200	12'0"
Fri. 8-17	2300	2400	1'0"
Sat. 8-18	0001	1100	11'0" (Off Day?)
Sun. 8-19	Off Day		
Mon. 8-20	2300	2400	1'0"
Tues. 8-21	0001	1200	12'0"
		Week Total:	**66'40"**

69

Hours Worked Per Week (Continued)

Date:	Start Time:	Time finished:	Total Hours Worked:
Tues. 8-21	2300	2400	1'0"
Wed. 8-22	0001	1100	11'0"
Wed. 8-22	2300	2400	1'0"
Thur. 8-23	0001	1400	14'0"
Fri. 8-24	0030	1400	13'30"
Fri. 8-24	2345	2400	15"
Sat. 8-25	0001	1500	15'0"
Sun. 8-26	0100	0300	2'0"
Sun. 8-26	0400	0530	1'30"
Sun. 8-26	0730	1500	7'30"
Mon. 8-27	0001	1400	14'0"
		Week Total:	**80'45"**
Tues. 8-28	0001	1500	15'0"
Wed. 8-29	0001	1500	15'0"
Thur. 8-30	0001	1600	16'0"
Fri. 8-31	0001	1400	14'0"
Sat. 9-1	0001	1400	14'0"
Sun. 9-2	0001	2400	24'0"
Mon. 9-3	0001	0145	1'45"
Mon. 9-3	0700	2400	17'0"
Tues. 9-4	0001	0930	9'30"
		Week Total:	**126'15"**
Tues. 9-4	2130	2400	2'30"
Wed. 9-5	0001	1200	12'0"
Wed. 9-5	2100	2400	3'0"
Thur. 9-6	0001	1630	16'30"
Thur. 9-6	2100	2400	3'0"
Fri. 9-7	0001	1600	16'0"
Fri. 9-7	2000	2400	4'0"
Sat. 9-8	0001	1600	16'0"
Sat. 9-8	2100	2400	3'0"
Sun. 9-9	0001	1430	14'30"
Mon. 9-10	0200	0300	1'0"
Mon. 9-10	2230	2400	1'30"
Tues. 9-11	0001	1200	12'0"
		Week Total:	**105'0"**

Hours Worked Per Week (Continued)

Date:		Start Time:	Time Finished:	Total Hours Worked:
Tues.	9-11	2300	2400	1'0"
Wed.	9-12	0001	1300	13'0"
Wed.	9-12	2300	2400	1'0"
Thur.	9-13	0001	1330	13'30"
Fri.	9-14	0001	1630	16'30"
Fri.	9-14	1900	2400	5'0"
Sat.	9-15	0001	0030	30"
Sat.	9-15	Army Reserve Day		
Sun.	9-16	0300	0400	1'0"
Sun.	9-16	Army Reserve Day		
Mon.	9-17	Off Day		
			Week Total:	**51'30"**
Tues.	9-18	0001	1500	15'0"
Wed.	9-19	0001	1300	13'0"
Thur.	9-20	0001	1430	14'30"
Thur.	9-20	2130	2400	2'30"
Fri.	9-21	0001	1430	14'30"
Sat.	9-22	0001	1800	18'0"
Sun.	9-23	0001	1330	13'30"
Mon.	9-24	0200	0300	1'0"
Mon.	9-24	0600	1500	9'0"
			Week Total:	**101'0"**
Tues.	9-25	0001	1730	17'30"
Wed.	9-26	0200	1400	12'0"
Thur.	9-27	0200	1400	12'0"
Fri.	9-28	0200	1200	10'0"
Sat.	9-29	0200	1400	12'0"
Sun.	9-30	0200	1200	10'0"
Sun.	9-30	1655	Fly to Detroit.	
Mon.	10-1	On Vacation		
			Week Total:	**73'30"**
Tues.	10-2	On Vacation		
Wed.	10-3	On Vacation		
Thur.	10-4	On Vacation		
Fri.	10-6	On Vacation		
Sat.	10-6	On Vacation		
Sun.	10-7	On Vacation		
Mon.	10-8	On Vacation		
			Week total:	**0'0"**

Hours Worked Per Week (Continued)

Date:		Start Time:	Time finished:	Total Hours Worked:
Tues.	10-9	On Vacation		
Wed.	10-10	On Vacation		Fly back to Houston.
Thur.	10-11	0030	1200	11'30"
Fri.	10-12	0100	1300	12'0"
Sat.	10-13	0200	2200	20'0"
Sun.	10-14	0400	1330	9'30"
Mon.	10-15	0200	0400	2'0"
Mon.	10-15	0630	1130	5'0"
				Week Total: 60'0"
Tues.	10-16	0200	2000	18'0"
Wed.	10-17	0400	1930	15'30"
Thur.	10-18	0500	1500	10'0"
Fri.	10-19	0300	2030	17'30"
Sat.	10-20	Army Reserve Duty		
Sun.	10-21	Army Reserve Duty		
Sun.	10-21	1900	2100	2'0"
Mon.	10-22	0600	1100	5'0"
				Week Total: 68'0"
Tues.	10-23	0200	1400	12'0"
Wed.	10-24	0200	1800	16'0"
Thur.	10-25	0300	1600	13'0"
Fri.	10-26	0300	1600	13'0"
Sat.	10-27	0130	1500	13'30"
Sun.	10-28	0001	0430	4'30"
Sun.	10-28	0630	1300	6'30"
Mon.	10-29	0800	0815 "Resigned!"	15"
				Week Total: 86'15"

You can see that during 12 weeks of actual work, I averaged working just under 84-hours per week!

Union Pacific (former MP) lift bridge over the Intracoastal
Waterway at Freeport, Texas on September 28, 2014.

(Back to July 31, 1973)

Shortly Mr. Jackson and Mr. Holloway left the
terminal and I spent the remainder of the day/evening
shadowing Mr. Adams. Mr. Adams finally sent me back to
my motel at 2:30 A.M., making it a 16-hour and 30-minute
day!

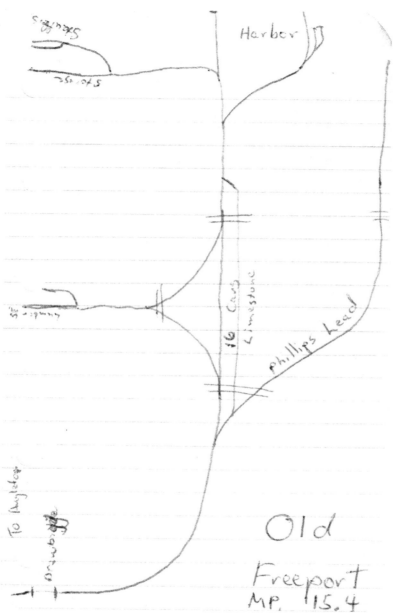

Old Freeport "across the river" track diagram 1973

"Soak It!!!"… and Other Railroad Stories

Later the second day (August 1st), I was declared "officially" a Missouri Pacific Assistant Trainmaster. Mr. Adams had me report at Noon and once again, I followed him around until 1:00 A.M., just a 13-hour day. (See track diagrams) We visited the *Freeport Harbor Terminal*, the Lumber Mill, and *Stauffer Chemicals* on the south side of the Intra-coastal Waterway. Mr. Adams even showed me the lift bridge over the Intracoastal Waterway. We drove out to the Phillips Lead in Old Freeport. Just north of the depot in Freeport the MP had an eight track yard, named Velasco Yard or Midway Yard. This facility had a railroad scale, which on a normal day would weigh over 200-cars! At its south end were the Rip Track and the Lead to *Dow Chemical's Plant A*. Oh yes, before I go any further at all, let me interject the fact that *Dow Chemical Corporation* alone, within their two Freeport Plants had 52-miles of track! Traveling a little further north on the Freeport Sub., we arrived at another small double-ended yard, at M.P. 11.4 known as Hoskins Jct. This was a six track yard with a wye where years ago a short branchline originated, serving a community known as Hoskins Mound. Sadly, this town and its adjacent industries were destroyed by a hurricane in the early 1960's! From Hoskins Jct. north to Angleton was a relatively straight shot with little additional industry along the way. Shortly I would learn that Angleton was really the key to keeping this entire operation fluid and even though it really only had a four track yard (at that time), every morning it would assemble three major northbound trains, and one more going south! Oh yes, let me interject three more key factors pertaining to the operation of this area…first, it was the world's largest producer of Sulfur! Second, it was the highest revenue producing point on the entire 13,000 mile Missouri Pacific System! And third, **NONE OF THE YARDS IN EITHER FREEPORT OR ANGLETON FUNCTIONED USING YARDMASTERS!** All of the operations were directed by Trainmaster Adams and two Assistant Trainmasters 24-hours a day, seven days a week! Now I was to become one of those ATM's, and there lies the point of our story.

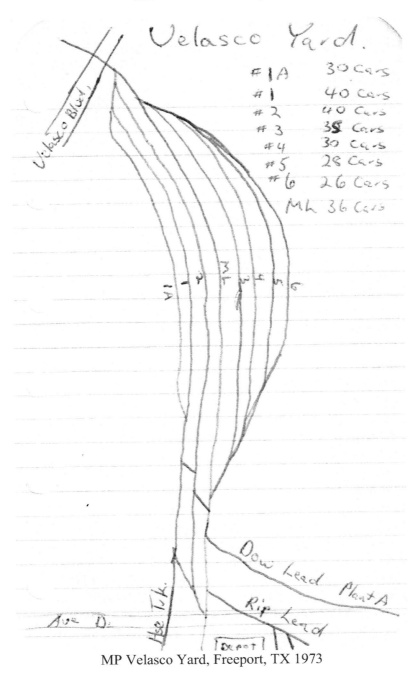

MP Velasco Yard, Freeport, TX 1973

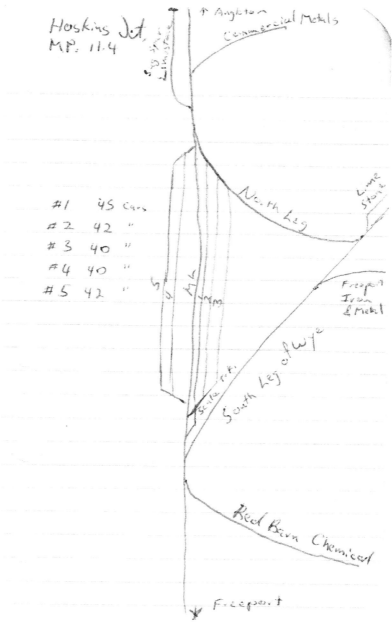

MP Hoskins Jct. track diagram in Freeport, TX 1973

Looking back, Thursday, August 2nd probably should have been marked down on the calendar as a Red Letter Day!

Charles H. Geletzke, Jr.

As instructed I reported for duty at 12:30 P.M., followed Mr. Adams around and was dismissed at 7:30 P.M., only a seven hour day, because I was instructed to report to Houston for a staff meeting the next morning at 6:30 A.M.

On Friday the 3rd I drove to the MP depot in Angleton and was picked up by Trainmaster Adams in the company car. Together we drove to the Houston Union Station where we attended a meeting of about thirty Gulf Coast District officers. Following the session, Mr. Adams took me to the office of the Chief Train Dispatcher and introduced me to all of the working Kingsville Division Train Dispatchers as well as the Chief. From there we went downstairs and walked by the track side of the station where I spotted two sets of Amtrak units, each with a passenger F7A and B unit still in Santa Fe paint! I vowed that I'd return and photograph them; but sadly, that never happened. From there, all of us walked to a nearby buffet for lunch.

While eating, Mr. Holloway, the Kingsville Division Superintendent, received a message that freight train 858 had derailed 13-cars at Vanderbilt, Texas and he was taking off to observe the mess…I was instructed to ride along! Believe it or not, it was a fairly quiet ride, as Mr. Holloway, who actually began his railroad career as an electrician in the Kingsville Shops was not a real big talker. I guess we arrived down at Vanderbilt (Milepost 240.1) around 3:00 P.M. and do you know that I just stood around observing the activity until the final car was rerailed and I was instructed to ride Train 858 back to Angleton.

The MP Hotel in Vanderbilt, TX as seen in September 1973. Unbelievably to me, at this date, this hotel, which housed MP train crews, was still segregated! (C. H. Geletzke, Jr. photo)

The crew for Train 858 (Engineer, "Radio" Richards; Conductor, Edwards; and Brakemen, Nesbit and Sims) were ordered out of the Vanderbilt Hotel for 11:50 P.M. The train had units 431 (GP18)-121 (GP7)-562 (GP9)-115 (GP7)-146 (GP7) and 147 (GP7) with 89-cars. I helped Mr. Richards couple-up and inspect the units. We departed at 1:45 A.M., encountered air trouble, and once again got underway at 1:55 A.M. We arrived at Buckeye (M.P. 272.2) at 2:50 A.M., made a set-out, and were underway at 3:20 A.M. Twenty-three minutes later at 3:43 A.M., we slowed down at Bay City (M.P. 283.8) and the Conductor put the waybills for the Buckeye setout in the bill box. At Allenhurst (M.P. 291.7) we slowed down to meet Train 395 the Extra 116 (GP7) South (with Engineer Wallace and Brakemen Lucas and Jones on the headend); but did not have to stop as they were "in the clear" in the CTC siding. I noted that they gave us a proper "roll-by inspection." We arrived in Sweeny (M.P. 300.8) at 4:35 A.M. and spent 30-minutes setting out. We finally arrived back at Angleton (M.P. 320.0) at 5:55 A.M. and I headed for my motel after being on the property for 23-hours

Charles H. Geletzke, Jr.

and 25-minutes and being not only hungry; but thoroughly exhausted!

Not stopping to eat, I reached my motel at about 6:30 A.M. and went directly to bed. I had previously been instructed to report back at the Freeport Freight Office at 1:30 P.M....seven hours later. After getting about five hours sleep, I woke-up, took a quick shower, dressed, and headed for a local restaurant. Arriving at the Freeport office at the appropriate time, I found that I would be working with friend and Assistant Trainmaster, Mike Pipkin that Saturday afternoon. Our first move was to drive the company car out to Velasco Yard or Midway Yard and pick-up the LFR (Little Rock-Freeport) crew and drive them to their hotel via the freight office. As a side note, Train LFR originated about 26-hours prior (12:01 P.M.) at Little Rock, Arkansas. The crew that we were taking to the hotel had relieved that train at Spring, Texas (M.P. 127.7 on the Trinity Sub. 22.4 miles north of Settegast Yard in Houston)...their portion of the route was 22.4 miles from Spring to Settegast Yard, 57.0 miles from Settegast to Angleton, and 15.4 miles down the Freeport Sub. to Freeport...a total of 72.4 miles. They would return via the reverse route in the morning aboard Train AA "Double-A" (Angleton-Alton & Southern), going on duty at Angleton.

Being a Saturday (August 4th) afternoon, the work was relatively light. We arranged for the 4:00 P.M. #3 Freeport TSE to go to Angleton to gather and pick-up all of the cars for Freeport. Afterward, they would weigh all required cars at Midway Yard. When finished, Mike told them they could go home.

I spent the remainder of the afternoon riding with the 3:30 P.M. Freeport crew doing the work "over the river" in "Old" Freeport, switching the Phillips Lead and *Stauffer Chemical*. I went home at midnight, having worked ten hours and thirty minutes.

Sunday, August 5th was another red letter day...I only worked at Freeport from 3:00 P.M. until 5:30 P.M. and actually spent most of that time taking photos around the Freeport roundhouse area.

"Soak It!!!"... and Other Railroad Stories

On Monday, August 6th, I got up early, ran to a laundromat and dry cleaner and later reported at Freeport at 12:45 P.M. My first task was guiding a Car Department crew out of Settegast Yard with their Cline Truck to a derailed loaded six-axle GATX tank car at the north end of Velasco Yard and watching how they rerailed it. To me this was extremely interesting, as I had never witnessed one of these trucks and their hydraulic-lifts working anywhere before. The car derailed at 2:30 P.M., was rerailed at 7:05 P.M., and the track was repaired at 8:45 P.M. I then worked with Mike Pipkin until 5:30 A.M., a 16-hour and 45-minute day, and then headed back to the motel.

Just to give you MP fans an idea of the yard power that we had available at Freeport that evening, we had the MP 1192 & 1144 (SW12's) and 1249 (SW9) on the 10:01 Freeport Job and the MP 1196 & 1198 (SW12's) working the 11:00 P.M. Freeport Job. Our extra engines were the 1143-1146-1160-1163-1166-1197 all SW12's.

During the evening of Tuesday, August 7th I had to drive a crew to Vanderbilt in our assigned company Chevrolet. Now it was not really a bad vehicle; but considering it was a 1969 with over 225,000 miles on it, I speculated it on borrowed time! That was a tremendous amount of miles on an auto with the original engine to still be operating during that era! On the return trip, the car overheated; so I pulled into a service station, which unfortunately was closed at that hour of the night. Sadly, even their water was shut-off; so when the car's engine finally cooled down sufficiently, I had to use my white MP hard hat to scoop water out of the nearby ditch in order to fill the radiator and restart the engine! Later, we will address other events concerning that vehicle.

Even though I had just passed a Rules Exam during the week prior to reporting to Freeport, on Monday, August 13th I was instructed to drive 101 miles to Bloomington, Texas (M.P. 219.3) to take another Rules Class and exam with the Kingsville Division Rules Supervisor, Bob Caldwell. Interestingly, I departed Angleton at 5:30 A.M. and returned at about 7:00 P.M., and then spent the night helping rerail a covered hopper at Freeport. This turned out to be a 24-hour day!

On August 16th I finally did a little searching and was able to rent a first floor furnished apartment in Angleton. I didn't realize it at the time; but it had one major disadvantage…it overlooked our mainline on the east side of town. Now I know the majority of you railfans would never consider that to be an issue! For me, it became a source of irritation when I was sleeping. When I would hear one of the southbound trains coming into town, I would always wake up, look out the window, and observe the cars on the headend that the train would be setting off and begin planning where they would go later in the day! I never did overcome that issue as long as I lived there!

In my earlier publications, I mentioned that I was a member of the U. S. Army Reserve's 226th Railway Shop Battalion. Let me explain a little about this, as I believe you may find it of interest. I was originally a "grunt" in the Marine Corps Reserves having enlisted in June 1970. In February 1973 I was notified by the U. S. Army that because of my railroad background, I was being conscripted into their 226th Railway (Reserve) Shop Battalion in Granite City, Illinois, effective immediately! Previously unknown to me was an agreement or law that permitted currently active railroad employees, who were members of an Army Reserve Railroad unit, to attend monthly drills with any reserve unit in the Nation; but would attend summer camp with their assigned railway battalion. In a case where the railway unit might be activated, the reservist would serve with the railway unit. I have no idea whether or not this policy is still in effect; but during my tenure in Texas I attended drills with the 348th Transportation Company (Term.) in Houston and yet was actually still a member of the 226th Railway Shop Battalion.

Before we go any further, let me give you a brief description of the Traveling Switch Engines assigned at Freeport and Angleton at that time.

Freeport Yard Jobs

8:00 A.M. #1 (off Sun.). Switches Velasco Yard, gets cut for "over the river," blocks cars for *Dow Plants A&B*, and South Cars (cars going south of Angleton on Kingsville Div.). Goes to Hoskins Jct., picks-up South Cars. Goes north to Angleton and switches *Marathon Tank Car Co.* Brings Freeport cars back to Hoskins Jct.

8:00 A.M. #2 (off Sun.). Goes to Hoskins Jct. switches cars for *Dow Plants A&B, Oyster Creek, Dow Badische* and takes cars "over the river" to be washed.

8:01 A.M. (off Sat.). Goes to *Dow Plant B*, switches plant, and brings outbound cars back to "town" (Midway Yard) when finished.

8:30 A.M. (off Sun.). Goes to *Dow Plant A*, switches plant, and brings outbound cars back to Midway Yard when finished.

9:00 A.M. (off Sun.). Switches Wash Rack at Midway. Switches out the *Dow Plant A* and Wash Rack cars, switches *NALCO*, weighs cars out of *Dow Plant A*, and inbound cars, and does all required weighing.

1:30 P.M. (off Sat.). Goes to Midway, picks-up Wash Cars for *Dow Plant B*. Works "new side" of *Dow Plant B* and brings outbound cars "to town" when finished.

3:30 P.M. (off Sun.). Goes to *GRP*, picks-up cars 8:01 Job has switched out that are ready to go and takes them to Velasco Yard. Switches out the "weighers" and puts them on a separate track. Goes to *Oyster Creek* and switches plant. Runs light to Hoskins Jct., picks-up cars for *Oyster Creek*. Then brings outbound cars to town, weighs cars on the headend, eats, then goes "over the river" to work *Freeport Harbor Terminal, Stauffer's*, and other industries.

Charles H. Geletzke, Jr.

4:00 P.M. #1 (off Sun.) Goes to *Dow Plant A*, works the "Loop," then brings outbound cars out of the plant and switches out the "spot cars," for the other side of the plant, and spots the plant.

4:00 P.M. #2 (off Sun.). Goes to *Dow Badische*, picks-up loads and takes them to *GRP* and then goes to Hoskins Jct. Picks-up inbound cars for *Dow Plant B* "Old Side," "New Side," *Dow Badische* cars, Chlorine cars, and takes them into *Dow Plant B*. After setting off, they pick-up the outbound cars that the 1:30 P.M. Job has ready, and takes them "to town."

4:00 P.M. #3 (off Sun.). Goes to Angleton, picks-up, and weighs cars at Midway.

10:01 P.M. (off Sat.). Switches Velasco yard, blocks outbound cars for Train "AA" and Houston. Takes train to Angleton.

11:00 P.M. (off Sun.). Takes "cut-cover" out of Velasco yard and goes to Hoskins Jct, switches outbound cars for Train "AA" and Houston. Takes "AA" to Angleton, brings back inbound cut of Freeport cars to Hoskins Jct., and switches them out if they have time.

Angleton Yard Jobs

12:01 P.M. Switches Angleton Yard.

2:00 P.M. Switches *AMOCO Chemical*, also Danbury, and Chocolate Bayou, and the industries around Angleton.

10:00 P.M. Switches *Monsanto Chemical* at Chocolate Bayou.

11:59 P.M. Spreads "AA" cars at Angleton, and finishes anything the 12:01 P.M. Job does not complete.

84

"Soak It!!!"… and Other Railroad Stories

For several days, beginning Saturday, August 25th another fellow, Andy Dietrich, who I had gone through the training program with was assigned to Freeport in the Mechanical Department, to fill-in for John C. Lambert, our Mechanical Supervisor, who was on vacation. I no longer recall where Andy was living (Probably in the Houston area); but he and I met for dinner that first night and later that evening drove over to Sweeny to inspect the switcher assigned there. During supper he informed me that his wife was pregnant and "due almost any time!" I felt so sorry for him, as a day or two later his wife went into labor and I don't believe that he was even able to be there for the delivery! He ran back and forth to be with her as frequently as he could; but I recall thinking to myself, "what kind of a way is this to celebrate the birth of your child!?!" If I recall correctly, he found a different job shortly thereafter.

After having been in Freeport for a little over three weeks, Saturday, August 25th was my first day to "solo" on my own at Freeport and Angleton. Not surprisingly, it turned into a fifteen hour day when I worked from midnight until 3:00 P.M.

Just to give you and idea of what constituted a normal night/day for me, here are my notes from Wednesday, August 29, 1973. Interestingly, I had John Smith, a Transportation Trainee assigned to work with me this one evening…looking back, I wonder what he thought? As was normal my night began by driving to the Freeport Freight Office and getting a "turnover" from Assistant Trainmaster, Mike Pipkin. I noted the following and continually updated details as the night progressed. Once we had all of the necessary information and after speaking with the train dispatcher in Houston, we drove out to Angleton, where we would spend the remainder of my shift.

Train 395 had been called for 7:00 P.M. out of Settegast Yard and departed at 7:40 P.M. with 19x29 (19 loads and 29 empties).

Charles H. Geletzke, Jr.

Train 858 was called for 8:15 P.M. out of Vanderbilt and would set-out 8-cars at Angleton. It arrived Angleton at 1:50 A.M.

Train 859 was called for 3:00 A.M. at Settegast Yard and departed at 3:25 A.M. with 25x41. It was by Liverpool (M.P. 333.4) at 7:25 A.M., and worked at Angleton from 7:50 A.M. until 9:25 A.M. picking-up 6x17.

Train 394 with the MP 751-749-769 (all SD40's) was called for 4:15 A.M. at Vanderbilt, by LaWard (M.P. 249.7) at 4:45 A.M., by Sweeny at 7:30 A.M., and arrived Angleton at 7:50 A.M. The three SD40's would become Train AA's power upon arrival at Angleton.

Train AA was called at Freeport for 7:15 A.M., worked at Angleton from 8:35 A.M.-9:50 A.M. and departed with 34x0 (Little Rocks) and 38x1 (Alton & Southern's), a total of 72x1 with 8,288 gross tons. The goal on Train "Double-A" was to try to run the train with one horsepower per ton! Since they would have 9,000 h.p. pulling 8,288 tons, we were in good shape! Incidentally, at that time, AA was probably the hottest train on the entire Missouri Pacific System! It was scheduled to be out of Angleton by 8:00 A.M....I can tell you in all honesty, we rarely made-it!

Train 860 was ordered at Angleton for 10:50 A.M. and its units were the MP 751 (SD40)-1901 (F7)-____. It departed with 27x0 Sandow's, 32x3 Fort Worth's, and 15x0 C&EI's, for a total of 74x3 and 8739 gross tons.

We also had a Ballast Train called out of Settegast Yard at 5:30 A.M. with units MP 548 (GP18)-939 (GP38)-656 (GP35)-T&P 14 (U30C) with 71x0.

An Extra HO (XHO) was called for 7:30 A.M. out of Settegast Yard at 7:30 A.M., arrived Angleton at 11:20 A.M. and departed at 12:10 P.M. after picking-up 81 cars.

Let me state that all of the crews that I supervised at both Freeport and Angleton were fantastic! On a normal night I would spend the bulk of my time right at Angleton working with the crew on the 11:59 P.M. job. On a normal day, this crew consisted of Conductor J. D. Hayes; Brakemen

"Soak It!!!"… and Other Railroad Stories
Clay Dove and Frank _____; and Engineer, Steven P. Merriman.

Now let's talk a little about Angleton. This small junction town had a depot as its only railroad structure, which was manned 24-7. On days, there was Agent Robert Dixon; an afternoon clerk, Able Comacho; and on nights another clerk, Mrs. Crowe. Additionally, Paul Glass was the Roadmaster and his office was located in a small cinder block shanty adjacent to the depot, which years earlier had housed a train dispatcher and a C.T. C. machine. Also stationed at Angleton was a signal maintainer, Mr. Walker, who patrolled his territory with a truck with a ramp on the back where he carried his motor car. Because Angleton just like Freeport provided LTL delivery service for local customers, we also had a contracted drayman stationed there who worked out of our freight room.

The yard trackage at Angleton was quite limited! Adjacent to the Kingsville Division C.T.C. Mainline was a four track yard bisected by a two-lane country dirt road. This added considerable problems when we tried to build two and sometimes three 100- car trains in the morning between 7 o'clock and 11:00 A.M.! Shortly after I arrived in town the railroad also constructed a new C.T. C. siding or passing track on the north side of the Mainline (compass direction), which truly helped to expedite train movements! On the Freeport or H&BV (Houston & Brazos Valley) side of the junction or wye were two double ended storage tracks adjacent to the Freeport Sub. Mainline. Just west of these was the *Marathon Tank Car Company*, which repaired and rebuilt tank cars. They had their own locomotive, a GE-44-tonner, No. 1204 (Builder's No. 12578, built in 1940). Interestingly, and truly adding to our switching problems in Angleton, *Marathon* had so many cars in town awaiting repair and on which they were paying Storage Charges, that #2 Storage Track adjacent to the H&BV Main was always full, as was No.4 Track in Angleton Yard! So, modestly speaking, we could state that we were denied the use of over 28% of our track capacity for building trains every single day!

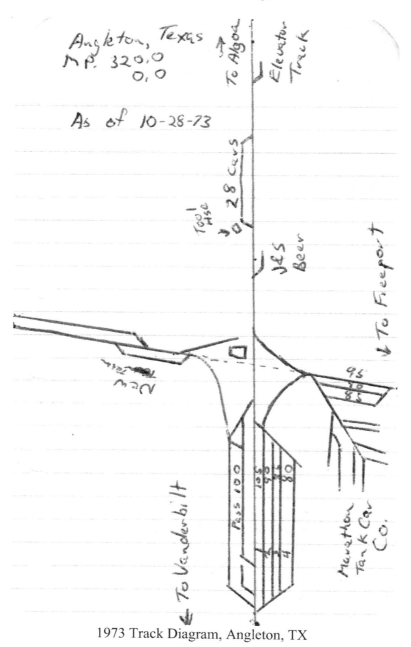

1973 Track Diagram, Angleton, TX

"Soak It!!!"... and Other Railroad Stories

Angleton Yard had one other physical disadvantage even though it was a double-ended yard. You see, just south of the south switch was a creek, which passed under the C.T.C. Main Track. Had they doubled the width of the bridge, they could have included a South Lead on which to switch without having to occupy the Mainline. Instead, anytime we wanted to perform any switching there, we had to obtain the dispatcher's permission and secure written "Track and Time" authority to occupy that track. When we did this any trains approaching from the south would have to obtain "Joint Track and Time Authority" and operate at Restricted Speed (not exceeding 15 mph and able to stop within one-half their range of vision) all the way from Sweeny (M.P. 300.8) to Angleton (M.P. 320.0)! Thus, we did very little switching at the south end of the yard. Instead we normally switched from the north end using the wye around the Mainline of the Freeport Subdivision as our switching lead. This worked fine most of the time; however, when we were lining-up cars to go south, toward Kingsville and Brownsville, it often forced us to hold onto extremely long cuts of cars, and this added a great deal of time that it took to perform each operation.

So now you can readily see that on most days, those of us working at Angleton were restricted to having only three tracks on the Brownsville Subdivision side open in which we could almost simultaneously build Trains AA and 860; after which, they would immediately go to work lining up cars in "station order" for Train 859.

So imagine this, they basically had three tracks to build Train AA with two blocks, Alton & Southern's and Little Rocks...usually about 100-cars. Then they would assemble Train 860 with four blocks, Sandows, Ft. Worth's, C&EI's, and Houston's...again another hundred cars! So, we generally had three useable tracks capable of holding 105 cars, 90 cars, and 85 cars, in which to assemble six blocks totaling 200-cars, while we simultaneously held-out another 50 or so cars to go south...not to mention having to find room for the local cars for Angleton and Chocolate Bayou!

MP Assistant Trainmaster, C. H. Geletzke, Jr. in the "Yellow Taxi" at Angleton, TX in October 1973.

The Company Car...a close call!

I have mentioned that yes we did have a "company car" assigned to us at Freeport. It was a 1969 Chevrolet in bright orange paint with a Missouri Pacific buzz-saw herald on each side. Now this vehicle had approximately 225,000 original miles on it and it still had the original engine! Because car washes were few and far between in the Freeport area, the vehicle was rarely clean! During the day shift, the car was generally driven by Mr. Adams. Mike Pipkin used it during the afternoons, and I generally had it all night. I have no idea how frequently the oil was changed!?! I'm thinking that for it to have accumulated that many miles during that era...the oil must have been kept clean!

Now around the late part of August 1973 we began having trouble getting the car to start. It turned out that it had a defective battery; however, I certainly could not get it replaced at night! We just continued to give it a "jump" when necessary. About this time I noticed that there was a crack around the Positive Terminal on the battery and that the battery post would wobble. One morning several days later at

"Soak It!!!"... and Other Railroad Stories
Angleton I went out to get the car; but as expected, it would not start. It turned out that J. C. Lambert, the Assistant General Car Inspector was in town and I asked him for a jump. While I was retrieving the jumper cables from the trunk, he immediately pulled his car up to ours. This was where I made a huge mistake and learned a valuable lifetime lesson! You see I attached the cables to John's car and then the white cable to the Negative Terminal on the Chevy and lastly the red cable to the positive terminal...at that point a spark ignited the gasses being emitted from the crack around the positive terminal and there was a huge explosion! The battery shattered into hundreds of pieces of shrapnel and battery acid flew all over me...especially all over my face! My face was covered with acid; but it was a miracle that none went into my eyes!

Later John drove me over to purchase a new battery and since that day when required to apply jumper cables to another vehicle, I always attach the cable to the positive terminal first. Yes, I was extremely lucky that day!

Several Notable Days

As I have explained several times before, I was not a Texan! I was born and raised in Michigan and while by 1973 I certainly knew how to railroad in the snow, I had no idea what I was about to face with *Tropical Storm Delia* headed directly for Freeport, Texas on Sunday, September 2, 1973!

For me, that particular Sunday began just like any other day at 12:01 A.M. and I was busy in the Angleton Freeport area of Texas just trying to "get my trains out of town." Since I was driving the Missouri Pacific's 1969 Chevy, which did not even have an am radio. I was not paying much attention to the weather and as I recall, when I began my shift and talked with the train dispatcher, the weather was not even a topic of conversation. (Let me state that we did not get anywhere close to the advanced weather information back then, that we receive today!)

Train 858 had been called for 10:00 P.M. Saturday evening out of Vanderbilt, was by Bay City at 1:15 A.M.

Charles H. Geletzke, Jr.

with 33x51 all for Houston, and went through Angleton at 4:50 A.M. and did not pick-up (this was unusual!).

Train 395 was called on Saturday for 10:15 P.M. out of South Yard in Houston and was out at 12:20 A.M. It picked-up 9x24 out of the south end of #2 Track at Angleton, arriving at 3:00 A.M. and departing at 3:15…a very quick pick-up!

Train 394 was ordered at Vanderbilt for 2:30 A.M., bye Sweeny at 4:55 A.M., and out of Angleton at 5:55 A.M. with 27x25 at 3,124 gross tons.

"Double-A" was called at Freeport for 7:45 A.M., arrived Angleton at 8:25 A.M. and out at 9:50 A.M. with 28x1 Little Rock's, 22x1 for the A&S, 19x0 Sandow's (cars for the Rockdale, Sandow & Southern), 14x0 for Ft. Worth, and 6x1 for the C&EI totaling 89x3 with 9,164 gross tons.

Things were looking pretty good and I was actually thinking that I might get to spend Sunday afternoon at the beach. Then things began to change…

Train 859 which had been ordered at Settegast at 4:45 A.M., worked at Angleton from 11:20 A.M. until 12:20 P.M. and picked-up 14x29.

Train LFR was called for 7:00 A.M. out of Spring, passed Belt Jct. at 1:10 P.M., and arrived at Angleton at 4:30 P.M. with only 9x4.

Lastly, I got word that an Extra Ballast Train was coming north and later arrived at Angleton at 7:45 P.M. and was pulled by four units…we just carefully headed it into the new siding still under construction, tied the crew up, and sent them home in a cab.

I headed for home (only two blocks away) and thought I would take a little nap; before I got out the door I had to drive to Freeport, where I wound up staying until 1:45 A.M.…just a 25-hour and 45-minute tour of duty!

On Labor Day morning, Monday, September 3, 1973 I returned to the Missouri Pacific depot in Angleton at 7:00 A.M. and relieved Assistant Trainmaster, Pipkin. Prior to my arrival, Train 858 pulled into town at 1:30 A.M. and spent one-hour picking-up and setting-out. When it departed, it also took the MP 653 a GP35 account their two units were low on fuel.

This was the only time that I encountered this on the Brownsville Division with Trains 394 and AA running in sections! Train First-394 was ordered out of Vanderbilt at 1:10 A.M., worked at Angleton from 4:20 A.M. until 5:55 A.M. and departed with only eight Houston's totaling 800 tons.

Train Second-394 was called for 3:45 A.M. at Vanderbilt and worked at Angleton between 9:05 and 11:35 A.M.

Interestingly, "Double-A" also ran in two sections! Train 1-AA with the 773-727 & ___ was called for 4:15 A.M. and departed Angleton at 8:10 A.M. with 14x0 Little Rock's, 11x0 for the Alton & Southern, 30x0 Sandow's, 9x3 Ft. Worth's, and 2x0 for the C&EI…the train totaled 66x3 and 6930 tons.

Train 2-AA was called for 9:30 A.M. on duty at Angleton instead of Freeport. They departed at 10:20 A.M. with 1x2 for the A&S, 21x0 Little Rock's, 4x0 Ft. Worth's, totaling 26x2 and 2,460 tons. The motive power consisted of units 720-711-706 three SD40's.

Train 859 worked at Angleton from 7:45 A.M. until 8:35 A.M.….I recorded no additional information.

At 6:40 P.M. Mr. K. M. Holloway called me at home (THIS WAS A FIRST!) and stated, "Alert all of your men to set hand brakes on all cars! We've got a hurricane coming in and I want you and (Assistant Trainmaster) Mike Pipkin to set handbrakes on EVERY car on the Freeport Subdivision!"

Enter Tropical Storm Delia (*WIKIPEDIA*)

Tropical Storm Delia was the first tropical cyclone on record to make landfall in the same city twice. Forming out of a tropical wave on September 1, 1973, Delia gradually strengthened into a tropical storm as it moved north by September 3. After reaching this strength, the storm turned more westward and further intensified, nearly attaining

Charles H. Geletzke, Jr.

hurricane status the next day. The storm peaked with winds of 70 mph. Several hours later, Delia made landfall near Freeport, Texas; however, the storm began to execute a counterclockwise loop, causing it to move back over the Gulf of Mexico. On September 5, the storm made another landfall in Freeport before weakening to a depression. The remnants of Delia eventually dissipated early on September 7 over northern Mexico.

Due to the erratic track of the storm along the Texas coastline, widespread heavy rains fell in areas near the storm and in Louisiana. Tides up to 6 ft. in addition to rainfall up to 13.9 inches caused significant flooding in the Galveston-Freeport area. Up to $3 million was reported in damages to homes due to the flooding with an additional $6 million to farmland and crops. In addition to the flooding rains produced by Delia, eight tornadoes also touched down due to the storm, injuring four people. Five people were killed during Delia, two of which were directly related to the storm.

I immediately drove over to the Angleton depot where I met ATM Pipkin. Before driving off in the old bright orange Chevy I obtained an old pick-handle, which I would use as a brake club. Mike and I then drove down to the middle of the yard in Angleton, and as instructed, began applying handbrakes on EVERY SINGLE CAR! We spent the remainder of the day working our way down toward Freeport.

Upon arriving at Freeport, Mike went into the office and contacted the dispatcher and Mr. Holloway. I went out and assisted the engineer on the 10:01 Freeport Job in coupling-up every unit at Freeport! The plan was to move them all to Angleton to keep them away from the rising floodwaters. When the crew departed at 1:45 A.M. they had the 1153-1201-1164-1199-1147-1149-1163-1166-1250 (SW9)-1145-1190-1192, a total of 12-units, all SW12's with the exception of the single SW9. To this day I regret that I did not get a photo of them all together; but it was dark out and it was certainly raining! With their departure, Mike drove me home to Angleton and I went to bed sleeping until about

6 o'clock. As tired as I was, I still have vivid recollections of the wind and pouring rain blowing down the street and hoping that all of the surrounding buildings could withstand the force.

The amount of rain coming down during the afternoon was unbelievable and we only had one yard crew working at Freeport. I spent the remainder of the day at the Freeport office just sending periodic reports to the Chief Dispatcher in Houston and to Superintendent Holloway in Corpus Christi. I finally headed for home at 9:30 A.M. on Tuesday the 4th after working 26-hours and 30-minutes….let's see, that now equated to 52-hours and 15-minutes on duty in only 2-1//2 days…very similar to the hours that my daughter would later work as a surgical resident!

We did retain one yard job to work on September 4th at Freeport in order to accommodate the needs of the *Dow Chemical Company*. This was the 4:00 P.M. #3 job. My notes show that Trainmaster Adams took them off duty from 5:00 P.M. until 9:00 P.M. to get the crew out of the extremely intense weather taking place at that time!

Nine hours later, at 9:00 P.M. on Tuesday, September 5th, I returned to the office in Freeport and relieved ATM Pipkin. I learned that we had a Train 395 ordered out of Houston at 9:15 P.M. with 37x44. The train cleared Brownie at 10:50 P.M., and arrived Angleton at 1:45 A.M. on Thursday the 6th. The train set-out 35 cars and picked-up. It departed for Kingsville at 3:00 A.M. Oh yes…sometime while I was home, all of the yard engines moved earlier to Angleton were returned to Freeport.

Let me state that by now the rain had subsided; but to say the least, there was water everywhere! Driving the old orange Chevy I had to be extremely cautious and stay on the highest portion of the roads. Fortunately, there was little other traffic competing for the roadways!

We also had a Train 858 ordered out of Vanderbilt at 9:50 P.M. It departed at 10:10 P.M. and arrived Angleton at 2:55 A.M. on the 6th where the crew set-out 27 and picked-up 14. I neglected to record their departure time.

Charles H. Geletzke, Jr.

It was now September 6th. Train 394's crew was ordered out of Vanderbilt at 6:30 A.M. on what turned out to be a sunny morning. They headed north at 6:50 A.M., passed Bay City at 8:05 A.M., and arrived Angleton at 9 o'clock.

Coming south, we had Train 859 called for 1:00 A.M. out of Settegast Yard and was shown departing at 1:45 A.M. They arrived Angleton at 5:30 A.M. with units 129 (GP7)-815 (F7A)-855 (GP38), set-out 36 cars and picked-up 39 more. The train departed at 6:55 A.M. While assisting this crew with their work, I encountered a problem...I drove the old 1969 Chevy through some water that was apparently a little too deep. When the exhaust pipe came in contact with the cold water, the vehicle immediately lost power! The cars engine still idled fine; but I could no longer get any power out of it. I drove to a local service station, which had been keeping the vehicle running for the previous four years and had them check it out. It turned out that the exhaust pipe was actually a pipe within a pipe, and when the exhaust pipe contacted the cold water, the inner pipe contracted and practically sealed itself shut! The mechanic replaced the problem, I signed the bill, and as I drove off he said, "I'll probably see you in a few days!"

At 6:00 A.M. a Train XHO South was ordered out of Houston with 115-cars...all Dow's for Freeport.

Double-A was ordered for 9:30 A.M. with three units lead by the 757 (SD40). The train departed Angleton at 10:55 A.M. with 36x0 for Little Rock, 45x0 for the A&S...a total of 81x0 and 9153 tons.

Train 860 got out of Angleton at 11:30 A.M. with 19x0 Sandow's, 35x0 Ft. Worth's, 22x0 C&EI's, for a total of 76x0 and 7797 tons. The train was pulled by the 335 (GP9)-641 (GP35)-424 (GP-18).

I learned that there was an Extra HO North to be called later. At 4:30 P.M. I headed for home, figuring 19-1/2 hours on duty was enough for one day and never did encounter the Extra. Let's total this up; since 12:01 A.M. on Sunday, I had now worked a total of 71-hours and 45-minutes...and it was only Thursday afternoon!

From here on the weather and working conditions

began to improve. Everyone still had to be extremely careful walking around the property as the resident diamondback rattle snakes were seeking high ground to avoid the water in the lowlands.

MP (former Houston & Bravos Valley H&BV) depot in Angleton, TX on October 27, 1973.

An Empathetic Friend

Please allow me to begin with an apology as I can no longer recall the man's name and I cannot find it anywhere in my notes; but he was the regular Conductor on the 2:00 P.M. Angleton Yard Job. Every afternoon, Monday through Saturday, this fifty plus year old man would line-up his cars at Angleton switch the local industries around town, and then head north to serve the *Amoco Chemical* Plant, Danbury, and the industries at Chocolate Bayou. This gentleman was all business, a true railroader, and well respected by all of the crews in the area. One day during a conversation I learned that he had previously been the Assistant Superintendent at Yard Center in Chicago, Illinois. This struck me as being quite funny to think that here I was, a 24-year old kid, supervising a former superintendent…twice my age! And yet, in all of these weeks, not once did this man ever give any indication of my lack of experience compared to his nor did he act like he was better then me. Why I would say that he set quite an example and had probably been one of my hardest workers. During our discussion I finally asked him, "Why on earth did you give-up your job as Assistant Superintendent?"

I'll never forget his reply, he said. "It was a beautiful Sunday morning and my family was all dressed and ready for Church…before we could even get out the door, the telephone rang and I was told that we had a major derailment and that I was needed immediately! Well, I went in and we cleared the wreck and at the end of the day, I told them that I was finished. I resigned right then and there and told my boss that I was going to return to Texas and exercise my seniority! Chuck, do you know that to this day, I have NEVER regretted that decision!?!"

Let me state that through all of the subsequent years, I have never forgotten those words of wisdom! I sure wish I could recall his name? I think his first name was Lloyd???

Physical Exhaustion

The hours required to get the trains "over the road" continued to increase. For those of you who were around in 1973, you will recall that it was the year of the BIG RUSSIAN WHEAT DEAL. The Soviet Union had encountered a poor wheat crop the year prior and so agreed to purchase a huge amount of wheat from the United States. For the next year, wheat was shipped in unit train quantities to ships at various U. S. ports and on to Russia. A huge amount of grain was shipped out of Corpus Christi and Brownsville. Interestingly, the north end of the Brownsville Subdivision did not handle the loaded trains; but we sure saw our share of empty trains being returned for additional loads!

The week after Delia hit our area I came down with a cold or flu and could barely function. I think I was about the sickest I had ever been. For some reason, three or four hours of sleep each night was not getting it! I recall telling Mike Pipkin how sick I felt and I will never forget him telling me to, "Take a couple of *Coricidin* tablets!" I recall later

98

stopping at an open pharmacy and purchasing a bottle. I have to say they helped; but I honestly felt like I should have been in a hospital! The problem was, there was no one there to relieve any of us, and as stated before; we did not even have yardmasters!

MP Train AA is ready to depart the east end of Angleton Yard with the 1932-_____-_____-_____ on October 27, 1973.

From Bad to Worse

The following week things actually took a turn for the worse! The only thing that saved me was that I was over my cold; but guess what? Mike Pipkin went on vacation for two weeks! And, you know how the saying goes, "when it rains it pours?" Only two days later a Trainmaster in New Orleans had a heart attack and since Mr. Adams had previously worked there, Missouri Pacific Management in St. Louis sent him to the Crescent City to run that operation. That left me in charge at only 24-years of age to run the entire operation at the highest revenue producing point on the entire Missouri Pacific System!

Now let me state that beginning January 1, 1973 I was informed that during the year 1973 I would be entitled to take four weeks paid vacation. Naturally, I had nothing special going on during the Management Training Program and did not feel any need for a vacation at that time. But at the end of working only two months in Freeport and Angleton I was ready for a few weeks off! About this time, Superintendent Holloway was in town and I asked if it would be possible to take two weeks of my vacation (After all, by this time there were only three months remaining in the fiscal year and as for the two days that I was supposed to have off every other week, so far, I had not had ANY!). I asked if I could have two weeks off from October 1st through the 14th. I was truly hoping to attend Homecoming at my Alma Mater, *Central Michigan University*, on Saturday, October 9th. I was really ready for some rest, to see my family, and have a little fun.

The next day Mr. Holloway got back to me as promised; but I will never forget what he said! He stated, "Chuck, you may have one week of vacation beginning October 1st through the 7th. We are so short of supervisors…I cannot permit you to be off for more than one week! Incidentally, you will probably be required to carry your other three weeks over until next year."

Seeing how things were shaping up, I knew that if I could not use that vacation time this year, I would never get to use it! I then told Mr. Holloway, "I was really hoping to attend my college's homecoming game on the 9th. I am afraid that if I don't get to attend this year, I may never get to go!"

Once again, he replied that he would check and see if there was an alternative available. Later that same day he called back and said, "Chuck. Well I pulled some strings and you can go for ten days beginning October 1st returning to work on the 11th. On the downside, you will not be able to use any of the rest of your vacation this year!"

I couldn't believe it! So far, since I had arrived in Texas I had worked only two days for less than 14-hours per day and had not had ANY days off! I just thanked the Superintendent and thought to myself, "you know there are other fish in the sea." I worked right up until Noon on Sunday the 30th of September and then flew out of Houston at 4:55 P.M. for Detroit.

On Tuesday, October 2nd I visited Bob O'Brien the

"Soak It!!!"… and Other Railroad Stories

President of my former employer, the Delray Connecting Railroad and Paul Weissert, the General Manager. We had a nice conversation where I explained what I had been doing. The following day, Mr. O'Brien called and offered me a job as Superintendent of the DC at the same money that I was being paid on the MP. I told him that I would get back to him.

On Thursday, October 4th I had an interview with Harland Reed the Superintendent of GTW's Detroit Division and pleaded my case with him. He too said that he would get back to me; but he wasn't sure if he could hire any more managers at the current time. Additionally, he suggested that I contact Mr. Clarence Frew, the President of the Detroit Terminal Railroad as he was in need of a Trainmaster. I immediately arranged an appointment with Mr. Frew and we met the next day.

Friday, October 5th I met with Mr. Frew in his office at Davison Yard and he took me out to lunch. He stated that he did indeed need a Night Trainmaster and that his Day Trainmaster would be retiring the following year. The President was extremely frank and following lunch stated, "as far as I am concerned you can have the job as Night Trainmaster; but I want you to know that our railroad is not in very good shape financially!" (At that time they were owned 50% by the Penn Central and 50% by the GTW.) He went on to say, "We almost made money about five years ago; but then we were sued following a major crossing accident and that killed our profit for that year! Like I said, the job is yours; but in all honesty, I think you can do better."

I really appreciated Mr. Frew's honesty! That afternoon I drove up to Mt. Pleasant, Michigan to attend the *CMU* Homecoming festivities.

With only three days left on my vacation, I received a telephone call from GTW's Superintendent, Harland Reed on Monday, October 8th. He stated that in all honesty he could not offer me a managerial position at the current time; but if I would be interested, he would put me on as a Locomotive Fireman, let me establish seniority, and then have me transferred to management when an opening occurred.

Charles H. Geletzke, Jr.

I told Mr. Reed that that sounded like a fair deal to me and he made arrangement for me to take a Pre-Employment Physical Exam the next morning. After passing my exam, Mr. Reed and I talked and it was agreed that I would return to the Missouri Pacific, give them two weeks notice, resign, and then return to the GTW to make my three Student Trips as a Locomotive Fireman working out of Milwaukee Jct. in Detroit, Michgan and establish my seniority. The GTW had always treated me fairly in the past and I was thrilled to be returning home!

On Wednesday, October 10th I flew back to Houston and drove back down to Angleton. At 12:30 A.M. on Thursday, I reported back for duty at Freeport and had quite a discussion with Trainmaster, Vern Adams. It was at this time that I gave him what would be my Seventeen Day Notice, telling him that my last day to work would be on Sunday, October 28th. I could tell that he was honestly shocked!

I then worked my shift from 12:30 A.M. until Noon…a relatively short day of only eleven hours and thirty minutes.

Friday morning, October 12th upon my arrival at Freeport at 1:00 A.M. in addition to Trainmaster Adams, I was greeted by G. M. Holzmann the General Manager of the Gulf District and M. G. Jackson, the Gulf District's Assistant General Manager. The three of them were very nice and reserved and just could not believe that I wanted to leave THEIR railroad! I will never forget Mr. Holzmann asking me, "What's the problem, aren't you making enough money?"

I don't believe that he knew what to say when I responded with, "No sir. I don't even have time to spend the money I am making now!"

The three men then went on to ask me questions about what I would be doing next. When I stated that I was going to give up the suit and tie and become a GTW Locomotive Fireman, Mr. Holzmann retorted. "If you want a job as a Fireman, I will put you to work here as a Fireman on the Kingsville Division right now!?!"

I tried to explain that it was not just the job; but I

"Soak It!!!"… and Other Railroad Stories
missed my family and most of all no one in 1973 should be
required to work hours in excess of 14-hours EVERY Day,
without Days Off, and then have to forfeit their vacation! I
went on to say that "in the three months that I have been
working here, I have only had two days off, and I have not
even had a single date nor even been able to go to church!" I
said, "I love the Missouri Pacific! I appreciate that you don't
care if it is a carload of automobiles or a carload of sand or
gravel…you WANT the business! To me, that is REAL
RAILROADING! But, having seen how this entire railroad
operates, Transportation Management is treated like crap and
life is way too short for this! At least working in the ranks I
can make plans and have a day off…once in a while!"

MP 11:59 P.M. Angleton Yard crew, Brakeman, Clay Dove
(standing); Brakeman,_____ (seated on step); Conductor, J. D.
Hayes (sitting on footboard), Engineer, Steven P. Merriman (at
bottom of steps); and Assistant Trainmaster, C. H. Geletzke, Jr.
(standing at right) at Angleton, Texas on October 28, 1973.

A Premier Crew!

During my last month and a half or so at Angleton I
became very close friends with the crew on the 11:59 P.M.
Angleton Yard Job. As previously stated this outstanding
group of guys was made-up of Conductor, J. D. Hayes (who

Charles H. Geletzke, Jr.

began his railroad career on the EJ&E working out of Gary, Indiana), Brakeman, Clay Dove, generally another spare man, and Engineer Steven P. Merriman.

This crew would generally begin their night by "taking up" all of the room in Angleton Yard. Next they would begin "blocking" all of the cars for Trains 859, AA, and 860. Generally, once we had trains 859 and AA out of town all of us would go to breakfast at a local diner. In time we turned a portion of our sessions into mock rule classes. About once a week I would ask them questions about the rules and different operating scenarios. If they answered the questions correctly, I would buy their breakfasts. If they missed any of the questions…they would buy mine! In the end, I am certain that I was ahead!

After several weeks, as I would drive into town in the orange Chevy, I would often hear one of them say over the radio, "Here comes the Yellow Taxi!" Later, they began referring to me as the "Driver of the Yellow Taxi." Occasionally, I would switch places with Steve, and I would run the locomotives…he in turn would occasionally drive around in the "Yellow Taxi." I recall one morning Steve allowing me to run three covered wagons as we put Train 860 together…one of my best times ever down there!

In conclusion just let me say that this was a fantastic crew that did their best to make me look good and during my final seventeen days there I knew that I was going to miss those fantastic guys!

Hand drawn "Yellow Taxi" gift card on gift given to Mr. Geletzke upon his departure from Angleton in October 1973, (which I still have in my collection!).

The Last 18-Days

My last days on the Kingsville Division were for the most part fairly routine. Well, one day was a little out of the ordinary. On the morning of October 16th the regular engineer on the 12:00 Noon Angleton Switcher booked-off sick. Now in most terminals this would not have been an issue; but because crews for Angleton were called off the Extra Board at Kingsville (202 miles to the south), that required that the replacement engineman must have 8-hours and 10-minutes travel time; thus he would not be rested until the next day! So where was I going to get an engineer?

I had reported for work at 2:00 A.M.; so theoretically, I could run and engine until 2:00 P.M. (Remember this was before the Laws of Engineer Certification). Since this was considered an Emergency, the crew of Conductor, Curtice Peavey; Brakemen, J. Severa and J. Sayles; and I were driven

Charles H. Geletzke, Jr.

out to Chocolate Bayou where we relieved the Traveling
Switch Engine (TSE) at Monsanto in Chocolate Bayou. I
inspected engines 1197 & 1143, obtained an Initial Terminal
Air Test, and brought our train of 30 cars back into Angleton.
For me, this was officially my first trip as a Locomotive
Engineer. Upon arrival I was relieved by Assistant General
Car Inspector, John Lambert and he finished the tour of duty
with Conductor Peavey and crew.

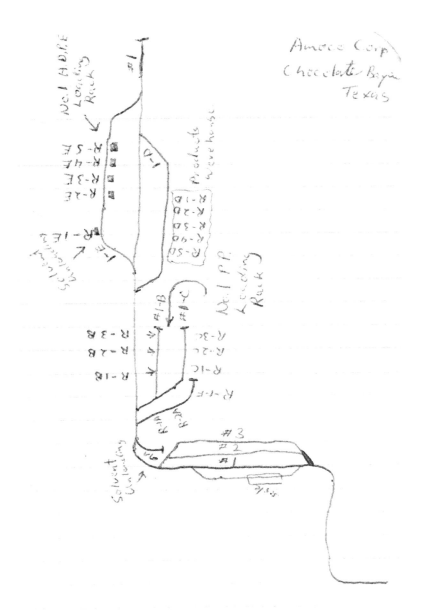

MP track diagram for Amoco in Chocolate Bayou, TX 1973

The very next day the *Marathon Tank Car Co.* went on strike and John and I had to switch their plant as we did again on Friday the 19th.

Charles H. Geletzke, Jr.

On my second to my last day, Mrs. Crowe the night clerk at Angleton, Conductor, J. D. Hayes, Steve Merriman, Clay Dove, and several others gave me a little Going Away Party in the Angleton depot. We all had a fantastic time and to this day it is hard to believe that such wonderful people that I had only supervised for a total of three months would treat me so lovingly! They will always remain dear to me in my memory!   On my final two days at Angleton I will never forget…I worked 36-hours straight, went home to bed for two hours and then came back for another ten…going off duty at 1:00 P.M.! By that time I was ready to go

The next morning I drove in to Freeport, turned in my keys, and said good-by to Mr. Adams.

I then returned to my apartment in Angleton, packed my few belongings, and thoroughly cleaned the interior. Interestingly, as I was walking across the apartment's courtyard I met a cute young lady…a little younger than me. She immediately stated, "Are you new here? I've never seen you before!" Before I could respond, she asked if we could have coffee one day!?!

I explained that I was leaving and thought to myself isn't it ironic that on my last morning here I finally meet someone!

Well, I finished loading my car and as I began driving out of town I turned on the radio. I will never forget that coming over the speaker was the song *"We May never Pass This Way Again*"* by Seals & Crofts. It was the first time that I had ever heard it; but I recall thinking how apropos!

"We May Never Pass This Way Again," single by Seals & Crofts released in 1973.

One More Story With an Angleton Connection

Sometime in 2000 I had to attend my Annual Canadian National Locomotive Engineer Certification Class in Flat Rock, Michigan. Let me state that these classes were formerly conducted by GTW Road Foremen of Engines and

"Soak It!!!"… and Other Railroad Stories

Supervisors of Locomotive Engineers; however once under the "leadership" of E. Hunter Harrison and the former officers of the Illinois Central Railroad all of that changed. Instead of being taught and examined by people that had a physical connection and a familiarity with our railroad, the CN brought in a contracted firm to teach these classes. The firm was known as *Rail Safety Training Resources*.

In my first day of class, the Instructor, who was also the firm's Vice President introduced himself to the group, saying "Hi, I'm Tony Crabb…" and then he went on to tell about his prior railroad career, which began on the Missouri Pacific along the Texas Gulf Coast. During our first break I approached Mr. Crabb and asked, "So you were a Kingsville Division Trainman?"

His eyes about popped out at my use of the "Kingsville Division" terminology. We then got to talking and came to the realization that Mr. Crabb had actually worked for me a few times at Angleton during my tenure there.

Today we are still *"Facebook Friends."*

Let's Wrap This Up!

In September 2014 my wife and I flew down to Houston to attend our niece's wedding on a Saturday evening. The next day we elected to take our rental car and drive down through Angleton, Freeport, and on over to Galveston. My wife had never been down along that portion of the Gulf and I had never returned to that area either.

Looking north or east from the south end of UP's (former MP) yard in Angleton, TX on September 28, 2014. It appeared that the yard had been expanded from four tracks to perhaps ten…but of coarse, I was not permitted to get close enough to check!?!

As we drove into Angleton, I drove by the apartment where I had lived (two years before we even met) and pointed it out to my wife. It pretty much still looked the same. I then headed over toward the south end of what was now Union Pacific's Angleton Yard, parked the car, and got out and looked toward the north. It appeared that the yard had been expanded to about ten tracks and I spotted a car inspector inspecting cars. As I walked over toward the tracks with my camera, the man started screaming to "GET AWAY FROM THE TRACKS…I SAID GET AWAY FROM THE TRACKS!" I took several quick photos, turned around, and walked back to my car. It then occurred to me how funny this was, that 41-years earlier this was "my domain" and that no one could remove me from the property, not to mention that I was free to take all of the photos that I wanted!

Leslie and I then drove to the north end of the yard and toward the site of the "former depot." In its place were

110

"Soak It!!!"… and Other Railroad Stories

two new buildings. I noticed a number of cars parked in the lot and I was about to go in and inquire, "Who is the oldest employee still working here?" That's when a UP Supervisor (with some unique modern non-railroady title) drove into the parking lot in a UP vehicle and asked me what I was doing. I told him that I had been an Assistant Trainmaster here 41 years before and inquired about the operation. He then became quite friendly. At the end of our conversation do you want to know what really amazed me? It sounded like this man was still working the same kind of hours that I was back in 1973! Apparently some things never change!

From Angleton we followed the line down to Freeport and I explored the area once again. I was not surprised to see that the former MP Freight Office was still in place and being used to run the operation, after all, the structure was only built the year prior to my original arrival. One major change of course was the fact that the railroad was no longer performing any LTL (Less Than Truckload Service). With Leslie waiting in the car, I walked into my former office and immediately located the "Supervisor." Here again we had a similar conversation and I learned of the many changes. It turned out that the switching at the *Dow Chemical* plants was now being performed by a switching contractor…not surprising! I was also not surprised to hear that the UP was providing remote control units with reduced crews to perform much of the other switching. The man seemed very friendly and more than willing to answer my questions. But once again I walked out the door with the same impression that I had gleaned during my Angleton visit…these young corporate officers were still working the same number of hours that I had a lifetime earlier…little had improved!

As we drove off toward Galveston I had the distinct feeling that I was reliving a bad dream and felt truly sorry for those young UP employees and their families.

Fifty years later I still wonder what would have happened and where I would be had I not resigned my position there!?! I recall being extremely impressed by the number of young officers about my age who stuck it out and climbed that corporate ladder…but then I recall those that too threw in the towel! When I think that I would never have met my wife, never have had the family that I have, that tells me that I made the right decision…yes, I still wonder; but I have no regrets!

The "Gluemaster"

By: C. H. Geletzke, Jr.

During the early years of my railroad career when I was working for the Grand Trunk Western Railroad in Detroit, Michigan we had a Trainmaster, Mr. Harold Woldanski who normally worked afternoons at Milwaukee Jct. He was generally an easy going friendly guy (a former switchman) and most of the men just called him "Waldo."

Now a big part of Waldo's job each evening was to drive around to the various on-duty points…Beginning with the Milwaukee Jct. yard office, and then onto the Milwaukee Jct. roundhouse, East Yard, Nolan Yard, Brush Street Depot, City Yard, D&M Yard, and Ferndale Yard where he would post the daily Operating Bulletins in each location's Bulletin Book. Additionally, he would post the job advertisements for any and all jobs that were up for bid.

Over the years all of the guys would see him as he drove from location to location with his stack of file folders and a bottle of mucilage. You can only imagine that over the ensuing years he eventually acquired the title of "Gluemaster!"

Not on Mr. Batanian's territory; but here is an AT&SF shot at Verdemont, CA on September 1, 1990. (J. G. Tyson photo)

The World Changed With the Birth of My Daughter

As told by: retired AT&SF Engineer; Road Foreman of Engines, Amtrak; BN and BNSF Engineer, L. E. Batanian

What a nice day it is today. I just got off the phone with my oldest daughter, Tiffanie. It is her Birthday! Spring is just around the corner. It's 55-degrees out in my shop and I have a nice fire going in my caboose pot belly stove. The wood trailer has been moved outside and the floor has been swept clean. *Clay Travis and Buck Sexton* are talking away on my 1981 *Pioneer* AM-FM Radio. Yes, it still works… I am sitting in front of the stove splitting kindling now. I can remember when Tiff was born like yesterday…She did not want to come out and meet us! She took her time. Once word spread around the railroad that we had a brand new baby at home, the guys down at the Red Barn, at the direction of Louie Sanchez, the 2nd Trick Foreman, passed the hat and chipped in…they bought Tiff an outfit. Don Ramariz's (a machinist at the shops) Mother even gave our baby an outfit!

113

She was something else! She also supplied those wonderful burritos we ate when we poured concrete.

The Santa Fe's Red Barn in Barstow, California was where all inbound and outbound power was cut-up, and made-up to go out again…that or they went up to the roundhouse for repairs. The Red Barn was a beehive of activity to say the least. They had a nice big pot belly stove there much like the one I am sitting in front of right now. Back then Barstow had 36 hostlers, working I don't know how many jobs…around the clock! Life was good.

Trains would come into Barstow and unless the power was to go through, either Eastbound or Westbound, the engineer and head brakeman would bring it up across from the White barn and spot them. Then they would go inside the White Barn and tie up.

Inside the White Barn sat the guy who made you money…the crew dispatcher! All engineers, Firemen, and hostlers were called from that building. Their names were written in chalk on a board on the wall behind the caller's desk. The conductors, brakemen, and switchmen were called out of an office down in the yard…don't ask me why! I don't know! It's just the way it was and it worked.

Once the power arrived from an inbound train, the Red Barn Foreman would instruct the hostler that was "first out" to go get the units and pull them down to the sand rack. If you were that hostler, he might tell you to stay with it and spot it over the pit located at the fuel rack…if he did, it was "nap time!" Nap time was important if you were doubling-over on 3rd trick. Inside hostlers could work 16-hours straight back then! (Editor's note: On the GTW we could work up to 24-hours or more in an emergency; but I never worked more than 24.) They just asked you if you wanted to double…it was not mandatory. Later they started a list for overtime. You put your name on the list, and all extra work was to be called off of it… No "buying the crew dispatcher an all meat burrito from *Del Taco*…Yea right…"

There could be power sitting over the pit and also spotted on the fuel rack. If so, things were backed-up and we could catch our forty winks!

114

"Soak It!!!"... and Other Railroad Stories

Once you pulled over the pit the process started all over again...you got off the units you spotted, then went into the Fuel Rack Shack and had a cup of coffee and could catch up on the latest.

One of the fuel rack foremen was a really nice guy named Ardell. He was always smoking a big fat cigar. Ardell liked to gamble up at the state line casinos. He played the one dollar slot machines. To hear him talk, he won all the time and boy did he like to talk about it! Ardell claimed the 97% payback on the progressive slots was the way to go! I never did figure out how Ardell got those machines to pay out...

Once the engines were done on the pit they would be pulled down and spotted on the fuel rack. There they were fueled and a laborer would walk through and sweep out all of the cabs. Next came the wash rack to wash off all the dirt accumulated between Chicago and Barstow. Then, we would take them west on the Lead stopping in front of the Red Barn for instructions from the foreman. Sometimes the power was given an air test and supplies might be put on either the west end or east end locomotive, depending on where they were going. More often than not the consist was cut-up and put in Tracks 12, 13, 14, or 15. Any units needing repair were taken up to the house and spotted on Triple Zero Track...from there they were now considered somebody else's problem! We might bring back a few engines that had been released from the Round House or we might walk back to the Red Barn and start all over again. Barstow was a pretty busy place back then! It still is; but now it's another time and another place...! Back then the employees RAILROADED! They got the work done. Tell them what you wanted, and then just get out of their way! They would do what you needed, when you needed it! Were there slackers? Of course! But the slackers did not get the breaks. Moving trains through the Old Yard in Barstow was an art and the Trainmasters and Foremen who ran the place used the old "Carrot on a Stick Method." Those who produced got the carrot. Sometimes the carrot was allowing a longer meal period on Saturday night, while one old engineer watched *Gunsmoke*! It did not matter. He wasn't coming back until the show was over anyway... Those who worked in the Mechanical Department punched a time clock. The carrot for them was...once they completed their work for the day, they got spot time. The Hostlers were Operating Department employees. It was pretty much standard practice to get an hour for lunch and most often an hour quit. Huh? Yes, it's true! It allowed me to go home to have dinner with my family, believe it or not. Even more of a quit was given if you worked through your lunch or longer...whatever it took! But, when done, we got the carrot! Maybe you did not receive the carrot right away; but those supervisors did not forget! They took care of their men and the Men took car of them!

The switch jobs in the yard worked the same way. I can recall walking in the door at the East Yard and hearing the switch list hitting the concrete floor with a thud! It sounded like the *LA County Yellow Pages* when it hit. It came down a tube from the tower where the yardmaster had his office and the East Barstow operator was located. Inside the Crew Room were wooden picnic tables and lockers for crews assigned to switch jobs on the east end. A speaker hung on the wall. It had a talk button that the foreman would push to talk to the yardmaster. Now when the list hit the floor with a thud, everyone knew what was next. The speaker on the wall would crackle and the yardmaster would say, "Do this and go home!" Once those words were spoken, out the door we would go to get on our engine and wait for the yard crew to come out. No games of Hearts or Spades would be played on this day. We knew that we were going to be going at it for 5-1/2 to 6-hours straight. And go at it we did! If we wanted coffee, we'd better have it with us; because we were not stopping unless we had to get in the clear for an inbound or outbound train, and there could be 20 or more of those a day!

Barstow had four yard engines a shift working in the Old Yard back then as I remember...two on each end of the yard. They started on the hour, 7 A.M., 3 P.M., and 11 P.M. Also, 7:59 A.M., 3:59 P.M.; and 11:59 P.M., seven days a week.

"Soak It!!!"... and Other Railroad Stories

There were also three locals that worked out of Barstow. The Saltus Local, which went on duty at 4:50 A.M., the Boran Local at 9:00 A.M., and the Parker Local between 9 and 11 A.M. Each had to be built every day except the Saltus Local. It was a six day job. In addition to the locals, several eastbound and westbound trains were built, and the rip track, where cars were repaired, had to be spotted and pulled. Cabooses had to be changed or added and Bad Ordered cars had to be thrown-out for repairs. It was a busy place pre-1976!

Railroading was fun. But then things started to change...the Bean Counters showed up!

"Huh?"

"The Bean Counters?"

"Yes. Mostly college boys walking around in white hats carrying stop watches."

"They timed our every move! How long it took to do everything!"

"Yes, EVERYTHING! They waited at the door... They followed us around like puppy dogs. One hour lunches and early quits went out the window when the Bean Counters showed up. Lunch was now 20-minutes. The Rule Book came out and each move in Barstow was done by the book. It did not take long to bottle neck the place. The carrot was gone. The yardmasters and foremen were pulling their hair out trying to move trains and equipment. I can't remember how long this went on; but it lasted until the Bean Counters left town. When they left, out came the carrots and things started to move once again. Life was good!"

"But let me tell you, somebody was somewhere counting all of those Beans that the Bean Counters had collected during their little stopover in Barstow. In fact, they were counting beans from all over the Santa Fe System!"

"Soon the New Barstow $50,000,000 Hump Yard would be constructed west of 'B' Hill...a 48-track classification hump yard with 550 employees. The north side of 'B' Hill would be ground into ballast for the 600 acre yard. I worked many shifts as the engineer on work trains spreading rock and laying rail to build the modern new yard."

Charles H. Geletzke, Jr.

"Little did anyone know that those 36 hostling jobs would soon disappear. The engineers on the yard jobs would soon be gone. The hostlers were bargained away. Anyone could now move engines in the Diesel Service Area after brief instructions. Hostlers were being paid a "Guarantee" every payday to stay home. Switchmen would soon be running engines from the ground with a Box of controls, hung around their neck, at walking speed. They were permitted to ride the end platforms of the engine; but not allowed to go in the cab. Had they entered the cab, which might have given the impression that someone was indeed needed to run the locomotive! There was no getting on or off moving equipment either! Instructions indicated "All movements must come to a complete stop!"

I wonder who thought of this stuff!?! They called it "PROGRESS!" I would take any bet as to who could switch a train out faster...the crew with the *LA County Phone Book* Switch List and a carrot out in front of them, or the ones with the black boxes around their necks walking next to their locomotive and not getting on or off moving equipment! All of this was bargained away for a few dollars...same as the firemen jobs in 1964. They went for $6 for every hundred miles run back then...or something close to that number (depending on the railroad). Someday soon, ALL trains will only have one person in the cab! They are doing it now in some places. I really knew change was coming one rainy night when several of us were crowded into the Hump Shack, right after the "new yard" opened.

Sitting at a desk overlooking the new several million dollar hump yard was Road Foreman of Engines, J. P. Herndon, from San Bernardino, California. The Santa Fe had brought in supervisors from all over the System to get this yard running...Mr. Herndon was telling the crew how the new yard worked and what was expected of them. As we listened to what he was saying, some idiot in the group said, "That's not the way we do things in Barstow!" You could have heard a pin drop... The RFE never even turned his head. He just said in a quiet, but firm voice, "You'll do it, or you won't be working here anymore."

118

"Soak It!!!"... and Other Railroad Stories

Following that statement, I slipped out the door and went back to my engine. It took years; but all the carrots eventually went away. Yes, things change...or do they?

As I was sweeping the floor in my shop today, I heard Buck Sexton and Clay Travis yapping away about people slowly returning to work after Covid 19. Clay was saying how people had gotten used to working from home. Do your work and get it done and then you were done. It was an incentive...a way to have more time with your family. Huh? Did I just hear the old Carrot on a Stick Theory? I did...

I guess we circled back on that one...different type of work; but still a carrot... One cannot help but think of all the industrial business that the railroads let go because some college interns were walking around in White Hats with a stop watch in hand... They turned in the Bean Report and somebody else counted them up. The next thing we knew there were very few commercial customers left...The Beans did NOT add up! Everything went to trucks! Now they don't have enough trucks or drivers to service what's left of the industry in this big beautiful country of ours...industry that was once serviced by the RAILROAD at one time no doubt!?!

I think I will go back to splitting kindling.

You can't make this stuff up...

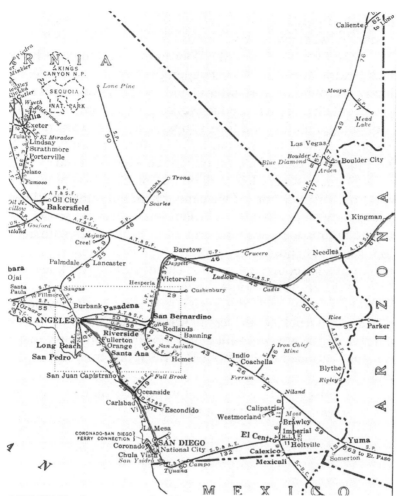

AT&SF Engineman worked between Barstow, CA and Seligman,
AZ. (*Rand McNally Railroad Atlas of the U.S.*- 1965)

May 15, 1973

By: L. E. Batanian

May 15, 1973…Fifty years ago today I hired out
firing on the Santa Fe Railway…three days before my 21st
Birthday. Little did I know that 14 months later, I would be a

"Soak It!!!"… and Other Railroad Stories
Promoted Locomotive Engineer at age 22! You can't make this kind of stuff up in life! It just happens…

Previously, I had been working as a laborer on the 3 P.M. Passenger Hostler Helper job at the Barstow Diesel Shop in Barstow, California. I also, still wore my nail bags when I could.

About 8 A.M., the bell on the small construction trailer started ringing. I was working a side job framing on the *Motel 6* outside the Main Gate on the *Marine Corps Supply Depot* in Barstow. I was up on the second floor laying our 2" x 12" floor joists. Those suckers are heavy, let me tell you! I could not wait for 2:45 P.M., when I would head down to the Shops for my 3 P.M. Hostler Helper Job. I hoped we'd make our moves and then get some "spot time!" All of a sudden, the Foreman came out of the Construction Shed and hollered up to me, "Hey Batanian, you have a phone call."

"Who is it?"

"Santa Fe Railroad," says the boss.

"HUH??? What do they want?"

He said, "It's the Trainmaster's Office. They want you down there to go take a physical."

I was thinking, how did they get this number? Then I realized that they must have called my house and Kathy, my wife, must have given them this number. My mind was spinning, trying to figure out what this was for. Then the light bulb went on…this must be for a Fireman job!?!

I threw my tools down off the second story and went down that ladder like my pants were on fire and went to the phone! I wondered why Sara Spink was not calling? She was the old gal who refused to hire me because I was in the *National Guard*.

Out the door I went and hollered over to the Foreman, "I gotta go!" I jumped in my *Datsun* pickup and was out of there in a cloud of southwestern desert dust. I went directly to the Trainmaster's Office. Sara was gone…she "pulled the pin" and retired. **My application was still on file! Dang!!!**

I was given my paperwork, along with instructions to go up to Dr. Sameroski's Office for my Physical. They took back x-rays, gave me a test for color blindness, and old Doc

Charles H. Geletzke, Jr.

gave me the "once over!" I liked Old Doc! "Burp!!!" Some say he drank a little…Really??? I never noticed…

Then it was back to the Trainmaster's Office where I finally met Mr. C. F. Lilley. He gave me the "Don't Screw This Up Speech" and a letter to take with me on my Student Trips.

The new clerk gave me a *Book of Rules*, *Air Brake Rule Book*, and an *Employees Timetable*. Then he handed me a "fill in the blank" book Rules Test. I had to complete this open book test before I could take my student trips! This was moving pretty fast! I sat down and went to writing the book. It was too much to complete before they closed up for the day; so I came back the next morning to finish. Then I stopped by the Diesel Shops and told Labor Foreman, Art Sanchez, "I had been called to go firing."

He was pretty happy for me.

I then went back to my side job and told them I was sorry; but I was moving on.

With all of my loose ends tied up, I was ready to start my Student Trips.

I went to the White Barn to see Junior, the Crew Dispatcher. He told me there was an eastbound sitting don in the yards, waiting for a crew.

Damn!

I went home, grabbed my knapsack, stuffed it with what I thought I would need, grabbed a couple blank checks, and wrote a note to my wife, who was at work at the *Cunningham Pharmacy* in town, on 1st Street and Main. After all, there were no credit cards or cell phones back then; and headed out the door.

I parked on Hutchinson St., across from the White Barn…little did I know how many more times I would be parking there! I went over to the White Barn, walked in the door, and found out the crew had already been there and gone. "Huh???"

The Caller told me, "No worries. Another Caller is in the Company Suburban, and will be here in a few minutes. You can catch a ride down to the train with him."

"Soak It!!!"… and Other Railroad Stories

As we pulled up to the lead locomotive, I noticed the Head Brakeman standing on the ground smoking a cigarette.

I only had an old Army knapsack with me…inside was my new rule book, a timetable, tooth brush, and a change of clothing. I got out and thanked the Caller for the lift.

To say I was nervous was an understatement. The Brakeman walked up to me and said, "Who are you?"

I told him I was making my student trips and that I had just hired out firing.

Next he said, "Who are you related to!?!"

"Huh?"

He said, "You got to be related to someone!?! Who is it???"

I told him that Bill Gust was my father-in-law.

He said, "No kidding?"

I said, "No, Gus is my wife's Dad."

I then asked him, "Who's the Engineer?"

He told me and I wish I could remember his name, because of what was about to happen next. I climbed the steps and went through the cab door. The Brakie was right behind me. I could smell the booze as I set my bag on the floor next to the electrical cabinet. Next I pulled out the paper Mr. C. F. Lilley had given me, to have each Engineer sign that I took a trip with.

The Engineer sat there looking straight ahead.

I introduced myself to him and he never said a word. He just sat there staring straight ahead.

Next the Brakeman intervened. "It's okay," he said to the Hogger, "he's Gus's son-in-law."

With that, the Hogger reached inside the old catalog style grip, that he and so many of the old-timers carried back then, and pulled out a ½ pint of *Jim Beam*. He slowly took the cap off, looking me in the eyes…then he tipped the bottle toward me, as if to offer me a drink…

I politely said, "No thank you."

With that he took a long pull for himself. I watched the air bubbles work their way to the top as he pulled that baby about 1/3 of the way down. He wiped his lips on his shirt sleeve, screwed the cap back on, stuck out his hand, and said, "Now let's have a look at your paperwork."

I had just been Baptized into the Railroad Brotherhood and did not even know it!?!

I told him that I had been working as a Hostler Helper at the Shops, that I had also been coming down "at beans" to ride with Gus, and that he had me running a switch engine.

He looked at me with one eye cocked and said, "Go check the power over." (As I write this, and think back to that moment, it comes to mind who he reminds me of...Rooster Cogburn! So, I may refer to him as Rooster from time to time.)

As I made my way back through the units, Ray Charles could tell they had already been walked through. All rain shields were down, the windows were closed, and everything was neat as a pin.

I cannot describe to you my level of excitement...probably "Hotter than a Bride's Breath," would be close!

When I came back in the cab door, I noticed Rooster had moved his grip next to the electrical cabinet. He was now standing next to the control stand. His body looked tired and worn out, from years of Railroading, and sitting in that seat. He looked at me and said, "Go on, get your ass in that seat," as he leaned over supporting his weight on the control stand.

"Huh?"

"You can't learn anything sitting over there," and he motioned toward the fireman's seat with his thumb.

I started to reach toward my knapsack to get my timetable.

He stopped me. "You won't need anything in there. Sit down."

"I was just getting my timetable."

"Look, you will have plenty of time to look at that when you are sitting across the cab, staring out the window," said the old man.

I thought I detected a slight slur of his words, to go along with the aroma of *Jim Beam*, and the fresh piece of raw garlic he just popped into his mouth. He reached toward the brake valve and pulled down the orders that had been neatly placed behind the valve. He handed them to me. He explained the Clearance Card and how each order had to be listed on there. It had to be signed and dated. He had written a number on each order and circled it. He told me, "They may not give them to you in the exact order in which you will use them…Burp!!! And numbering each one helps you to keep track."

"Good idea." I thought.

"Now look them over," he said, and watch for the Car Knocker…he will be here soon. When he gets here, he will tell you 'Set 'em up.' You will do this with every train. When he does, make a 20 pound reduction with the brake valve," he said…as his breath passed over the control stand into my face.

I did not know what was stronger, the sound of my knees knocking or the aroma of garlic and *Jim Beam*!?!

"Once the air quits blowing and everything settles down, wait 45 seconds, and then cut-out the brake valve. Then check the leakage for one minute. You got a watch, don't yah, kid?"

"Yes." (I stopped by the *Railroad Approved* Timekeeper's Shop and bought one on the monthly payment plan.)

"Did you check the time at the Crew Office?"

"No." I replied.

"You will need to do that each time you sign the book." He said. "Here, let's compare time."

We did…the glare off my shiny new watch almost blinded him as he again cocked his eye to look at it.

The Car Knocker showed-up and hung the Blue Flag and told me to "set the brakes."

I set 20 pounds, and he was gone in a cloud of dust. After the exhaust port quit blowing and the 45 seconds ticked by, I cut-out the brake valve and checked the leakage for one minute…only a couple pounds leaked off.

"Good," he said. "You are allowed six pounds."

Pretty soon the Car Knocker called and said, "Release the brakes."

Charles H. Geletzke, Jr.

I could see the Car Knocker working his way up the train checking each car in the rear view mirror. I loved those mirrors! How much of my time would be spent looking back through the mirror? I hadn't a clue. There is a certain view only a Hogger will know…You are screaming along at 70 mph and you glance in the mirror, as your train starts into a slight curve on your side…you see your trailing units dancing back and forth gently rocking to the music. They may be dancing with some piggybacks…rockin' and rollin', having a good time while they work. It is a view only a few have seen…I don't think the new container trains know how to dance…they just wait their turn…slowly moving ahead…One BIG LONG storage building for *Walmart*! Like the Coal Train of Wyoming…inch by inch, waiting, waiting, waiting…I do not even know if they run Hot Shots anymore? No more Shut-Down trains for *Pico Rivera*…Nope! That plant is long gone…

He soon got to the headend, stopped his little "tote" that he used to get around in the yard. It had a little box on the back where he kept air hoses, a pipe wrench, gaskets, and an insulated box with a hinged lid where he kept burritos. His wife would make fresh tortillas and stuff them with whatever she may have…beans and cheese, egg and potato, egg and hotdogs…they were 25 cents. We ordered three! He and his wife had a "side job…"

And with that, he said, "The Release was good to go" and reached-up and handed me the Air Slip, and removed the Blue Flag.

Rooster picked-up the radio handset, then burped again. "Santa Fe xxxx to the East Yardmaster. We are ready to roll."

The Yardmaster told us to, "Come on out when we can take you." He then called the East Tower Operator, and he said, "The Dispatcher is ready for you."

My knees were knocking harder now!

"Okay Kid, let's get these hogs moving!!!" He handed me the radio. "Tell the cab we're ready."

I called the cab. I had heard how this was done so many times before on the radio. I had even called the tower needing a signal when I was down running a switch engine spending "Lunch with Gus." I told them, "We are ready to go."

The Conductor said, "Roger that. Who is this?" He did not recognize my voice.

I told him and ALL THE WORLD that I was making my Student Trips.

"Oh Great…, let's go," was all he said.

I cracked the throttle to Run 1, then 2, then back to 1, slowly stretching it out. Rooster still had that eye cocked, watching me as I took the slack.

"All Moving, Santa Fe xxxx."

"All Moving." I replied. My life had just changed forever! At that moment, I did not know how much.

I was instructed to keep it at 10 mph until the Cab was "by the tower, then open her up." When I began advancing the throttle, those old Hogs came to life! They had been patiently waiting…lying in the mud. They were on their feet now. Black smoke began to pour out of each stack. If sitting idle, waiting to go to work, will do this to a tired old engine, it will do it to anybody…

There would be a Zero Board by the sewer ponds. Rooster the old Hogger told me, "When the cab calls out Zero Board, look out the window and you will see a board that has a number on it. Call out the number to them and don't exceed 50 mph until they call it. Then let her rip!"

He told me to, "Blow the whistle at the crossing for the Town of Daggett, Daggett Airport, Minneola Road, and Newberry Springs. At any other cow crossing only blow if you see a car or truck."

I reached for the whistle handle at Daggett and blew as I looked over to the south side toward *Daggett Elementary School* , where I went through the 5th grade. I looked at the café, the *Shell Station*, on the left *Scott's Market*, and *Fout's Garage*. Soon I spotted *Coolwater Ranch* where my childhood buddy lived.

Rooster said, "Set the first notch."

Charles H. Geletzke, Jr.

I did and baled-off the locomotive brakes as instructed. When I let off, a WHOOSH of air released into the cab.

With the sound of the air, Rooster reached into is pocket and pulled out a little tapered piece of wood. "Here, stick this in Little Jeff. I don't want to hear that crap all day! I know you know how to do it, if you've been helping up at the Shops.

I did…

We would stick a wooden plug found on each unit, or Reverser Lever, into the Independent Brake Handle in the Released and Baled-Off Position, to move engines around. This prevented the brakes from setting-up…a little trick in the "Not to Do Book!"

Rooster turned and went for the new plug sticking out of the tool rack.

So many memories there at *Coolwater Ranch*… Three young boys racing around those Alfalfa fields on a two-seater homemade go cart with a huge gas engine from some piece of farm equipment. Their Dad had welded an old tractor seat with a bent spring on it that curved up over the engine. Two boys up front and one on the spring seat for the "E" ticket ride…we fought for that seat!!!

On we went…

I blew for the cow crossing between the big high tension power lines. The road wound off to the north toward *Hill's Ranch*.

Rooster barked. "What'cha blowing fer?"

I told him the School Bus crossed this one…I knew because I rode it!

"Release the air," was my next order, as we eased out of the sag.

Next was *POP's*, a bar on Old 66 on my right. My parents and other workers at the airport hung out there sometimes. As kids from the base we would ride our bikes up there and play shuffle board with our parents or shoot pool. The *Hamm's* Bear hung on the wall paddling along watching over the place. I blew for the Airport crossing and watched a

Cessna take off to the east into the wind. "I used to live there," I said to Rooster.

He looked up from the end of the wood plug he had been fiddling with and said, "Where?"

"The Airport…"

"The Airport?"

"Yes, I grew up there."

"No Shit," he said. "What'cha doing living there? He asked.

"Well, my father worked for the *FFA*. He was a Flight Service Specialist. Gave weather reports, talked to air planes, filed flight plans…that sort of stuff."

"He still live there?" He asked.

"No. He lives back in San Diego, where he started during World War Two, when he was in the *FBI*. He works at *Limburger Field* (*Lindburgh Field*) now."

"G-Man, back then…Huh?" He asked.

"Yes, sorta…I guess."

"We got us a G-Man running engines! Tommy Barrett. You'll hear his stories…You'll like old Tommy." He said.

I blew for Minneola Road where a few years from now I would be stopping my train to pick a few watermelons.

Rooster handed me a plug, just like his, to block down the Independent. He had whittled on it, to clean up the part he had broken off. "You'll be needing one of these! Let me have mine back before we forget."

On we went through Newberry where soon I would be picking-up old rusty water cars on the Parker Local for the thirsty desert towns like Amboy and Cadiz.   Soon we were starting up Pisgah, where famous Second World War Pilot, Howard Fogg painted the picture, "Crossover at Pisgah." That man could sure paint… I wish that I could find a print of that picture!?!

Rooster said, "Up here, as we go around this next curve, start easing off the throttle. We will be going into Dynamic Brake. Do it slow. Yah don't want to knock them guys around back on the caboose."

I started notching down.

"That's good." He said. Now flip that lever." He said, pointing his finger.

I did and things started clicking and snapping in the electrical cabinet.

"That's good. Now start coming out slowly on the throttle…Burp! Easy now…yer bunching them up. Now, when we get 'em all bunched up you can control the speed, if it will hold 'em? If not, we will set the first notch. This is a good place to see how good them Dynamics are. We're gonna need them down Ash Hill."

"You notice those red reflectors on the telephone poles a while back?" He asked.

"Yes I did, what's that?"

"An Engineer named Phil, came out here to all the sidings, he counted off the poles for a mile before each headn'n switch, on each siding, in both directions, and hammered up them reflectors. Those things are going to be real handy as you learn the road. You'll be headin" in at night and be thankful to have 'em alright. They don't look kindly on laying out the Hot Shots or Amtrak! By the way, there are 36 poles to the mile. Don't ever forget that! Everything out here is based on that. Yes sir, you will be glad old Phil did that. You'll see him out here. He likes to take pictures…just give him a toot!"

"Up around the next left hand curve is an "S" curve…Ludlow. Blow for Ludlow! There are section men who will be around…they live there. You'll be bringing water out here for them. That Café over there ain't bad…guy named Luther Friend owns it."

"Yes, I have heard of him. I have a friend from school who works for him."

Old Rooster looked at me and cocked that eye and said, "You get around, don't you?"

"I've made a few friends." I said.

As we rolled into Ludlow I blew for the crossing and he says, "Now start easing off them dynamics. When you get rid of them, hit the selector I showed yah and go back to power. Then start coming right on them. Blow for Old Highway 66."

"Soak It!!!"... and Other Railroad Stories

We are in Run 8 and they are screaming at the incline ahead of us. I heard the Conductor say, "Straight track, Santa Fe 55-East."

"Straight track," Rooster replied.

Our rear had just come around the 50 mph curve coming into Ludlow.

Rooster excused himself. "Keep pushing that Alerter. I will be right back." He opened the nose door and climbed down to relieve himself.

I could smell the *Jim Beam*/garlic aroma mixed in with those crappy tablets they dropped in the toilets.

As he climbed out and shut the door, he returned to leaning on the control stand. "Yah doin' alright?"

"Yes sir."

"Okay then. Now when we top over Ash Hill the first curve to the right is 45 mph. We're going to be going back to dynamics as we get some of the train over...too little of the train over and you will stall out! As we go around that curve, it will really drop off! I am gonna tell yah, this is no place to Hot Rod a heavy train! Those piggy-backs, you can drag 'em over. Set a notch and go to dynamics. Hot Rod the piss out of 'em...you won't spill the Skipper's coffee. With these heavy trains its best to balance it out and get ahold of her. You understand what I am saying?"

"Don't Hot Rod a heavy train here!" (Boy was he right!!!) I learned the hard way one day on 901!!! Rooster's words would haunt me! (But that's another story for another day.)

"Let's start gathering them up. As you get to 36 or 37 mph, start easing off the throttle. As they top over, we want to catch 'em...like Dominos...Got it?"

"Yes sir." I followed old Rooster's instructions, over the top and down the Chute...I could not believe this man put me in the seat...what was he thinking???

He told me at the Bottom is Bagdad. You will be going back to Power. He said there used to be a café there along the highway...pretty good food! I told him, "My best friend, who is now in the Navy has a father who drives for *Yellow Freight*, used to stop there for coffee." I said, "The owner used to upholster car seats. He reupholstered my 1967 *Jeepster.*"

"Yes, that's the guy." He said. "Navy huh? What's he do in the Navy?"

"Boiler Operator." I said. "He's off the coast of Vietnam right now."

"I was in the Navy." He said. "World War II. I am not so sure we should be over there now…They have f__ around long enough…Yah think them people in Washington would learn. They did the same thing in Korea. I say we either are in it to win it, or don't go at all! He looked at me with that cocked eye.

I backed off the Dynamics…slowly went to Power, and started tugging as we came out of Bagdad.

"Yer getting' her kid!" He told me after I got back up to track speed to set the first notch coming into Amboy and blow for the crossing. "Get her through Amboy and kick her off. You will be going by Saltus. We haul salt out of there on the Saltus Local. If you been down running a midnight Goat with Gus, you have built the local. She goes on duty at 4:50 A.M."

I told him "I probably had; but I was just following the lantern."

"After we go over Bolo we will be coming into Cadiz. Just keep right on doing what yer doing. I am going to set my rear down, as we go up the hill to Goffs. You good with that?"

"I hope so…your the boss!"

"Oh hell kid, yer going good. Yer doing Okay!" He hollered over the engine noise so much information, it would have taken a tape recorder to capture it all…

On we went as we started chugging up the hill to Goffs.

I think, if I could dig deep enough into my "Bank of Bad Habits," I could write something about each siding I was then seeing for the first time. Whether it was something I experienced, or something that was passed on to me by someone who had.

"Soak It!!!"... and Other Railroad Stories

Soon I was blowing for Goffs. There was so much history there. The General who kicked Rommel's ass in North Africa and moved his troops across Germany at record pace to the Battle of the Bulge, trained his Army here! Bonnie, my Step Mom lost her first husband at the Bulge, while she worked at *Convair* in San Diego, California. My Father knew Bonnie from high school in Ohio. They were both working for the War effort in the same town, a mile or so from each other...my Dad at the FBI and Bonnie working for the aircraft company. There lives would not cross for 25 year, when my Dad returned after leaving Barstow.

"How yah doing over there?" Said the Rooster as he made his way over to the control stand.

"Good, I think."

"Just do like yah did when we dragged over Ash Hill...same drill."

I did as he instructed...as the dominos came over the hill behind me. As I went into Braking, I could feel the slight bump they made telling me they were there. Soon the Dynamics were howling as loud as they could as we wound down the hill. As we approached Ibis, I told Rooster, "I worked on that freeway bridge!"

Again that eye cocked and he said, "That was in 71, right?"

"Yes. I was staying over at Sam Martin's then."

"You know Sam?" He asked.

"Yes sir, I do."

"Best flop house in town!" He said. "Old Gus was always making home brew over there." He said, as he smiled.

Before long he called out the "Switch Time" and told me to set the air. Our train gradually slowed down as we came rolling into town...dynamics SCREAMING by the depot!!! He walked me through applying the Independent Brakes, just a wee bit to hold the head end to slow her down a bit more. "Be prepared for the dynamics to give up on yah...and YOU got to hold THE SLACK!"

I did as I was told, my heart racing, my mind spinning, and my soul praying! I was about to make my first

Charles H. Geletzke, Jr.

spot on the East End fuel Rack with my train standing on end…on the hill, behind me! "Oh please let me make it!!!"

"That's good…that's good. You got it…You Got it…Little more of that Little Jeff, Burp!!! Rooster said, as we slid to a stop.

I was shaking…I sat for a few seconds to soak it up…

Rooster said, "Good job. Don't forget your plug!"

As he made his way out the door through the brake shoe smoke…"Phew!!!"

I grabbed my bag and climbed down.

The outbound crew smiled at me as my feet hit the ground. "How's the power?" One of them asked…I assumed he was the Engineer.

"Ahhhh, good, real good!" I said. My life is changing, I thought.

I had to jog a bit through the brake shoe smoke to catch up to Rooster. It looked like fog as the lights of the platform shined through it.

I thanked him for taking the time to help me.

He said. "That's the way it is…I'm at Bat, and yer on Deck. You got to take batting practice, and you just did. You will do alright. Just step up and don't be afraid to swing!!!"

I said, good-by, thanked him again, and walked around a bit. I went out in front of the depot, and found a bench under the swaying palm trees. I put my knapsack on the bench and stretched out using it as a pillow. I laid there, staring at the stars above Needles. With the cool breeze and the swaying trees, I fell asleep thinking about the trip.

I woke up to the Mojave Desert sun shining in my eyes. I went inside of the depot and met Doc, the 1st Trick Crew Dispatch. I asked him if he had called any eastbound trains.

He said. "A Hotshot will be here in an hour or so."

I thanked him and asked where the "head" was. He pointed down the hall past the Wall Clock… the same Hall, Leo Kowalski would be tip-toeing down when we would come in ahead of "the advertised"…on a date in the future!

I went in and washed up. I was amazed how clean everything was! The floors in the hall and the head had a shine to them…the walls even shined! Somebody took pride in their work! I finished up and walked uptown for some breakfast and coffee. I ordered a lunch to go; then headed back to the depot.

When the Engineer showed up, I told him I was a student fireman, and asked if I could go to Seligman with him. I remember his wire framed glasses for some reason, *Kromer* railroad hat, and bib overalls. He was neat as a pin! "He said, "Sure, why not."

I don't remember a whole lot about the trip, other than he sat halfway out the window most of the trip…kind of cocked in the seat. I guessed he was an old steam hogger. He was very polite, explained things as we made our way up the hill, 149 miles to Seligman. He did not put me in the seat; but he was a fountain of information. His name was Mr. Plaster.

A few years later, when we moved to our home on Community Blvd., I met the neighbors, Will and Betty Horan. Best neighbors I ever had! They were members of the Barstow Class of 1947 and drove a 1947 Packard to their 30th High School Reunion…turned out, Mr. Plaster was Betty's Uncle! R.I.P. Will and Betty!

The Railroad World is really a small one…

As we rolled into Seligman, Mr. Plaster told me that I could get a room in the *Harvey House*. "Just tell the Crew Dispatcher and he will set it up."

After the night on the bench in front of the depot in Needles, I was ready for a bed. It turned out to be a flea bag and that was the last time I ever stayed there!

I figured I would get rested up and stay on whatever I caught in the morning through to Barstow.

Mr. Plaster made a perfect spot.

As we climbed down another old thin hogger in bibs was standing on the platform. "Who yah got there?" He asked Mr. Plaster.

"New hire Fireman. Leon, meet George Story."

I put out my hand and shook George's hand. He looked to be in his 70's.

"You shoot pool?" He asked me.

"I do." I replied.

Charles H. Geletzke, Jr.

"Well, after you get settled, why don't you meet me at the *Black Cat?*" He said, as he raised his arm with his thumb pointing over his shoulder.

The *Black Cat* was where the Rails drank in Seligman.

I said, "I will; but just for pool. I have to get over my Derail."

He smiled and said, "Okay, I'll meet yah there."

It was a very pleasant evening…shooting pool with the old Hogger…listening to his stories. He introduced me to some others whose names I have long forgotten.

Crew Dispatchers came in and out looking for crew members to give them their calls. The place was a beehive of activity.

Several years later, George got into a Track Gang's limits. No one was hurt. He got stopped in time…he walked into the Trainmaster's Office and made a deal to take the heat for the whole crew. They fell for it…and George retired!

I shot pool with a Class Act guy in my opinion…

The next morning I went down to see what I could catch going west. The line-up was dead! Dead that is, except for one train, the 891. The 891 was THE HOTTEST train on the Santa Fe Railway! You could get a few brownies if you laid this guy out!

I went to eat, then got my knapsack, and was there when the crew went to work. I introduced myself and got the "old who are you speech" again. Dang!!!

After I finished the name dropping, the 891 came rolling in. We climbed on and were out of there so fast we were a blur to anybody watching! No BSing on the platform today. This was all Business!!! Santa Fe Business!!! Everyone was proud of the 891/198! In 1976 the Company even painted a number of 5700's, Red, White, and Blue and these were primarily used in captive service on the "Super C, as the 891/198 was called. I am extremely honored to say that I have run them…

AT&SF 5704 & 5694 westbound at Joliet, IL on March 21, 1976.
(J. G. Tyson photo)

Anyway, I rode this train all the way to Barstow...didn't take too long. Everyone was getting in the hole for us. Man oh Man this thing was HOT!

Upon arrival back in Barstow I went to turn in my student trip paperwork to the Trainmaster. The light was on in his office. As I handed Mr. C. F. Lilly my paperwork and he examined it. It turned out I had missed the spot for riding a switch engine. Mr. Lilly looked over the top of his glasses and said, "I guess all them nights you have been running with Gus will take care of this." And he "OK'd the line with his name!

Sharp Shooting Son of a Gun...

By: L. E. Batanian, retired Santa Fe, BN, BNSF, Locomotive Engineer, and Amtrak RFE-Rocky Mt. Division

It was no secret that the Switchmen in Barstow (CA) had this little gig going on, where they bid from job to job...sometimes working seven days a week or bidding days off. This kept the extra board flipping, plus gave the crew dispatchers job security. It was interesting to watch.

Now, sometimes sitting on an Engine, an Engineer has time to think...

Barstow had 36 Hostler jobs, three locals, and maybe 12 to 15 yard jobs...also, the Pool jobs in Needles and the Amtrak trains.

As long as the Hostler jobs did not go "no bids," a guy could do some "Sharp Shooting..." The crunch from Firemen entering the training program, the number of Engineers retiring, and vacations all added to the equation. Vacations created what they called "Hold Downs" (We had those on the GTW too.-CHG) If you could get out on a job before someone else "older than you" (seniority wise), you "owned" the job! The only way to get knocked off it was if someone had a regular job "bump." This was how I managed to get more experience under my belt.

I started watching the bids and vacations a little more closely...of course there was always the *Del Taco Burrito* for the Crew Caller too! That being said, I managed to shoot my way onto the Fireman's job with "Tiny" Thompson on the Saltus Local. If you saw "Tiny," you would know why they called him that!

There is a story that Gus (my Father-in-law) used to fire for "Tiny" on an afternoon "goat." Now before Gus married my Mother-in-law he would wear old kaki pants, a sweat shirt, and an old straw hat. One day Gus got off the engine and was walking around looking for God only knows what...picking-up ballast and throwing it...you know, just killing time. So the "Cinder Dick" pulled up in a cloud of dust and said. "Okay Buddy, let's go. Yer outta here for Trespassing on Santa Fe Railway Property!"

"Huh?" says, Gus!!!

"I said let's go...NOW!"

Gus said, "I'm the Fireman on that engine over there."

The Cinder Dick walked over and looked up at "Tiny" and asked, "You know this man?"

138

"Soak It!!!"… and Other Railroad Stories

"Tiny" replied, "I have never seen him before in my life!!!"

And off they went to the railroad police officer's office.

It took Trainmaster, Mr. C. F. Lilly to get him released.

Years later, the BNSF at Klinefelter, CA April 2, 2013. (Jeff Mast photo)

So off I go with "Tiny" on the Saltus at 4:50 A.M….the "Salty Dog." We picked-up water cars at Newberry for the thirsty towns…Newberry Springs was known for its good water. We would switch the *Barriod* Plant on the way back. Then we headed to Saltus for the MONEY MAKER!!! *Morton Salt* ran this little operation. We would pull in, set out the empties, and grab the "cash" for the Santa Fe. These cars would be weighed back in Barstow at the scale house. Soon we had our train "built" and Conductor Jerry Cason went to the phone. It was time to get permission to crossover and head back to "B" town (Barstow).

Shortly, Jerry came up to the headend and said, "There's been a derailment west of us. We are to crossover and put the train in the Westbound Siding at Amboy." (This

Charles H. Geletzke, Jr.

was the same siding Gus and I tore out in the derailment of the 348.)

"Then what?" says I.

"I don't know," says Conductor Cason.

So we got crossed over and tucked away in the siding, and waited...and waited...and waited...

Roy's Café in Amboy, California. (L. E. Batanian collection)

I decided to walk over to *Roy's Café* for a piece of pie. Isn't that what the Fireman job is?

Roy's was known for its homemade pies after all!

So, I was sitting on a stool in the beanery having my pie, when in walked a Track Supervisor from Cadiz. We shot the breeze and he told me, "both Mains were torn out at the derailment and it will be a day or two before it is clear."

"This don't sound good…" I paid my tab and made my way back to the train with the latest dope.

I told "Tiny" and Jerry who was now sipping on a Lemonade and Gin…Jerry's favorite beverage, what the straight dope was. After all, it had to be true…I heard it in the Café!

With that, Jerry walked back to the phone at Amboy. There was no use trying to use the radio…it had too much traffic due to the derailment…why a safe cracker could not break in!

Soon our Conductor returned and says, "We wait!" And he prepared himself another Lemonade Cocktail. He even offered me one!

It looked refreshing in the desert heat.

I declined…

By now the two Brakemen had disappeared to the caboose. More time passed. I looked at my watch. We will be "Dead" at 1650. Jerry and "Tiny" are in no shape to go anywhere…I decided to go to the phone. (That phone hangs in my office today!) "Saltus Local to Dispatcher…"

"Dispatcher."

"Dispatcher, we are Dead in 30 minutes."

He then asked me if the motel at *Roy's* had any rooms?

I reply to him, "I will go find out."

Then the Dispatcher said. "If they have rooms, just tie-up there and we will find you when we need you."

"Roger that! Amboy out."

"Dispatcher out."

The AT&SF phone from Amboy, California is now in Leon
Batanian's collection.

So back to *Roy's Café* I marched. "Hello again. Do
you have five rooms?"
"We have three rooms available."
"Doubles?"
"Yes."

"I will take them…you can bill the Santa Fe Railway!"

"Of course."

Then, back to the train I went…I told the crew that the DS said to "Tie up here."

"We can't do that!" They said.

"They did." Said I. "I got us three rooms."

We tied the train down and made our way to *Roy's*. The two Brakie's doubled as did "Tiny" and I. Conductor Cason was on his own. After everyone was squared away the crew realized they were out of cocktails! One of the Brakemen went into the *Café* to see about refreshments.

"Nada, none, zippo!"

BNSF along Route 66 in California on April 2, 2013. (Jeff Mast photo)

The closest place was east of us at Cadiz. There was a store there that sold beer.

They were now working on a plan… "Problem was, they close at 6 P.M.! The clock was ticking…the store was 13 miles away!" One of the Brakie's spotted a Santa Fe truck parked in front of another room. He knocked on the door…a guy opened the door…the Brakie came back with the keys…The Brakie's were then eastbound on Highway Route 66 bound for Cadiz! They returned with four cases of *Coors*

Charles H. Geletzke, Jr.

Beer on ice in the Santa Fe ice chest from the back of the borrowed Santa Fe truck…

I went to the *Café* for dinner…pretty good cheese burger and fries and a couple glasses of Sun Tea.

When I returned, the crew had assembled some chairs and were sitting around drinking their dinner.

Conductor Cason had managed to find out more information. He said, "It will be later tomorrow!"

I had a couple of cold *Coors Beers* with the crew as the sun set. *Coors Beer* that no doubt came out of Boulder, Colorado on a westbound 408 train. The 408 was known for hauling *Coors Beer*.

We weren't going anywhere tonight!

Sometime after dark "Tiny" and I headed to our room. The old hogger was done…He told me stories of the old days as he drifted off to sleep. That was a big mistake on my part…Not getting to sleep before "Tiny," was brutal to say the least! I thought he was running a chain saw, while he chewed and clicked his false teeth. My Lord, why didn't I put him in with Cason, I do not know!?! They both would have passed out sawing away. I tried to sleep for about two hours. I could not…no matter what! "Tiny" was clicking those teeth so hard, I thought his jaw had come loose! Finally, I got up and shook "Tiny" awake. I said, "Tiny, either swallow those teeth or take them out, and please lay on your side."

With that "Tiny" removed his teeth and gently placed them in his boot.

"Huh???"

In his boot!!!

I finally got to sleep; but was woken up at about 7 A.M. by a scream from "Tiny" as he hopped around the room! He forgot that he had put those choppers in his boot. Never a dull moment on the railroad, I tell you! I laughed till I cried.

Later in the afternoon we got word to triple-up the two westbound's that were parked back to back on the Main with our Local on the Siding. I guess those boys went back to Needles in the middle of the night?

This took some ciphering on the part of Conductor Cason. We managed to get everything together and ended up with 16 units on the headend! "Tiny" and I hooked the whole thing together. **We did not want to loose any Weight on Drivers!**

It was my turn to run, so after we got word from East Barstow we headed west.

"Tiny" dropped off and caught the rear unit as I eased them ahead. He started isolating units as he came back to the head end. When we got to Bagdad he went back and put a few more "on line" to help us up Ash Hill.

When we got to Barstow we had to double into three tracks. I was all the way out on the Mojave River Bridge. As we backed in the clear, the Outside Hostler and Helper met us. The Red Barn wanted all those units as quickly as possible. They needed power!

As I say, you never know what might happen while Sharp Shootin' the boards. You can't make this stuff up! It was Railroading…back when it was fun!!!

U.S. Army Corporal Leon S. Batanian on Reserve duty in the mid-1970's. (Batanian collection)

It was Railroading!

By: L. E. Batanian, retired AT&SF, BN, BNSF Locomotive Engineer, Amtrak Road Foreman of Engines-Rocky Mt. District.

Bam, Bam, Bam!
"Batanian?"

"Yah."

"You're called…788 Train…11:35 P.M."

I flew out of my bed at the *Canyon Shadows Motel* in Seligman, Arizona and went to the door and opened it. There stood Tommy the Crew Dispatcher.

And there I stood in my U. S. Army issue Boxers left over from National Guard Boot Camp!

"I said you're called!!!"

I said, "Yeah Tommy, I got that; but did you say 788 Train?"

"I did, what's the problem?"

"Well Tommy, Mr. Mulligan has not ridden with me on the Coal Train." I said.

"I know. I figured that might be…guys try to dodge The Coal Train all the time; so I called the RFE. He said you're good to go! At least you're an honest kid." With that he was gone as I quietly closed the door to block the cold December wind.

Tommy also had a side business…He and his brother cut Christmas trees. You could order a tree in the morning, and the Santa Fe would deliver it to Barstow the following morning **on Number 5…Merry Christmas!** They also ran a slaughter house and butcher shop.

Gus and I would stop in there on our way to Colorado…hunting. They would load us up with the best BEEF I ever ate…ON THE HOUSE!!!

Gus had some connections!!!

On one trip we stopped to see Tommy and he had a pot simmering on the stove. I asked, "What ya cooking, Tommy?"

He said, "Son of a Bitch Stew! Try it, if you don't eat it, you're a Son of a Bitch!"

I did not even ask what was in it, as I ate a bowl.

Seligman, AZ is almost a mile higher than Needles, California. What this meant was…this 22 year old Locomotive Engineer was about to crack the throttle on a RCE (Remote Control Engine) 12,000 ton Coal Train…nearly down hill for 149 miles. I had only been promoted for six months!

Charles H. Geletzke, Jr.

I am being honest...I was scared sh-- less! I ran the coal train a few times, while training on the West End, Needles to Barstow...Never on the East End. I even dropped off the headend one night while firing for an Oldhead 1940's Hogger. The RCE failed. I dropped off the head end and caught the rear locomotives and shoved that old Hogger to Barstow...that was Railroading! I was not even promoted; but I was shoving him like I had been doing it all my life, with him coaching me through it over the radio...we got over the road. I remember him telling me his son was an Alaskan State Senator! I do not remember his name; but I am very thankful he trusted me to do that. You learn more by doing on the Railroad, than you do by watching.

You also earned the old head's respect. If you climbed on and went to the second unit and went to sleep on someone, you lost respect!

I am not saying I never slept on the second unit. I would be lying. But if I did, it was because we split the trip or I was watching a unit or Deadheading.

When I got Promoted, my check ride was on the 668 Train...a westbound Smoker!

Mr. Mulligan the RFE asked me about the Coal Train. I guess I had all the right answers because of the situation I was now in!?!

I went in and took a quick shower, packed my grip and went down to the only café in town. I set my thermos on the table and broke-out my Air Brake Book. I found the section on RCE Train Handling. I skimmed through it. I had no fireman to drop-off and catch the rear units if things went wrong. There was nothing else left to do, but face the Music! So, I finished my meal, paid my tab, and walked to the depot.

My Conductor was "Shoe Fly" Miller. I had worked with him before. Shoe Fly was not from around Needles...I think Texas or Oklahoma originally. I think what would have best described Show Fly was Slim Pickens. You will know why I said this, when we hit the switch at needles.

I signed the register and checked my watch. Shoe Fly got our orders and gave me a copy. There was really nothing out of the ordinary...we were good to go.

148

"Soak It!!!"… and Other Railroad Stories

Shoe Fly looked at me, his cowboy hat tilted back on his head, spit, and said, "It's going to be a good night. I'll let you know when we're on." Then he gave me a big grin.

A few minutes later Westbound 788 came rolling in. They ran the Coal Train back then with nine SD25's…five up front and four on the rear with an RCE car. The RCE car was a converted B-unit packed with Radio equipment. It was not uncommon to lose continuity with the rear units going around curves, or through cuts or tunnels. Lose it too long and everything would shut down!

I got a quick "turnover" from the inbound Hogger. I asked if the train was bunched and he said, "Yes."

Then I climbed up on the old 46__ and put my bag down and sat down in the seat. The brakeman came over to the control stand and said, "I will handle the radio if you would like?"

I said, "Sure thing."

He called the cab and told them that we were ready to go. We would be pulling down to allow the Conductors of both crews to get off and on. Seligman is in kind of a slight bowl or basin.

I pressed the Release button to release the brakes on the train. Then I held in the Independent Motoring button and went to Run 1 on the rear. I held the headend in tight with the Independent Brake Valve after backing off a little. I turned the bell on and gave a quick "Toot-toot." Then Run 2 for a bit and then back to 1. There it was…a slight bump on my seat and the Inbound Conductor said, "All moving."

I was in no hurry. I slowly walked her down. As the headend started up the hill toward Yampi, I released more engine brakes and added more rear throttle. I was trying to shove in and out of Seligman. Not too much, just a bit…

Soon the radio said, "10 cars 46__"

I pinched her down some. Soon I heard Shoe Fly say, "Highball Santa Fe 46__ West." Shoe Fly was a stickler about train identification! He would "Santa Fe" us all the way home on the radio!

I brought the rear power up a notch. I slowly let-off the rest of the engine brakes and when released, I went to

Run 1 on the headend. Then I let it settle, then Run 3 on the rear...then 2 on the headend...back and forth...back and forth. Soon I had them all talking in Run 8! We were on our way up and over Yampi!

At Yampi, as the headend topped over, I started slowly backing-off the lead locomotives. As the speed increased to about 20 mph, I went to Dynamic (Brake) on the headend to start bunching them up as they came over the top. Slowly the speed crept up.. Slowly, I cut back a notch on the rear. I was in Full Dynamic on the headend by this time. I kept notching back the rear and when it settled down back there, I put the rear in Dynamic and looked up as the speed was inching up. Soon the rear was in Full Braking and I watched my speed as it leveled out. I had good dynamics! I backed off the rear a bit and inched up to 45 mph. Then back a little on the rear and it was holding pretty good. My ass let go of the seat...we were on our way!

Shoe Fly was on the job. He Santa Fe'd the restrictions and green boards all night long.

I was glad!

We worked our way down the hill through Peach Springs, across the flats coming into Kingman, doing all of my moves in reverse of the last one. Kingman was going to be a little different. It was like stepping off the Grand Canyon past the depot! Surprisingly, it wasn't too bad! I ended up with about 10 pounds set and rode it out 'til the grade let up and on we went...

BNSF 775 at Needles, CA on November 3, 2013. (Jeff Mast photo)

When we crossed the Colorado River at the Topoc Bridge, I got the rear shoving. I figured I would keep the headend in Dynamic and work the rear. The units did not have Extended Range Dynamic Braking; so I had to be ready for them to fade out! I did not want to miss the "Spot" sign at the West End Fuel Rack in Needles!

Soon we called the switch and Shoe Fly let out a big "Yeeee-Hawww" and repeated the time and said, "GOOD RIDE Santa Fe Extra 46__."

That is why he reminded me of Slim Pickens. Think of the movie "Dr. Strangelove" as Ole Slim rode the Nuke out the bottom of the B-52.

I said a "thank you" prayer and breathed a sigh of relief as we slid to a perfect spot! "Phew!!!"

22 years old!!! Who would let a 22 year old do that!?!

The Santa Fe Railway, that's who!!!

They put a lot of faith in us to get the job done! It was Railroading!

Charles H. Geletzke, Jr.

"Destination Wedding"

By: C. H. Geletzke, Jr.

This was a "one of a kind trip!" On Saturday, September 20, 1975 I was called off the GTW Brakeman's Extra Board at Milwaukee Jct. in Detroit, Michigan to work "Extra" Trains 830 and 831 on duty at 11:30 A.M. Working with me this day were Engineer, Glenn Hansman; Fireman, Jim Miller; Conductor, G. O. Potter; Brakeman, Joel Kruskie; and I was the other Brakeman. When the crew dispatcher called, he instructed Mr. Potter, Mr. Kruskie, and me to all "wear your passenger uniforms!" Now this was extremely unusual and being a railfan, I was totally unaware of any pending railfan trips being planned or scheduled at this time!

When all five of us reported for duty we were informed that we would be deadheaded by company van to get our train, thus we would only actually be working Train 831. None of us wasted any time and we immediately climbed into the van and headed up I-94 toward Port Huron.

Upon arriving at Tunnel Yard in Port Huron we were informed by the Trainmaster there that we would be working a special passenger extra, consisting of one privately owned railroad car, the *Jean Pierre*. The car was sitting out in front of the 32nd Street yard office where it had just arrived…having come through the St. Clair Tunnel from Canada. At this time also, Engineer Hansman, Fireman, Miller, and Brakeman Kruskie were instructed to go to the roundhouse and get the GTW 4917, a passenger equipped GP9.

While they were getting the engine out of the house, the Trainmaster, G. O. Potter, and I went out to the privately owned "business car." Sadly, the car had not been turned and the open platform end was still headed west. At the cars open platform end, we introduced ourselves to the owner of the car and his wife. I am sorry, I can no longer recall their names; but they seemed to be very pleasant people! Also with them were their infant son and I believe a car attendant or two.

152

"Soak It!!!"... and Other Railroad Stories

Shortly, Joel Kruskie appeared and tied the locomotive onto the single gorgeous car and two of the Port Huron Car Inspectors gave us an Initial Terminal Brake Test. Following the successful brake test, I gave Engineer Hansman a "Go Ahead" signal and we headed for the Top End of the yard at an interlocking tower known as Tappan (Milepost 55.5), where we would pick-up our train orders. While pulling west on the Westward Main Track the car owners gave us the "cook's tour" of the car and then we all took seats in the lounge at the west or head end of the car. The owners told us that they had arrived from Montreal (I believe) and were on their way to a wedding in Grosse Pointe, Michigan. (Actually, there are five cities in Michigan, all in the same general vicinity with similar names...Grosse Pointe, Grosse Pointe Farms, Grosse Pointe Park, Grosse Pointe Shores, and Grosse Pointe Woods...generally the entire area is just referred to as Grosse Pointe.) We were instructed to stop at Seven Mile Road (Milepost 8.9) in Detroit, where the car's owners would be met by a limousine and chauffeured to the venue and wedding celebration...all of this was spelled out on a message from the Train Dispatcher and attached to our orders.

While it was a cloudy gray day, the trip down to Detroit was nonstop and went without any difficulties. Following about an hour of pleasant conversation, we stopped at Seven Mile Road and allowed the wedding guests to detrain. We then took the "train" on down to the roundhouse at Milwaukee Jct. (Milepost 4.6), where we headed right into the roundhouse with the private car attached. I regretted that I had not brought my camera on this trip; but fortunately, while we were lining the roundhouse switch, GTW Conductor and fellow railfan, Dennis Smolinski happened to be working right there and he took photos of us on our train.

We tied-up at 5:20 P.M. I assume the family was returned home the next day following the celebration; but truthfully, I never heard any details regarding the reverse trip. For me this was an adventure of a lifetime; but even now, I cannot begin to envision how much an outing like that must

have cost!?! Honestly, I cannot conceive a Destination
Wedding ever topping this one!

Looking east from Johnson Ave. at the east end of GTW's Pontiac
Yard on October 29, 1969. From this location there were 12 grade
crossing within the next 2-1/2 miles. The crossing towers had been
removed by the date of the incident .

Run-Away...and not by Del Shannon

By: C. H. Geletzke, Jr.

I have explained before how in January 1975 the U.
S. economy took a real hit and I was furloughed from my
Locomotive Fireman job on the Grand Trunk Western
Railroad in Detroit, Michigan. Fortunately, because my
brother and I had a side business doing grading and
excavating, we were able to put one of our trucks on the road
hauling perishables and other commodities. Throughout the

year the railroad would call about once a month or so and ask me to work "in emergency" as a Hostler at Milwaukee Jct., which was nice because it kept my medical benefits current! Then an unexpected surprise occurred on July 6th…I was asked if I would like to be added to the Milwaukee Jct. Brakemen's Extra Board! I readily accepted the invitation and immediately marked-up. I then continued working (off and on) as a road brakeman into early January 1976 when I was promoted into management.

Now let's get to our actual story…

On the morning of Tuesday, October 14, 1975 I was ordered to deadhead the 67 miles from Milwaukee Jct. (M.P. 4.2) to Durand (M.P. 69) at 1045 along with Trainman James "Jimmy" Lett to work Train 410 and 411. Our on-duty time at Durand was 1215. Our crew consisted of Engineer, Pat O'Hearn; Conductor, Bill Cottenham; Head Brakeman, Jimmy Lett; and I was the Flagman. Going east out of Durand, down to Dearoad (D&TSL M.P. 46), we had two GTW SD40's the 5914 & 5906 and 117-cars. At Dearoad we swapped trains with the Detroit & Toledo Shore Line (D&TSL) crew on Train 411, which originated at Lang Yard (D&TSL M.P. 2) in Toledo, Ohio. That train also had two GTW SD40's, the 5900 & 5909 and headed back to Durand. All day until we arrived at Pontiac Yard on the return trip, things had gone extremely well. However…

As we pulled up to the west end of Pontiac Yard (Milepost 28.8), Conductor Cottenham dropped off at Johnson Avenue (Milepost 26.8) and a clerk drove him to the West Tower. Brakeman Lett dropped off to make the cut on our 25-car set-off at the west end of the yard. Simultaneously, I too dropped off the caboose near the middle of the yard and began climbing through the cars sitting in Tracks 1-16 in order to reach our pick-up of about 25-cars in Track 17. When I reached the east end of our pick-up I began walking toward the west end of the yard, making certain that all of the air hoses were coupled, that the angle cocks were all open, and that there were not any handbrakes applied to any of the cars other than a few on the headend. Oh yes, did I tell you that Pontiac Yard was built on a hill!?!

Charles H. Geletzke, Jr.

Well, I am guessing that I had examined approximately 15-cars when all at once the Yardmaster called over the radio and announced, **"TRAIN 411...YOUR TRAIN IS ROLLING AWAY!"**

I immediately called Jimmy Lett over the radio and instructed him to "cut away from the set-off! Go back to the Mainline and pick me up, and we'll go after the train!"

Now let me state that James Lett was a good man, a Viet Nam War Army Veteran (who would later succumb to the effects of Agent Orange at a young age), and a hard worker. That said, Jimmy was a new man...only having worked on the railroad for several months by this time and apparently no one had ever told him that with the new ABD and ABDW brake valves, **YOU DO NOT EVER SAVE THE AIR!**

Apparently, that was exactly what happened...when Jimmy made the cut on the 25-cars he was going to set-out, he closed the angle cock on the head car remaining on the Mainline...leaving 23-cars and the caboose sitting there and he never applied even a single handbrake! Then, over the next several minutes the air stored in the reservoirs began to cause a release of the brakes in all of the cars equipped with the relatively new ABD and ABDW brake valves.

Now, let's take a look at this in detail...when James Lett brought the two SD40's out of the yard lite, he stopped clear of the turnout at the west end of Pontiac Yard right at Milepost 28.8. He then threw the switch and gave Engineer O'Hearn a signal to back-up...fast! In the meantime I cut back across the seventeen tracks in the yard as fast as I could run and jump out to the Main Track and they slowed down and picked me up at approximately Milepost 27.5. We then raced after our runaway train as fast as we could! We finally caught up with it at approximately Milepost 25.7, coupled to the train, and brought the 23-cars and caboose to a rapid halt. We then opened the angle cock and cut the air back into the train. Oh yes, let's look at one more detail...while we tied-on and got stopped pretty close to Milepost 25.7 or Wessen Street in downtown Pontiac, the tailend of the train probably came to a stop at or near the Saginaw Street crossing at

156

"Soak It!!!"… and Other Railroad Stories

Milepost 25.0. Looking at a track profile, that means that our caboose and the attached cars rolled unattended across 11 or 12 public crossings at grade! It was a true miracle that no vehicles nor pedestrians were hit at any of those crossings and thank God, there was not another westbound train or yard job following closely on our heels! Looking just a little further east in another half-mile or so was the crest of "Pontiac Hill," and had we not caught our train when we did, it would have taken off on the descending grade averaging about -.67% and probably would have rolled all the way to Brush Street Depot, in Detroit at Milepost 0.00, at unthinkable speeds! Yes, the Lord was watching over all of us that evening…and do you want to know what was the most unbelievable thing of all? We pulled back up to the west end of the yard, completed making our set-off, picked up, and went on to Durand…and to this day not any of us on the crew ever heard anything about the incident from GTW management!

Brakeman Lett and I then tied-up at Durand, deadheaded back to Milwaukee Jct., and went off duty at 0110 on Wednesday, October 15th. And yes, I am certain that Brakeman Lett learned a valuable lesson that night!

"Book Me Sick!"

By: AT&SF Switchman, NYC-PC Conductor, GTW-CN
Conductor & Trainmaster, L. D. Akers

Effective April 1, 1976, I had to make the choice of either transferring to the Grand Trunk Western Railroad (GTW) or going with the newly formed Consolidated Railroad Corporation aka Conrail as a Conductor. I made the right choice and decided to go with the GTW.

Within a year on the GTW I was promoted to Assistant Trainmaster-Saginaw, Michigan. With the formation of Conrail, the GTW acquired various territories of the former Penn Central (PC) and Bay City and Saginaw were two of them. Before the acquisition, PC had more

157

Charles H. Geletzke, Jr.

traffic and industry in the Saginaw Terminal than GTW. For example, the GTW yard crew worked about three hours on an average day, whereas the PC crew normally worked 12 hours! Following the acquisition, Saginaw had two yard assignments...both working days. I recommended that the former PC job should work the day shift on account of the number of industries to service and that the GTW crew work an afternoon shift with lesser businesses to take care of. Needless to say, I was overruled!

On my first day as the Assistant Trainmaster-Saginaw, I was challenged by the GTW crew regarding the amount of work issued to them. The Conductor that day was Bob G., who walked into my office and threw down on my desk...all of the switch lists for the industries he had to service! Next he said, "Book me sick!"

I looked at him and started rubbing my stomach...referring to stomach problems; but he responded by patting his heart! He then stormed out of the office!

I immediately called the Crew Dispatcher in Durand who handled this territory and requested another employee. At the same time I also instructed the Crew Dispatcher that Mr. G. must see the Company Doctor before he would be allowed to return to his assignment.

The next day, Mr. G. called me and told me that he could not pass a physical exam to enable him to return to work. He asked if I would change or rescind my instructions and just allow him to return to work at once. That did not happen! It took Mr. G. 30 days to get his blood pressure down to the level of the Company Medical requirements for a man his age. The bottom line with me..."If you are sick, you ARE sick! But never book sick with me 'cause you think that you have been assigned too much work to do!"

What do you think?

Never in my entire railroad career did I book sick because of the amount of work to be done! In the case of Saginaw, in 1977, I wanted to prove a point...that is...if you are sick, be sick! If you are not and just want to get out of doing too much work, that is completely different!

158

"Soak It!!!"… and Other Railroad Stories

I was never considered a "Hard Ass Supervisor!" But, I expected the employees to do their work. My Motto was, "I never expected you to do more than I would do!" One day in 1979, I was told by a yard conductor, after telling him my motto…"That was unfair, because you do everything!"

Similarly, Rule G. 99 out of 100 Rule G violations are caused by the employee's own fault. In my railroad experience, it is not the carrier who traps the employee…the employee comes to you and fires himself! In most cases, the drunken employee approaches the supervisor and starts an argument and his drunken demeanor gets him terminated!

LDA

I was new to the railroad…

By: Joseph DeMike

I was new to the railroad on Erie Western. On one of my first trips, the engineer, Dave Winkelman and his brother, Paul, working as conductor offered to let me run a while. It was my first time in an RS-3 and I was excited to learn. We were moving along about 30 miles an hour west of Huntington, Indiana on what was once the Erie Lackawanna main line. Dave put the throttle to Idle and gave me the seat. "He said, "Open the throttle and let's go!"

I grabbed the big handle Alco used for the throttle and moved it up to notch 6; but nothing happened.

Dave looked at me and said, "Close it back and let me try." He reached over the control stand and moved the throttle to notch 6. The RS-3 responded with a big black cloud of smoke as the diesel roared to notch 6. "Strange" David said as he moved the throttle back to Idle. "Try again."

I opened her up and nothing happened. And again, Dave reached over, notched it out and the Alco responded as before. What in the world was I doing wrong?

On the fourth attempt, Paul who was standing with his back to the electrical cabinet burst out laughing. It turns out RS-3's have a throttle limit switch on the wall inside the cab and Paul would switch it to "0" when I opened the throttle, and set it to "8" when Dave would show me how.

After we got done laughing, the brothers told me how lucky I was. They loved to get a newbie on one of the Alco yard engines. The S-1 had the hand brake wheel inside the cab, and the newbie would be told to steer and make sure to keep everything on the track!

D&TSL Bicentennial GP7 76 (former 46) is seen departing Edison Yard in Trenton, Michigan with Train 708 in December 1979. (E. M. Gulash photo; Geletzke collection)

Bicentennial Slide Show

By: C. H. Geletzke, Jr.

Looking back 1975 and 1976 had to be two of the greatest years ever for railfans in my opinion! During that time span virtually every railroad in North America painted up a locomotive in some form of red, white, and blue and the vast majority of us fans did our best to record as many of them on film as possible.

Now let me state it was not only diesel locomotives that were the focus of attention. If you were alive at that time you will recall that many cities painted fire hydrants as little patriotic Minute Men. Aircraft, trucks and trailers, fire equipment, buildings and bridges, benches, lamp posts, construction equipment, clothing…you name it! And, we did our best to photograph it all!

"Soak It!!!"... and Other Railroad Stories

In May of 1976 I was appointed as an Assistant Trainmaster for the Grand Trunk Western Railroad at Tunnel Yard in Port Huron, Michigan. My assignment worked from 11:30 P.M. until 7:30 A.M., Tuesday through Friday and also on Saturday afternoons from 3:30 P.M. until 11:30 P.M. Thus, when I completed my tour of duty on Saturday night, I was finished until 11:30 P.M. Tuesday night, giving me three full days off! This was practically unheard of in the railroads' Operating and Transportation Departments and for the most part, other than occasionally working and extra half hour or so, was quite consistent.

In a previous story I discussed our Detroit Metropolitan Area slide group and I mentioned that we always got together at various members' homes on the first Tuesday of each month. Naturally with the excitement of the upcoming Bicentennial Celebration on July 4, 1976 we planned to have a Bicentennial Slide Night, Each of us (and we generally had about 15 or so present) would meet at the late Ray Sabo's home on Tuesday, July 6th, and were encouraged to bring and show the best of their Bicentennial slides that they had taken over the preceding two years. As I recall, all of our regular members were in attendance in addition to several invited guests. I brought my Dad along. I previously mentioned in my book, *Go Ahead and Backup and Other Railroad Stories* that as far as I knew, my father was never a railfan; but on several occasions even to this very day...I sometimes wonder!?!

Normally our meeting would begin at 8 o'clock; but due to the number of presenters and the anticipated number of tremendous slides to be shown we began an hour or so earlier. Let me state that ALL of the slides were OUTSTANDING! Naturally, they were not all just of locomotives and the creativity displayed was astounding! Norfolk & Western Railroad (N&W) Tugboat Captain, Ted Hanifan showed two slides that I will never forget! Apparently one day he was driving his car and just as the vehicle's odometer hit 1776 miles, he stopped and photographed it! Similarly, he did the same thing when the car turned over 1976 miles...none of us could believe it! Yes,

Charles H. Geletzke, Jr.

there were locomotives, cabooses, freight cars, railroad signs, action photos, tugboats, Great Lakes Freighters, aircraft, practically everything!

If I recall correctly Ken Borg was the last to present his program of outstanding material. He even went the extra step and played recorded music with his presentation. All at once as he neared a conclusion, the music's volume increased and Kate Smith began belting out *God Bless America!* Before the end of the first note, my Dad, a World War II Veteran (who spent over 2-1/2 years in the jungles of New Guinea) jumped to his feet and stood at ATTENTION! Seconds later, all of us stood, even our Canadian members, and placed our right hands over our hearts. It was really something to witness and an event, which I am certain will never be replicated. Thank you Ken Borg and Kate Smith!

Playing Tag With Railroad Dick...

By: Pennsylvania Railroad Freight Car Expert, Richard J. Burg

I was born at a time that presented me with the worst chance of seeing great railroads. The railroads in the Northeastern United States were falling apart by the time I was old enough to explore them. The great stations were in ruins, steam was gone, the tracks were a wreck, and long trains of bedraggled box cars rolled through town with what would appear to be three times the head end power as would be needed. Maybe five engines, no two alike, a couple of road switchers, a yard unit, and two aging cab units...each with only one or two traction motors cut out...rolling down track on rotted ties, loose spikes, swaying from side to side wildly. You didn't stand too close to the track for fear one of them might tip over; but somehow they all stayed on the rails...often going by at what seemed to be foolhardy speeds! The Alco's smoked like they were on fire. The EMD's sounded like they were about to throw a rod. The cars were no better. The loud clunks of flat spots on their wheel rims,

162

"Soak It!!!"… and Other Railroad Stories
where they'd slid down the tracks at some time with their
brakes locked on or brake shoes mal-adjusted, sometimes
smoking as they passed. Occasionally, a "ring of fire," that
glowed in the night as it approached, sometimes with the
brake shoes on a given wheel all but locked up…wheeling
toward you like a wheel of fire in the dark night.

Such a wonderful mix of old cars though, nearly
every car Pennsylvania RR…almost all colored "rust," and
doors all open if they were empty.

Ever since I was a kid, I'd for some reason fallen in
love with the old freight cars! I could see passing trains out
the study hall window in high school and I knew every road
name that passed. Once I had my 1963 *Evans* bike I would
often ride over to a small local park on the "Shirley
Greenbelt, which was along the Pennsylvania Railroad's line
through West Detroit, where I could watch the local
switching job sort out cars to be spotted at a half dozen local
industries…a nice mix of cars, forty-foot boxes, reefers, an
occasional gondola, or flat car. None of those sixty-foot
monsters there…never an auto rack, and who needs
passenger equipment anyway? Hopper cars? Never saw one
until I was an adult! This spot was lost in the past. Just
banged-up rusty cars…with character; but every now and
then a string of all identical cars in fresh paint would roll into
the little yard. Old cars, empty cars, they were coming to
have their refurbishing finished. New wood linings would be
applied at the local lumberyard. Oh yes, and I can't forget
that strange three-dome tank car that came home about every
two weeks. It was assigned to *Nelson Chemicals*, just down
the old Pere Marquette belt line a quarter mile east. Today it
is in *Henry Ford's Greenfield Village*, a 1936 antique. (I sent
them my "in service" photos, so they could get the painting
right.)

As an adult with a decent job, I worked pretty much
all the time. At the beginning it was six days a week, and
often over 11-hours a day. Finally, in 1976, a new union
contract set a ten hour limit to shifts (more if you wanted it),
and you only worked two Saturdays in a row, and then had

one off. Between that, and holidays, I almost had a life…almost!

By that time, I'd gotten up to two weeks of vacation. Then I discovered a *Pennsylvania Railroad Technical & Historical Society (PRRT&HS)* flyer in a local hobby shop. I joined and decided to take a mini-vacation to one of their annual meetings in Altoona, Pennsylvania with a new *Minolta* camera in hand. Penn Central had just died and the government had taken over the bankrupt railroads…a lot of them, and glued them together into a massive wreck! The whole mess had only 66,000 freight cars and probably 40% of them were stenciled PENNSYLVANIA RR. Almost all were colored "rust" with their doors all open if they were empty sitting in "Bad Order" yards awaiting repairs or the scrapper's torch. Most were awaiting the later! For perspective, the PRR alone in 1936 had over 500,000 cars and they were not all sitting rusting away in bad order yards!

Altoona was the "bone yard" of thousands of cars…they didn't even move! A car sitting in a given place in 1977 probably was still sitting there, or within a few yards in 1980. It was a mile long and eighth of a mile wide sea of cars.

The railroad was bankrupt and security was lax, or non-existent. One guy kept an eye over miles of the mess it had all become. No human could do that job; but he'd try…we called him the "last Railroad Dick!" I soon became very aware of his presence and often, he was well aware of mine! The cat and mouse game we played was heavily stacked in my favor…one Dick, and thousands of freight cars to hide in, under, and behind. To his credit, he did finally catch me, once, and gave me a lame lecture about safety, and asked where I was parked. I replied, "A long ways away across the yard."

"Go back over there and leave!"

"Sure sir." It was now a "catch and release game!"

I can't count all the times I knew he was around and I just crawled up into an empty car and sat quietly in the darkness as he walked by looking for me. Once he was gone, I continued poking around the dead cars for another couple of hours looking for those real beauties on their death beds with stories to tell. A few thousand portraits of them survive in my den…sometimes shots of intimate details, a gondola without a floor, a tightlock type-F coupler, or maybe a hopper car's interior…even the body of a gondola, lying upside down on an equally ancient flat car. Then I'd find one…a normal looking car; but one I knew was super rare! They only built five of these! Here is one of them sitting in decent shape in a sea of junk. I'd climb up into that gondola, or perhaps stand back as far as I could in a box car doorway to get enough distance to shoot a photo of it. If I must, I'd scamper up a car's ladder and even stand on the car's roof to get the shot! Can't do that, Dick will see me. After a few years of this I think Dick started to get an M. O. (Method of Operation) on me, he knew my age, and maybe where I was from even!?! A couple of times he'd spotted me driving my '68 Volvo (Dorian); but never caught up with me on the ground again. He had a rough idea where I'd park the car; but he was based on the other side of the yard and it was over a mile away to drive to me. I kept an eye on the cars over there and if the one I thought was his left…I left too!

Dick wasn't the only problem. I was here; but asked for the days off months ago. We could ask for a day off; but we couldn't ask for good weather! On some visits, there was constant drizzle. It would subside and I could quickly shoot my photos. If it came down hard, I could take cover in a boxcar. On one occasion I didn't get into a boxcar during a downpour. I knew the cars around me were buried deep in the yard and couldn't be accessed without hours of moving stuff. Since they were not moving anywhere, I climbed under the boxcar and laid on the dry ground looking up at the car's underframe. It was a class X52, one of the first two car classes that were built or converted to cushioned under frames! The Pullman Standard sliding center sills were fairly new in 1958 when the work was done and there was a lot of customer pressure for cushioned cars. By 1963 practically every new boxcar was built with them, although the Pullman Standard design was not what most of them got. And here I

Charles H. Geletzke, Jr.

was laying a foot below one of them getting to see the details and how it actually worked!

You'd think that I hated those rainy trips; but the exact opposite was actually true! I found that on days like that I got the best photos. There were no shadows and I could stop down the lens and use a tripod. The depth of field was far better and contrast could be added later when I printed them. Everything was the same dim lighting, even in obscure places. I learned that the camera could see through that, if I just gave it a longer exposure time. Without a tripod I could use the side of another car to steady the camera, while I shot the car I wanted. And, I also learned that Dick didn't go out in the rain!

On sunny days I'd bring lunch in a little *Oscar* cooler. I'd walk out along the sidewalk to a street bridge over the yard and slip down the embankment to the riverbank. Calling it a river was a stretch…I was near the head waters of the Little Juniata, which would eventually become the Juniata River. But at this point, it was only about four to five feet wide and only inches deep…crystal clear, and so nice and cold on a hot day! A few hundred yards north up the bank I'd get to my favorite place on earth! There was a little island in the "river." It was only about a yard and a half wide and maybe 20-feet long; but supported some plant life and had little pools and eddies along its banks at some places downstream. The pools would be teaming with little fish…maybe two inches long or less. Upstream was the real fun! Once I got to the island I always took off my shoes and socks and rolled up my jeans. It was beastly "high noon hot" there in the sun! I'd apply a bit of sun screen and take a walk…right up the middle of the stream. The water was clear as glass and below it was something you will find nowhere else…probably…a sidewalk! Apparently, the Little Juniata was relocated back circa 1900 when they built the yard. I was walking in a long gone neighborhood, full of fish, and the water was ice cold with my shoes tied by their laces around my neck and my socks in my pockets. That sidewalk was still in nearly perfect shape yet!

166

"Soak It!!!"... and Other Railroad Stories

Time for lunch...then off to hunt "big game" in Altoona. I opened *Oscar* and dug out a cold *Yuengling* can and opened a package of cheese and a bag of chopped slices of turkey. I had a few slices of bread in a baggie. I hit the beer a couple of times and made a flat spot in the sand to sit it on. Then I ate a few slices of cheese. About now I noticed I was being watched! A family was coming down stream toward me; but they paused about five yards upstream and just looked at me eating my lunch on "their island." Mom, Pop, and four kids. They swam closer and assessed me for a moment...the kids swimming behind their parents. I tore off a couple pieces of my bread and threw them out to them. Both parents ate them immediately and Dad let out a vocal approval. They liked it! I didn't need bread anyway; so I threw a couple more pieces out. Gone instantly! But then they surprised me. They parted, and the little ducklings swam out to see what was going on. I tore-up a bunch of smaller pieces; but couldn't throw them that far, so I leaned forward to toss them into the water. There was a feeding frenzy with the babies, while the parents watched. I leaned back to break-up more bread. Mom and Dad actually herded the ducklings onto the shore in front of me and swam off a yard or so away. Then, they started looking for food in the stream. I broke bread with the babies. They were insanely trusting, occasionally bumping into my knees while I fed them. I doubt I will ever have a relationship with an animal family like that ever again in my life. I'll always wonder what I did to so completely convince Mom and Dad to trust me with their children? Looking back, I wish I'd brought the whole loaf! Sadly, I never took a photo of this wonderful experience. I guess I was too busy being in the moment.

With food gone, beer empty, duckies fed, and the jungle full of "big game" just across a couple feet of shallow water and up the hill, I waded across, and put on my shoes and socks. I kept a keen eye for snakes as these places were full of them, or rats or both. Yes, these were my neighbors! But I hadn't seen anything that would look like that moving through the tall grasses. Once up on the tracks, there were never any such things alive. It was way too hot and dry...not to mention the oily ballast. I rarely even saw an insect in this wasteland of steel. This was now the big game called, "What Can I Bag Today?" There were no limits!

I crested the rim of the river valley and could finally see the sea...yes, layer after layer of rusting steel on wheels as far as I could see. The first good view of it always froze me for a few moments with that feeling...when you suddenly find a new can of worms...so many of them I could not even imagine seeing them all, much less knowing all of them! It was like a tribal market place, where members of dozens of tribes come as old men to trade their last stories....then get "called home," often with all of their close friends down the track...waiting to meet the torch. Was it torch season? Is the price of scrap steel up? They looked so wonderful when they were young, brand new, and had a purpose. But, look at them now...go look in a rest home sometime, and you will get the idea.

Once I came out of that temporary dream state, I focused on the closest freight cars, scanning up the line from the south. I made it to 11 o'clock in the morning and my scan stopped. There sat an old Delaware, Lackawanna & Western (DL&W) twin hopper car! It was in nice condition (given its age). It had been converted to a little twin outlet ballast car at some time years ago. Things like that increase my heart beat! I quickly moved through the underbrush to a small clearing, about ten feet away...just the right distance and angle to photograph the car. The sky had conveniently clouded over allowing the option of using my tripod, which I quickly set-up...almost as if I was afraid it might move, or run away before I could capture it! I snapped off a couple of good shots at slightly different exposures and lens settings. Then I stepped back to admire the car some more. As I bent down to take my camera off the tripod, I first saw him...a rather large black snake, asleep directly in the area between the three legs of the tripod! Somehow I'd not seen him when I set it up!?! There was no way he came over while I was setting up my exposures to take a nap in "his place" while some crazy human set up a structure over him! I was most apologetic. He had dibs on the spot and I was happy to give it back to him.

"Soak It!!!"… and Other Railroad Stories

The organization of the yard seemed haphazard; but some clerk, somewhere, probably had that as one of his jobs. Everything to be complete anarchy; but every here or there I would run across a long string of nearly identical cars, that had all been called out of service together. Twenty-five X53 plug-doors, insulated box cars in a long row…perhaps. Maybe *Campbell Soup* stopped using rail service because it was going to hell!?! They no longer wanted the cars built for them in 1960. Seventy ton H39's; not much demand left for those small capacity old hopper cars. I'd aimlessly wander around out there for hours looking for gold…sometimes finding it; but often it would be in a spot so congested that I couldn't get a photo angle safely. I may have missed the era of the great railroads; but I thoroughly enjoyed my time at Altoona studying the freight car relics and the game of "keep away" with Railroad Dick!

Ship and Travel by Rail…From an Extremely Technical Perspective!

By: David Dykstra, retired Deputy Director-Equipment Project Engineering, Capital Engineering, Metro-North Railroad (MNR)

I did not join the railroad until just before my 30th birthday; but that didn't mean there was no contact. My first train ride was one where I had no view; I can't tell anything about it other than Mom and Dad wanted to take a vacation and Mom's doctor advised her that she needed a smooth ride due to her delicate condition! They took the New York Central (NYC) from Buffalo to New York City and back. That was August 1949 and the start of my connection with the Railroad. That started me down the slippery slope that resulted in the following notes…

My exposure to the railroad continued at a slow pace. I have vague recollections of leaving my baby brother with our grandparents and Mom and Dad and I taking the DL&W, the "Lackawanna" Phoebe Snow on a day trip from Buffalo

Charles H. Geletzke, Jr.

to Corning to see the *Corning Glass Works* in 1954 and once again, Dad, Timothy, and I (sparing Mom) again made the trip about 1957. On the latter trip, I do recall dinner on the train on the return trip!

Back to my misspent youth. My grandfather, Arthur Ebling, spent 50 years on the Erie and Erie Lackawanna. As the eldest grandson and only one insane enough to want to be part of the Railroad, I have inherited his gold pass! He never owned a car or even held a driver's license. As a result of a fall off a locomotive one winter night about 1930, he sustained a broken arm and when set, his left elbow was frozen at about a 100^0 angle; he was taken off road service and became a hostler at the Buffalo Engine House and later Bison Yard. On occasion, we would drive him to work at the old Erie Yard. That required taking a bridge over the Nickel Plate yard, still filled with steam engines. One evening as we crossed the bridge, I made a comment, "Look at all the neat steam engines!"

With great disdain, my grandfather, who I never heard say a cross word responded,, "The Erie is a modern Railroad...we no longer have steam engines!"

Perhaps 15 years later, steam engine construction was still used in my Mechanical Engineering courses to explain calculation of forces for riveting and bolting plates together and balance of rotating machinery via counter weights on wheels to balance the loads of the drive rods.

The summers of 1968 and 1969 found me earning money for college at *Republic Steel's* South Buffalo plant, the first in the Bar Mills and later in the Open Hearths. The plant was serviced by the Erie-Lackawanna off the old Lackawanna line. One day I walked into the plant, past the bar mills and saw a new Penn Central gondola. In preparation for writing this, I looked in my *1970 Car Builders Cyclopedia* and found two Pennsylvania designs. Inquiring with Scott Ornstein, a fellow MNR retiree and current President of the Penn Central Historical Society, was sent the freight car roster from the New York Central East Rochester Dispatch Shops, which lists the more likely G43C steel floor gondolas being out shopped at that time. There was not a

170

scratch on the car. I watched for the car each day as I went to work or headed out at the end of the shift. Six weeks later, as I was leaving to return to school, I observed the beat-up wreck of the same car that looked like it had seen 20 years of hard service! It as enlightening for a young Engineering student as to what cars can be exposed to.

During my first two years of college at *Purdue*, we were precluded from having cars in Tippecanoe County. I preferred to take the train! There were still two a day to Chicago and three a day from there to Buffalo via Cleveland and two via Detroit. My parents tended to discourage this since the best train each way was the ghost of the 20th Century and served Buffalo about 2:30 A.M. in both directions. Several trips were uneventful. On one, we caught a ride home from Chicago with my cousin who was coming in from Wisconsin. We pulled out of Lafayette and my traveling companion, an Aeronautical Engineering student suddenly noted…"The train is moving!" Such was the skill of the engineer that there was no slack and no sudden movement. On another trip, I met an upper classman who was headed for Rochester and was familiar with the route; we traveled together the rest of the trip. Coming into South Bend, a rather rowdy group from *Notre Dame* got on the train; some were in Army ROTC uniforms; but not properly presented (coats open, ties loose, etc.). We conversed with them the remaining seven or eight hours, never letting on where we were coming from.

My last trip was a wild weekend in Chicago. Amtrak was not six weeks old and had a mix of equipment including an improvement in service…a former New Haven "American Flyer" (Pullman/Osgood-Bradley) car, baggage café with first class seats. I went for the car not knowing what it was and remained there the whole trip! To this day I am not sure if I was supposed to have a business class ticket or not. The conductor did ask if I would not rather sit in the coach with others; but did not ask me to move. A week later, I graduated!

I was known as the guy who knew about the train schedules. While passenger service was still Penn Central, another man in my dorm was sent to me. He was trying to get to Syracuse and had been told at the Lafayette station, he would have to take the train to Indianapolis and catch a St. Louis-New York train over the former Pennsylvania Railroad and change again in New York…across town, for a train to Syracuse. It would have been a two day trip each way. A new agent, an older woman returning to the workforce was the agent. I visited the station and got the same answer from her, though I knew better. One last try; I spoke with a friend from church, the late Dick Neumann, who worked part time there (Later with the CN family and was this book's editor, Chuck Geletzke's boss, for part of that time and later worked for a couple of short lines.). He unsuccessfully tried to convince the new agent, "You go north through Chicago!" He ultimately spoke with the Station Master who convinced her of the realities. If you wonder why rail travel was failing, this was one example!

In 1975 I would see a bit of this again when trying to buy tickets in Baltimore in advance for the *Montrealer* from Wilmington, coach and sleeper from New York to Burlington, Vermont. I was in the Army, stationed at Aberdeen, not a stop at this time, with my new wife with the purpose of visiting Dick Neuman, now with Central Vermont and his new wife. We would return on the *Adirondack* and a corridor train. The agent was an old *Pullman* man who was having a very hard time with the brand new Amtrak ticketing system. It would have taken two minutes with the old manual system; but closer to half an hour with the computer. I would later learn that to err is human; but to really foul things up, it takes a computer!

Ten years later, I was in Conrail's Mechanical Department training program in Altoona, part of the largest class ever to go through the program! We were 12 in all and quickly became "the Dirty Dozen." The second phase of the program was at the Samuel Rea Car Shops at neighboring Hollidaysburg. In addition to basic Railroad indoctrination, we were given Engineering projects as a sort of term paper. Mike Givler and I were tasked to design common box car door opening/closing and locking adaptors that would work with and replace any of the six different designs of pairs already in use on doors and side sheets of box cars as well as accept various "Come along" mechanisms used to open and close the doors. While gathering information on the use and abuse of these items, we interfaced with both Mechanical Engineers who were in the process of designing the next version of gondolas to be built at the Shops and the Industrial Engineers who would create the tooling and processes for manufacture of the cars. They each gave us their long, sad stories of those foolish guys next door.

The basic design of the new car was at least 40 years old, originating at the Pennsylvania Railroad. The Mechanical Engineers were concerned about the longevity of the cars and repair of in service damage. I could attest to this from seeing the damage a new car sustained at the hands of my fellow steel workers. They wanted to weld two angle irons together to form a box as the top chord as it could be cut out or straightened to be repaired. The Industrial Engineers objected to some 280 feet of welding needed to build top chords for a 60 foot car; they wanted to use square tube. The tube would have to be replaced over the entire length of car once it was damaged. The top chord serves to stabilize and strengthen the sides and seals the tops of the vertical stays. It traditionally has a rectangular cross section.

Mike held a Civil Engineering degree and I had worked two other summers forming steel for buildings. While the gondolas were not part of our assignments, we discussed the debate we were witnesses to and posed the question to each group…why not use a Ship Channel shape that would yield the same strengths and be wide enough to serve as the cap for the vertical stays of the car sides? It was a less expensive shape to purchase, needed no welding other than for installation, gave a stronger connection to the side panels and was repairable. Neither group would even entertain a suggested solution from trainees! I never did hear of a negative to our suggestion and went on to passenger car design.

Charles H. Geletzke, Jr.

European Adventures

In January 1972, I reported to the Army's 21st
Replacement Battalion in Frankfort, Germany and was
subsequently sent to Schweinfurt. It was Saturday, so I spoke
with the Duty Officer who was also the Personnel Officer
and was not expecting me. He would get someone to
Frankfurt to pick me up. No problem, the Army gave me a
ticket; I would be arriving by train in a couple of hours and I
would be met at the Schweinfurt train station. I took a cab to
the Hauptbahnhof (Main train station) Frankfurt and found a
seat in a first class compartment on the next train headed
toward Nuremberg. Note: most mainline passenger cars were
sectioned off into compartments with an aisle down one side
of the car. There were three seats facing three seats in each
with first class having a bit more room and better cushioned,
reclining sliding seats and more leg room. We left the station
and three GI's and a wife joined me in the compartment.
They were glad to have an American to talk to. I found out
the wife was newly arrived and her husband and two of his
buddies had come from Weiden to pick her up. Being junior
enlisted on a budget and in civilian clothes, they had second
class tickets, I was traveling in uniform.

The Conductor came through collecting tickets. He
took mine and thanked me and noted I would change trains at
Wurzburg. He took the group's tickets and spoke to them, as
he had to me in German, which they did not understand. It
was my first use of the German language in four years and
then only in a third semester college course. After he left, I
explained, as best as I understood, that they had second class
tickets in a first class compartment…a No-No! Worse, they
were headed for Weiden; but the train split at Nuremburg and
our car was headed for Regensburg. They had to move or
wind-up in the wrong city. When I changed trains in
Wurzburg, they were still in the same seats. I observed the
sign on the outside of the car and it did read as the Conductor
had said, "Frankfurt to Regensburg via Nuremberg."

174

"Soak It!!!"... and Other Railroad Stories

On the platform, I now had the challenge to find my next train. It being a known short connection, I started to panic! Seeing a uniformed Railroad employee I mustered the courage to ask in German. "Where is the train to Schweinfurt?"

He simply responded in kind..."There," and pointed to the train on the opposite side of the platform. It was then that I realized this could be a fun couple of years riding trains. I quickly learned to look for the poster beside each door that gave the route and destination of the car.

A year later, I needed some leave time and chose to visit Dick Neumann, in the Navy at Naples, Italy. As a bachelor lieutenant, I had money to spare and it would be a long drive! So, it was back to the train with a first class ticket. I was surer of my German; but still made mistakes. I asked for a ticket on a fast train and was ticketed through Bamberg and Nuremburg to Munich with a change there to Naples over Brenner Pass. It was a 24 hour ride and no sleeper. I had lunch in Munich Hauptbahnhof and hoped to have dinner in the diner...there was none! There was a cart at the Austria/Italy Border crossing with snacks. A couple in my compartment laughed the next morning when I woke up...I slept through Rome!

The return trip was to be the reverse route, only starting in the evening. The train was packed and there was just a half car of first class. One compartment was reserved and another filled with smokers! I showed the Conductor my ticket and asked where to go. He looked and found an Italian Army Private in Tyrolian uniform, complete with a full brim hat with feathers and told him to leave. It turned out the rules were military personnel could ride anywhere where there was a seat; but had to make room for paying passengers with the higher grade ticket. To my amazement, the guy went out the window, not the door and not at the platform we were boarding from! I shared the compartment with a Guest worker who was returning to Munich after the Christmas holiday visiting family. We visited most of the evening and noted our traveling companions were a well presented Austrian family...the Mom and Dad told the daughter, a young lady of about 20, not to talk to these foreigners! I have always wondered if they knew how much we understood or what their response would have been if they knew I was a degreed Engineer and an officer in the American Army.

While changing trains in Munich, I discovered there was an ICE, a real express train operating at higher speeds that would get me to Wurzburg and with another train change, there to Schweinfurt. It was a good chance to try the better service. The service was only first class, which my ticket qualified for; but there was also a 6 Mark daily fee. It was all of $2.00 and I was on vacation; it was a great ride, well worth the money! The Bundes Bahn put schedules in the first class compartments that showed connections as well as the train's schedule. I found a time table for this train that revealed ICE schedules. On my outbound trip I should have taken a train to Stuttgart and an ICE from there to Naples. It would have been an overnight with sleeper and diner and about four hours less day travel. I made note, ask not for Schnellzug, a fast train or E class; but a Trans Europa Express TEE or ICE train (now IC in Germany and EC when crossing borders) train.

The Army moved tracked vehicles by rail whenever it was practical. My first year in Germany, I was with Third Infantry Division's cavalry squadron (3rd Squadron, 7th Cavalry). We moved to border posts twice and to Grafenwehr and Hohenfels once each. One night one of the Troops was making the move, loading at Oberwerrn, the small town outside Schweinfurt where two other lieutenants and I lived. Bob was the Squadron Duty Officer, just like the day I had arrived. He called the house, "There is an emergency, go check it out!"

I went to the freight track, next to the passenger station and found two cars with four of our tracked vehicles on the ground. The railroad crew had planned to attach the passenger cars for the troops to the freight cars; but did not pay attention to the length of the siding! The vehicles were properly tied down and held in place…no damage. There would be a delay in movement. I could report back to Bob who relayed the information to LTC Ameel, who while not happy with the activity was relieved he still had a full compliment of people and equipment, Having responsibility for wheeled vehicles, I never got to take a troop train.

In 1977 I was Motor officer for 1st Battalion, 76th Artillery at Ft. Hood, Texas. We had an eight inch artillery piece with problems that was sent to Picatinny Arsenal, New Jersey. It was lost for a couple of weeks on the return trip, somewhere in Kansas. (Note my previous writings for Chuck Geletzke, where passenger cars and car shells too went missing enroute.)

Moving on to the railroad…

From 1980 through 1984 I occasionally rode the same tavern/lounge observation cars in commuter service on Conrail/Metro-North's Hudson Line to or from work; there was something familiar about them. Later, when the *Bombardier* Shoreliner cars arrived, Vice President-Operations and later President of Metro-North, Don Nelson, took the two cars as part of a three car Inspection Train. He also wanted a theatre car arrangement and asked for the rear ends to be cut open to create a full width floor to ceiling view. As the Senior Mechanical Engineer for the Mechanical Department and primary Engineer for Car Structures, I advised this would not work because, unlike conventional stainless steel cars, the corner posts on these cars were not major structural elements, rather the door posts were. Removing the door posts for the view would not work and cause the end of the car to collapse. Rather, we should use one of the newer (1950's) coaches for this. This advice was taken; but the full window car was never attempted.

What was likely my last trip in those cars was on the annual Christmas Train in 2012 when then President, Howard Permut asked for a briefing of status on the M-8 electric multiple unit cars. The only time available in his schedule was aboard the movement of the Executive Train from Grand Central Terminal to Harmon. I as Program Manager and Tim McCarthy as Vice President-Capital

Charles H. Geletzke, Jr.
Programs, jumped at the chance…it also took us from the office toward home in the late afternoon!

MNCR southbound train passing Bannerman's Island, NY on April 9, 2011. (David Dykstra photo)

Car Equipment Engineering

I had intended to write more about travel by rail and Car Equipment Engineering at a later date; but was stimulated by a small article in August 2022 *Trains Magazine* about M-8's entering Shoreline East service. I was MTA Metro-North Railroad's Program Manager from the conception of the project until promoted, turning the day to day management of the project over to my Project Engineer, Amir Rahimi. By this time most of the cars were accepted and in the Warranty period.

The article in *Trains* dealt with the long planned employment of the M-8 cars on the State of Connecticut's Shoreline East service. From the start of writing the Specification in 2004 for M-8, it had been planned the cars would work in this service and also in Penn Station. Both required cooperation with Amtrak, which was the Contract Operator for Shoreline East and owner of the former New Haven Line from New Rochelle, New York over Hell Gate

178

"Soak It!!!"... and Other Railroad Stories

Bridge to Herold Interlocking where Long Island Rail Road (note the historic difference between their designation and Railroad) enters the picture. As of this writing, the Penn Station access is still in the planning stages. We knew and planned for a change in power voltage east of New Haven, 25,000 volts, 60 cycle power instead of MNR's 12,500 volts, 60 cycle power. At Herold Interlocking we chose to adapt to the Long Island Rail Road over running 600 volt DC third rail, not Metro-North's under running third rail. Overhead wire from Sunnyside Yard was 25 cycle, requiring twice the iron core in the transformer and not worth the weight penalty. This did preclude the hoped for run through to the *New Jersey Meadowlands* for sporting events with the cars.

The *Trains* article noted clearance issues, which were third rail shoe induced. This had been dealt with on the former New Haven lines west of New Haven at the time of purchase of the M-2 cars in the early 1970's. Previous New Haven equipment relied on retractable third rail shoes. Station platforms and bridge reinforcing plates had to be modified. Platform clearances were dealt with in major part by installing high level (floor level) platforms required by the car designs of MTA/CDOT designs from the M-1 in 1971 and onward. The Americans With Disabilities Act (ADA) would later require this anyway.

What the *Trains* article did not note, was a Power Department concern. Amtrak told Metro-North the M-8 cars would bridge the phase breaks between substations. That was explained in detail to Amtrak that unlike the ACELA trains, M-8 cars were in pairs only. A single pantograph on each pair could not bridge the phase gap! They insisted they would! After several months of back and forth in e-mail and phone conferences, a meeting was convened by the *Connecticut Department of Transportation* (CDOT) who was most anxious to resolve the issues. Use of M-8's on Shoreline East was essential to free the CDOT cars the in use there for overhaul and employment on the New Haven-Hartford-Springfield Line, which was under renovation.

A rare consist of all Connecticut cars (no MNR cars!) are seen at Marble Hill, NY. (Ron Yee photo; Dykstra collection)

I, as a car guy, sat opposite the Amtrak Power guy, out of Boston, in New Haven. There is nothing like looking the other guy in the eye rather than over the phone. We were each adamant in our positions. The others in the room were sure we would come to blows; but we were each intent on getting the job done. Finally, something snapped and we realized we were talking past each other. I knew MNR's AC power phase breaks were as built by the New Haven, a cut in the wire where the pantograph left the wire on one phase and reentered the next. The Amtrak Power Representative knew his system was like the Pennsylvania Railroad system; the pantograph always had wire above it. He drew a sketch and the problem became obvious to me. A dead wire runs along side of the one circuit's power wire. The power wire ends. A distance after the first live wire ends, a second dead wire runs beside the first dead wire for another distance and the first dead wire ends. Finally, the power wire for the second circuit runs for a distance beside the second dead wire, which then ends.

"Soak It!!!"… and Other Railroad Stories

The ACELA train set takes power from either or both pantographs in the consist. The Engineer is required to drop pantographs at the Phase Break and command up to the local pantograph after entering the second circuit; this is why there are occasional losses of lighting and air handling on ACELA.

M-8 cars are of just the right length that pantographs on any two pair will bridge between two wires and the second pair will be in position to bridge between the second and third wires at the same time. When a third pair is added to the consist, its pantograph is simultaneously in the correct location to bridge between the third and fourth wires. Power then flows from the first to the second, second to third, and third to fourth wires through the three pantograph shoes. A loud bang will be heard and darkness on the railroad follows…not a good thing! We looked at the effect of a single unpowered car, then under construction, added to the consist and the dynamics did not change.

One solution would have been to lengthen or shorten the phase gap structure; but Amtrak was not interested, nor did CDOT have a budget for this. A second option was to run consists of four cars. This is currently the plan for CDOT; but growth of service is always expected. An additional concern was the full knowledge someone would not know or remember the situation and grab a six car or longer consist! The ultimate and safest solution was to modify the M-8 cars. Amtrak was fully prepared to accept that there Engineers were responsible enough to properly operate through the phase gaps as they were required to do with ACELA. A change in Pantograph logic was made. In addition to All Pantographs Down, All Pantographs Up, a Local Pantograph Up command was added. Now the Engineer will command Pantographs Down as a phase gap is approached. Upon entering the next power block, the command "Local Pantograph Up" is given. When clear of the Phase Break, the "All Pantographs Up" may be initiated. As an added safety, we added logic from the GPS locater that is part of the Automatic Announcements System that created a wall at New Haven State Street, east of which, the All Pantograph Up could only be commanded when fully stopped or when well clear of the phase breaks, the location of which were also entered into the GPS data base in the same manner as stations are for announcements. Software and computers complicated car design, but also allowed more flexibility.

Cooperation between railroads is frequently difficult to achieve; but when it happens, everything becomes possible!

Technical note: The morning after writing the above, it occurred to me many readers will have no idea what a Phase Break is or why it is used. The phase break is a physical separation of two power circuits; think of your house having a number of circuits, each protected by a fuse or breaker. The same principle applies on an electric railroad. There is an additional problem in that power must be transmitted over long distances, which have resistance and resulting drop in voltage. To overcome the losses, higher voltages are used for transmission, reduced to operating voltages and power is fed from the wayside at intervals based on the expected number of trains, the voltage, and frequency supplied. For alternating current, there is also concern that the power from each source be of the same frequency and be in phase with each other. Power plants in a grid first bring their machine up to speed to produce the standard frequency, then phase match to the grid before attaching to supply power. Once connected, all power producers fight each other to stay in the same cycle. Distance between source and use provides resistance and more correctly, impedance, which causes small shifts in the current cycle. Even though the railroad is being supplied power from the same grid and therefore theoretically in phase, slight shifts occur due to capacitance and inductance. Each step down of voltage from the commercial feed and wayside tap causes a phase shift. The result is the need to isolate one source from the next to keep the maximum power being fed to the trains.

Sometimes even the same department of the same railroad cannot be brought together. While reviewing proposals for the M-7 car one supplier brought in a computer generated structural analysis that had been prepared for an earlier car of similar design and been updated. One of the key changes was to be a roof mounted unitized air conditioning unit. They decided the best distribution of air would come from placing the units at the quarter points of the car length, over the doors. Due to clearance limits, the HVAC units had to be within the roof line, not on top of the car.

The original analysis showed the roof over the doors had high structural loads. This was obvious since the holes in the car sides for the door openings meant all the load carried by the sides had to be transferred to the floor or the roof. Most everyone was impressed with the quality of the presentation until I asked the embarrassing question: "All the stress in the original design was transferred to the roof. Your design eliminates the high stress area. Where did the stress go!?!"

I had previously worked with some of the presenting staff; they knew I pulled no punches and expected the same in return. There was a brief pause in discussion, a quiet chuckle, and the replay…"I guess we need to revisit this!"

Three of the five builders did not return for phase two of choosing a builder; but the embarrassed bidder did…with a new location and new stress analysis. The air conditioning units were ultimately placed nearer the ends of the car. On the following M-8, the end of the car had to contain the pantograph and the air conditioning was moved to the center. Since the M-8 was an MNR "only" car, there were fewer clearance issues and the HVAC units sat on top of the car.

All good ideas need to be checked using common sense reviews.

The bidder's name has been withheld to prevent needless embarrassment; they know who they are.

First set of MNR M-7's arriving at Croton-Harmon, NY. Notice the elevated structure paralleling each track, for those who are not familiar, these are the electric "third rails." (Dykstra collection)

In 1997 Metro-North was preparing a specification for the M-5 car: I was the Program Manager. I returned from vacation to find our President, Don Nelson, had determined it was advantageous to have a joint procurement with the Long Island Rail Road. Since we were working on an M-5, they dubbed their effort M-7. The M-5 name was never used. The LIRR had money allocated; so they went first in acquiring cars. MNR held options and ultimately purchased 336 cars. *Bombardier* won a contract for 198 cars, built as pairs, and wound up building some 1600 cars with all options exercised and a few more added. Since the combining of efforts, I have thought it would make an excellent cost analysis exercise for a business school to compare costs of two designs to the increased cost of construction from compromises based on two variant sets of needs.

The first three pairs of cars that were completed went to Pueblo, Colorado and the AAR test facility to test systems in an out of the way place. This allowed more time to test since there was no rush hour traffic to be avoided. The second three pair went to the Long Island for additional testing under actual railroad conditions. Following the Pueblo test, the cars were moved to New York to accelerate testing under actual railroad conditions. After the Long Island Pilot Tests were completed, the most current designed two pair was sent to Metro-North to check operation on our railroad. The other cars were returned to *Bombardier* for modifications.

One of the earliest tests was compatibility with MNR's power systems. My Director, Tim McCarthy, an Electrical Engineer, came out for the test and Mike Savchek, Tim's equivalent for Electric Power, joined us since the compatibility with and behavior of the substations he had built needed to be confirmed. MNR had far newer designs than LIRR, except for West Side Yard, which was of the same generation as LIRR substations. Mike and Tim were both good guys who I enjoyed working with; but they were like oil and water…it was to be a strictly working night!

All went well until about 2:00 A.M. when the substation reset feature was checked. If there was a fault, the substation would trip its breakers…cutting power to the section of track. It was a built-in safety feature like the breakers in your house…only industrial strength in capacity. The substation was manually tripped and the automatic reset was allowed to proceed. The substation would not reset…it was manually reset and immediately tripped again!

Mike knew the procedure. After a trip, the substation would automatically send out a lower voltage, low amperage test signal. A small power loss was considered normal grounding losses. A large draw meant a train was in the circuit and in either case, the substation resets. The range of draw between a small and large draw was presumed to be a safety hazard, perhaps a trespasser's fishing pole (our tracks are up against the Hudson River) or a child's bicycle. The possible presence of a trespasser is subject to electrocution; 600 volts DC will ruin your day! A dead short will also re-trip the breaker because that is a safety protection people working on the right of way use, grounding the third rail in

Charles H. Geletzke, Jr.

the area of work; but that is a scheduled event. The automatic reset test was repeated three times, then the system shut down until manually reset. The fact a manual reset failed meant trouble! There were no signs of life on the tracks. Fortunately, and by plan, the last revenue service train had cleared the area before we began this test.

For the next two hours we played with the equipment trying to restart and figure out what had gone wrong. This had not happened during testing on the LIRR. As we went through the process of how the substation reset, the question of how the M-7 started was raised. It turned out the Auxiliary Inverter on the car that converts the incoming 600 volts DC to 120 volts single phase, 240 volts 3 phase 60 cycle and 74 volts battery charging power, continuously monitored power available from the third rail. It commenced operation at a lower voltage, less than the substation test voltage. The test voltage was enough for the Auxiliary Power Units to start functioning and its load was more that a normal ground loss; but less than a functioning train. The two systems were confusing each other! We had to put shoe paddles between the third rail shoes and the third rail, had the substation restarted, and then removed the paddles so the train would take power. It was a long night, not just because of the hour; but the professional rivalry on a hot muggy night without fresh air or air conditioning was too much for the participants!

Bombardier representatives were present and naturally said it was the Railroad's problem, since it had not happened on the LIRR. In the light of day, our consultant, Jack Ronalter, of *LTK Associates* produced a document MNR had provided all bidders on the operation of MNR's substations. It helped that Jack had worked on every electric car series on Metro-North since the M-1, circa 1970. About half-way through the document, some 70 pages long, was a single paragraph describing substation reset. It was *Bombardier*'s problem. They had not fully involved *SEPSA*, the Auxiliary Power Unit's designer and manufacturer. Tim McCarthy gave them the answer, so again *Bombardier* tried to say we were now specifying the design and it was a

"Soak It!!!"... and Other Railroad Stories
"Contract Change Order" and the Railroad's financial responsibility. Ultimately, the simple answer as Tim suggested, a timer was built into the Auxiliary Power Unit that delayed start up from when power was detected until the substation reset.

Sometimes too much information is as bad as not enough!

The testing of the Long Island cars continued into the winter. Joe Riley was my "go to guy" for all things Transportation. He was from the lower Mohawk Valley and understood what winter was; I being from Buffalo noted a distinct lack of winter in the Hudson Valley! I approached him with an idea for a Snow Test. He in turn had already planned for such an event...great minds think alike (but so do sick minds). Previous electric cars had cam controllers, located under the cars in fiberglass enclosures. Sealing was always a problem. Snow would enter the boxes, start to melt and then refreeze. The controllers then locked up with ice. The new AC propulsion used variable voltage and variable frequency to make transition through the operating speed range, all controlled by computers and using solid state devices. There was only a main contactor to pass electrical power or isolate the propulsion system. Sealed aluminum boxes contained the propulsion gear.

With the promise of a snow storm, which in New York is a couple of inches at best, we went out to "play trains." We simply ran up and down the Hudson Line while the white stuff fell and checked the operation. At one point Joe was operating and I was standing at the front door. We knew where the Home Signal was coming out of Yonkers Station; but could not see it until it was about 100 yards away. Not much had fallen; but what did, came at a sufficiently intense rate enabling us to check the survivability of the equipment.

Propulsion and brakes all worked as intended. Carbody seals were fine. The doors functioned; but on all but two, snow accumulated at the seal between the door and the door frame. On closer inspection, I heard a whistling at all but two of the doors. Most of the doors had to be adjusted to hang properly. We now had another acceptance test criteria that would work at any time of the year!

We also found the fresh air intakes were plugged with snow. Fresh air came in vertically through the roof, made a 90 degree turn along the length of the car, through a spin filter, made a 180 degree turn parallel to the floor through a paper filter, and entered a plenum where the heater element and cooling coils were located...there they mixed with the return air and entered the car! The inlet and ducts became packed with snow. Our Canadian representative from *Bombardier* also understood winter and immediately accepted there was a problem and agreed to fix where needed. The LIRR had clearance restrictions at the Atlantic Terminal and East Side Access to Grand Central Terminal that limited raising the roof; so they did not get the fix! Air scoops were added to the MNR HVAC units that took in air from the side, even requiring a minimal upward flow before entering the existing inlet duct. The fix was inexpensive and quick; something car builders like!

Additional extemporaneous test were sometimes the fastest way to find a problem!

About a year later, the New York City area experienced their idea of a blizzard...18 inches of snow in 24 hours. MNR cut service to once an hour with diesel trains only. The MNR President at the time was Pete Canito, who hailed from South Buffalo and just four years my senior. When together, we would speak of the "good old days." After the event, I asked why service was cut and my weather hardened equipment removed from service. His answer was simple: "We ran out of customers!" The diesel trains made it a one crew and a one seat ride for the whole line.

Our on board public address system provides automated visual and verbal announcements triggered through GPS maps. Shortly after MNR cars went into service, trains sitting on the platform at Grand Central reported, "This is the train to Ronkonkoma," an impossible move for electric cars. The software was configured when

188

two or more pair of cars was coupled together, the most recent software would automatically propagate throughout the train. An MNR pair had been mated to an LIRR pair at the *Bombardier* modification facility and the LIRR pair had a higher version software; it was accepted by the MNR pair and brought over when the cars were returned to service. It began to spread through the MNR fleet as consists were broken-up and put together. From then on, each railroad was issued a different series of software, so only their own would propagate.

Everyone had agreed MNR cars and LIRR cars would never run together…Mr. Murphy was proven right again!

A new glitch appeared a few months later; but only on Hudson Line trains, near Spuyten Duyvil during the evening rush hour. The U. S. Air Force was responsible for maintaining the GPS satellites and has provisions for 32 active units. They normally had 27 active; but added a 28th unit. The additional unit became visible to MNR cars only at that location and time, confusing the system with too many signals. The software was changed to accept the addition of up to 32 signals…proving improvements have consequences!

Language frequently became a barrier. While purchasing Multiple Unit Electric Cars, we had to consider many factors. As noted above, Transportation, Communications, and Power people had to be included in the team. Maintenance of Way people were never directly part of the team; but did give us clearances and track conditions. The Cab Signal supplier had criteria not just to receive and process signals; but evaluated train performance. If the train was not responding to a down grade in signal indication at a fast enough rate, it had to announce this and if not responded to by the Engineer, to step in and add brake force, usually by applying the Emergency Brake. This required the use of accelerometers to feed information to the system. The earlier systems used "slosh tubes," a U-shape filled with mercury that as it tipped would connect the circuit, activating the system. The new systems are computer controlled and have electronic decelerometers. Each required calibration, which entailed testing on flat track.

The Track Department was asked to supply "level" track, which they willingly did. Unfortunately, "level" for track people means cross level, which means both rails are at the same altitude across from each other. What had to be asked for was a "no grade condition." The cars could not be calibrated until we started speaking the same language!

Mechanical Management

Management was not always the most subtle or civil. Several of us arrived under orders to help the Conrail Metropolitan Region "clean up its act." The people were not bad, generally willing; but poorly led and with less organization. Only two of the twenty or so of us sent knew anything about railroad or maintenance. The remainder were mostly right out of college and the Management Training Program. One of the more dedicated was Jim Chew of Pittsburgh. He was deeply interested in the machinery of the Railroad and was most willing to get dirty on the job. Given the condition the equipment was in, he was a great addition to the team! Each night he would report to Poughkeepsie, check out the four trains then based there and ride in the most likely to fail in the morning. Jim dressed the part of a Conrail Mechanical Department system mechanic...work boots, dungaree pants, bloused with issue bands marked "Conrail-Safety First," plaid work shirt, hooded sweat shirt, safety glasses, and helmet. At the end of the run, he would report to our future Regional Chief Mechanical Officer, Richard C. Kirner, with the Report of Equipment Status. He took the elevator to the Mechanical Department offices in 450 Lexington Avenue and walked to R. C.'s (Kirner) office, leaving greasy footprints all the way on the beige carpet! At the time, Charlie Cole was the Regional CMO (Chief Mechanical Officer) and was finishing out his career. Lee Lytle was the Assistant CMO who, in addition to Jim Chew, was also being bypassed for his boss's job when the CMO would retire in a couple of months. Lee was displeased with the dirt Jim brought in and spoke harshly with Jim. Jim turned to him and informed him, "If the engine rooms of your locomotives were kept as clean as they should be, I would not be dragging dirt into the office!"

Lee was dumfounded and R. C. repeated the story for several months, whenever the occasion arose.

Jim didn't last long. His mother had died several years earlier and his father became ill. He left Conrail, joined *WABCO* and lived with his father.

Just before Christmas, R. C. Kirner was visiting Harmon Shop. I stopped in to the Shop Office and had a brief conversation with him. He asked about the family and I told him I would be leaving that evening on the *Lake Shore Limited* to join my wife in Toledo, then return with her before New Year's Eve. Everyone knew R. C. had come from Ohio; but it was Cleveland and to "New Yawkers," there was an amorphous mass of land out there that was all the same. They also knew he had adult children. R. C. announced, "That is right, you be sure to take care of my daughter!" There was a sudden panic that a new family was taking over. Charlie Cole's two sons-in-law were both working as General Foremen at Harmon. While they may have gotten their jobs through "Dad," they were both fulfilling their responsibilities well! It turned out, R. C.'s eldest child was a girl, the same age as my wife, though I do not recall ever meeting her. It was R. C.'s way to keep the help off balance, so they would stay alert.

When I returned a week later, it was again via the *Lake Shore Limited*. I walked my wife Ruth through the shop as it was the easiest way to the car. R. C. was again in the Shop Office and so was Charlie Cole, whom I had yet to meet. I stopped to say hello and introduced Ruth to my fellow managers...that was the Army way. R. C. and John McNulty, the Shop Manager, boss and later friend, were gracious. Charlie Cole quipped, "This isn't the same woman you introduced as your wife last week!?!" Fortunately, two years of pre-marriage exposure to the Army society and four more as wife, including one as the wife of the senior married officer of a battalion had hardened her to crass people. I do believe both John and R. C. were embarrassed by the comment.

Things did get better after that and by the time we formed the Mechanical Department Engineering Office, we had family gatherings. Most of us were at the point of having children, which helped. There was always the danger of wives comparing notes and realizing they were all suffering from our inordinately long days of work!

MANUALS

By: David Dykstra, retired Deputy Director-Equipment Project Engineering, Capital Engineering, Metro-North Railroad (MNR)

Working in Maintenance I quickly learned that Manuals were a vital source of information. When I joined the Army in 1971, the Manuals were written at the 11th grade level. By my departure in 1978 they had been rewritten to the 9th grade level and were in the process of being rewritten to the level of 6th graders. There were times when I had to sit beside equipment with my mechanics and read the manual, directing them what to do because no one had ever dealt with the particular situation. When I joined the Railroad I found things were even worse…manuals were frequently not to be had! Several others observed this as well, so when a new set of equipment was ordered one of the main things we insisted upon was proper manuals! Sadly, it seldom came about because too many on the Railroad were too anxious to get the equipment, and builders gained nothing by supplying manuals, they are rather an expense and the builders have no experience with maintaining what they build and sell.

MNS M-1's at Harmon, NY in the late 1970's. For those who are not familiar with electrically powered railroads, the elevated structures between the various tracks are the electrical "Third Rails." (David Dykstra photo)

I had been Shop Engineer at Harmon, New York for about six months when I was called upon to provide documentation support and evaluate a poorly remanufactured part. An N-2 coupler used on M-1 and M-2, and later M-3 cars, had been sent out for renovation. The supplier had done a number of these without problem; but this time, the renovated coupler had been installed in a car and would not couple to another car. It was removed and turned over to me for evaluation. I had been visited and established good relationships with several vendors; so I asked for and received a visit from the vendor in question. Upon inspection it was obvious the coupler shank was twisted! It was necessary a plain be established between the centers of the pin and cone on the front face…that was perpendicular to the axis of the mounting pin and the centerline of the shank, which were also perpendicular to each other. The vendor noted he had fully complied with the builder's (*WABCO*) instructions for inspection and repair. There was no mention

193

Charles H. Geletzke, Jr.

of the possible deformation of the casting. The vendor said he would be glad to add this to future work if he was given some criteria.

It turned out *WABCO* protected its information as though they were State Secrets! They would not offer such information! I contacted Ted Price and John Fulton, in CONRAIL's Passenger Engineering Section and Charlie Smith who had recently left to join L. T. Klauder Engineering; these three had all the passenger information that had to be had on CONRAIL. Unbelievably, no one had the numbers. When I asked about an in-house Specification, I was allowed to create one, which I presume was later shared with New Jersey and Philadelphia who had the same device and were also CONRAIL people. It was the first "Manuals" item I created. Fortunately, the American Association of Railroads (AAR) had Shop Manuals that included procedures for straightening and even welding cracks in coupler shanks. I had witnessed this work the previous summer while in training at Altoona. I referenced the AAR Shop Manual for the "how" and developed limits for both defining "worn" limits and "renovated" minimums for the dimensions.

Twenty years later, *WABCO* was supplying the N-6 coupler, the same design; but the next larger size coupler on the M-7. When confronted with this lack of information and with the power on a Contract Specification behind me, they still could not supply dimensions, only an in-house jig, which they would gladly sell us. They were also mystified as to why we could possibly need this information. Our reasoning was simple: "How do we know what you are sending us is any good? And, why should we send this casting back to the manufacturer to simply qualify each piece?"

Next

After fifteen years of use, the cab drop sash windows on the M-1 and M-2 cars were failing. At each stop, the Conductor had to open one window to look out on the platform while operating the doors. They were also frequently opened by the Engineers. If not properly closed,

194

there would be a draft in the cab, so it became necessary to replace the windows. There were two manufacturers who had each supplied some of the windows; but to the same design and dimensions. One had recently gone out of business and the other, recently sold. The new owner of *U.S. Seating and Sash* was Ulf Hammerskjold, an entrepreneur, businessman, and engineer. He was interested in the challenge and developed a new design with better seals and return springs. His first attempt was a handmade demonstrator. To make it presentable, he painted it black. Upon presenting it to our Chief Mechanical Officer, R. C. Kirner, he looked it over carefully, then noted Ulf had painted it black because black is sexy and sells. Ulf was dumbfounded; but he had made the sale!

Having provided the car dimensions, I now had to write the Modification Instructions. I sat in the car and observed the situation and reviewed the drawings documenting the car construction. After drafting the instructions, several of the more skilled craftsmen and I tore apart a car and installed the first window. There were a few false starts and a trick or two noted; but after a day of work, the first window was installed. I made the corrections and improvements to the instructions and we tried again on the next car. It only took a couple of hours. The other side of the car was done next with a few notes as to the differences made and we were off and running! It was only by working with and observing the craftsmen that a truly useful instruction could be written.

Next, I took the instructions to New Haven and attacked an M-2 in a similar manner. There were just enough differences in the cars that there was need for specific items to be changed for that car. Again, the observations and comments from the craftsmen resulted in an effective and easy instruction.

About a year later, I was back at New Haven Shop with Ulf. One of the foremen saw me and came to complain, "You were responsible for the new drop sash windows…they don't fit!"

Charles H. Geletzke, Jr.

I enquired as to what the problem was and he repeated, "they don't fit!"

When pressed, as to a description as to where the installation problem was, he gave an impossible situation. I asked if he had read the instructions and got the same comment. The third time I asked the question, he admitted he had not read the instructions. Dick Renbarger ran the shop most efficiently; so we inquired of him what the situation was. No one else had a problem and that particular foreman was know to be a complainer!

There had been a problem. The third batch of 40 widows was delivered to the Distribution Warehouse in Croton and when two were drawn out, they did not fit! I was called and measured the legs that were also the lower track onto which the glazing rode while opening the window; they were six inches too long! We put the batch on hold and I called *USSC*, asking for Ulf by name. By this time he had grown the company and his clerks stood between him and irate customers. He was busy. I gave them my name, office number, and home number because it was important. About 7:00 P.M. that night my home phone rang: "Hi, David. This is Ulf. I noted he sounded like he was far away…yes, he was in Australia visiting his older son. When I explained what had happened, he told me his younger son, Christian, was running the company and would be up the next morning to recover the defective units and give me a schedule as to when the new units would be delivered. The next morning Christian drove up in the company van, we met, measured the window frames again, and packed half the order that would fit in his van. He promised a week turn around and came back a week later with the corrected units and took the other half of the shipment for their change out. Ulf called again from Australia to make sure all had gone as planned.

Fifteen years later Christian was sitting in front of the committee to determine vendors for the M-7 car. Ulf was still the head of the company. The Long Island Railroad people were attacking what was by then *USSC*, questioning their capability. I had to defend them, noting that if anyone could pull off the design and manufacture of seats and windows,

196

Ulf could! After the meeting, my own boss, Tim McCarthy, noted my defense of *USSC* about put him in tears. They still make all Metro-North's Engineer's seats!

And another...

MNR FL9 2008 is seen at Harmon, NY. (Ron Yee photo; D. Dykstra collection)

EMD had an excellent system for improved instructions or modifications. They put out a full index of their instructions, noting changes each quarter. The unfortunate part of this was, if you were not on the mailing list, there was no way of knowing something had changed. Railroad Mechanical Department Headquarters were notified; that did not mean the information made it to the working level. In 1957 and again in 1960, the New Haven Railroad took delivery of a total of 60 FL-9 diesel-electric-electric locomotives, the only ones ever built. They were F-units, lengthened six feet over FP-units, which had been lengthened nine feet over the original F-units. The first extension had been to accommodate boilers for heating passenger trains. The second lengthening was to accommodate the third-rail electrical gear to allow for electric operation in third-rail territory. This increased the

Charles H. Geletzke, Jr.

weight of the locomotive putting it over the authorized limit to operate on the New York Central's Park Avenue Viaduct leading into Grand Central Terminal in New York City. The design was further modified to use the SD-three axle truck, which had been designed to accept three traction motors for heavy haul, low speed freight operations. This spread the load and made them acceptable for the service the locomotives were designed for.

By 1962 SD-7 and SD-9 freight locomotives were experiencing fatigue cracking where the pedestals met the mainframe. *EMD* created a modification to repair the faults and prevent this from occurring. Shortly after the creation of Penn Central, the State of Connecticut paid for all of the units to be processed through Altoona for a mid-life overhaul. No one paid attention to the fact there were modifications outstanding against the B-end trucks! In this service, the loads were lower, so no defects were found. Metro-North received a Federal grant to create an experimental AC propulsion locomotive, designated FL-9AC. The locomotive shell and trucks were about all that were used in the ten units built. By that time the locomotives were over 30 years old. The trucks had started to show signs of fatigue the freight units had experienced a quarter century earlier. *Brown Boverei (BBC)* started the work and quickly found defects. Charlie Smith, Metro-North's consultant with *L. T. Klauder* remembered the problem from his time on the New York Central. The EMD modification document was still listed and readily supplied by *EMD*. The correction was straight forward, made during the locomotive conversion, and subsequently applied to other locomotives in the Metro-North FL-9 fleet.

One more…

I moved from the Mechanical Department where I was the representative for the FL-9AC project to Capital where I was the Project Engineer. As the Project was winding down, I became the Program Manager. The Manuals were not finished, in part because the locomotive was experimental and was being modified often. Bill Woodring was Metro-North's Manuals Manager. He formed an excellent working relationship with the Technical Writer at *ASEA-Brown-Boveri* (*ABB*) that held the contract originally signed by *BBC*. They could confer on how the manual would be formatted with *ABB* providing content. Bill would then send the draft letter to me for finalizing and issue.

I reviewed the Manual as each section was sent to me. I made my own comments, originally not knowing the existing arrangement. Since I had been involved in much of the design and all the changes, I made technical corrections. When the letter arrived at *ABB* in Elmira, there was confusion and consternation: why was the manual not acceptable as agreed? After this happened a couple of times, Bill put the pieces of the puzzle together and called me. He agreed, the Manual should also be technically correct, and that was beyond his knowledge; he had trusted *ABB*'s engineers had proofed the technical side.

In the end we had a good manual and a locomotive that was retired within three years! It had been designed with the idea the technology was changing rapidly as it was cutting edge. The control and power electronics were "plug in" and would be replaced by more current equipment. By this time, now *ADTRANZ* had grown tired of burning through money and upgrades were never considered.

One more once…

General Electric had perhaps the best instructions, well written and professionally presented. Because they utilized components from all over the company and used everywhere, they were component level instructions. They also converted instructions of any purchased parts to the *GE* format; so our criteria, that the instructions appeared to have been written by a single hand was also met. The weakness was there was little overview to tell how all the components worked together. Early on, I even had access to S-2 locomotive documentation from 1903!

Charles H. Geletzke, Jr.

Pullman Standard had built our oldest fleet, the Air Conditioned Multiple Units (ACMU) or 1100's built in 1962. *Budd Company* built our next oldest, M-1 from 1971. Each company took vendor documentation and inserted it into their manuals. The M-1 Air Brake Manual had a free standing manual labeled RMC-1. After hearing this quoted so man times, I asked what it stood for. It was Richard McCarthy's first manual and utilized his initials! Rich was the local *WABCO* representative and had gotten so little from his company that he wrote the manual. He too recognized it was essential for full and proper documentation to be available to the maintainers. As the Customer Service Representative, he felt it his duty to assure that documentation was on hand!

The second overhaul...

The first program I managed from start to finish was the second overhaul of the M-2 fleet by *Morrison-Knudson* at Hornell. It called for a number of Metro-North generated modifications to be applied and another group of modifications that *M-K* was to create using their Engineering talent. There were to be two binders, one with how to apply the modifications and a second noting the required maintenance...Repair, and Parts Lists for the *M-K* modifications.

As the project progressed, each Modification and Maintenance document was reviewed. As they were approved, they were entered into the volume. Toward the end *M-K* was facing financial distress and eventually became *AMERAIL*. Selected people were moved to keep them employed. One was a woman engineer who had been head of Door Engineering. She knew she was one of the select few and was put in charge of Manuals. Unfortunately, she knew little of Manuals or our car systems. I reviewed and commented on sections and found my input was ignored. The key item was air compressor settings, which the Metro-North Air Brake Supervisors had determined and explained to me. John Casale and Chris Stuckard were two experts I had come to trust implicitly! When our settings were not noted for the

200

third time, I utilized tools I had found through my school teacher wife. There were two rubber stamps; one was an unhappy face and the other a cut-off unhappy face with the word "INCOMPLETE" under it. I used the two as appropriate throughout the manual. Everyone on both sides of the project, except she and I knew what was going to happen when we met. It was not civil! She left her technical writer to finish the job noting she could not work with someone like me! After she left, my resident inspector, the four *M-K* project people, and the technical writer all expressed relief.

The Technical Writer was a man who had graduated high school about the same time as I had, gone to work for the Erie Lackawanna, then in turn *General Electric, M-K*, and now *AMERAIL*…all at the same facility! He was a competent mechanic who had been promoted to Foreman and was now composing manuals. He, our Resident Inspector, Don McFadden, who was also an MNR Electrical Engineer and I sat down together and went through the Manual. Don and I had worked together in the Mechanical Department and between us had most of the known answers for MNR rolling stock. I gave the *M-K* Technical Writer his marching orders.

- You are a competent Mechanic who knows nothing of the Equipment.
- What do you need to know to Inspect, Evaluate, and Repair the Equipment?
- Include necessary parts and tools.
- Compose it in a manner your High School English Teacher would expect of you.
- If you have technical questions, ask Don, myself, or Brian Edwards and Sam Knight (the AMERAIL engineers).

The next iteration we needed to make spelling and punctuation corrections and the Manual was done, complete, technically correct, and understandable to mechanics.

When all was done, I had delivered a personal copy to Mike Dorsi with whom I had worked for the previous 15 years; he was running the New Haven Car Shop in which the cars were maintained. A year later he complained he had no idea what modifications had been performed and how they were to be maintained. I visited his office, took the two booklets off his bookshelf and opened them. "These are the modifications and how they are performed. Here is a list of cars they apply to. Here are the maintenance requirements. Manuals are ultimately only useful if they are opened and read." This manual was a success because it was written by a mechanic for mechanics!

It is possible to go too far…

Tokyo Car built the M-4. The Japanese take things very literally. I was shown their manual and asked what I thought of a particular instruction. It started out with the instruction to turn the bolts counter-clockwise to remove them. They took the "step by step" instructions to the extreme until they could be told to cut-back the obvious tasks.

We see author, David Dykstra and Steve Krayer, *Kawasaki's* Project Manager with the first Metro North Railroad M-8 train on February 28, 2011. (Dykstra collection)

Final project…

M-8 was my final project. During the opening reviews we insisted *Kawasaki* must have the Technical Writers present at all second and third stage design reviews and First Article Inspections. They needed to bring draft Manuals to the first Article Inspections. As typical, the Car Builder hired most of the writers from a service…not their own employees! John Freund was assigned to head the writing; even he was a consultant; but at least he was imbedded in the pages of documentation on a myriad of subjects. It was expected that several of the major suppliers would have in-house technical writers, many of whom would already have prepared documents for their systems that could be modified to match the *Kawaski* format. Like the car builders, the component systems manufacturers wanted to sell product and be done with it! To make matters worse, the Japanese philosophy is not so much to overhaul but replace; so while Maintenance could be discussed, Repair and Overhaul were foreign concepts.

Mitsubishi was the Propulsion supplier. This was the most comprehensive set of equipment and one that interfaced with most every other system on the car. *Kawasaki* had full faith in *Mitsubishi* and gave them free hand. As a result, there was little oversight for integration of systems and no one to write on how the system was built into the cars! Even within the *Mitsubishi* Systems, there was no one present or presented who seemed to understand the system components.

During the final days of system by system review, there was an M-8 pair at *Kawasaki's* Yonkers facility with a failed transformer. *Mitsubishi* sent an engineer from Japan, had Jim Speasce, their Head of Field Service and an excellent Field engineer, one of his technicians, John Freund, taking notes for Manuals writing, and myself, all working on this car. We tested the system to find the fault, identified the component to be replaced, and did the replacement… taking the better part of two days. John took about three times as many pages of notes as were in the original documents. We started, hit a wall, had to undo some of what was done, and take a different path several times because the existing instructions were misleading or incorrect. That was the old saw, three steps forward, two steps back. After the component was changed-out the unit was tested with no change in status…the wrong part had been determined to be faulty!

MNR's John Hogan is seen working on one of the M-8 cars at the *Kawasaki* plant in Kobe, Japan in June 2011. (Dykstra collection)

The *Kawasaki* Program Manager still insisted the Manuals were done and our many pages of noted defects were irrelevant! Poor John was embarrassed; but fell back on "I can only do what I am told I am allowed to do!" Jim was frustrated beyond belief; he fully understood his company needed to put forth better effort and the engineer who had been sent from Japan was probably the junior man who had a passport and was volunteered.

Back at the Metro-North Shops, we needed to do some truck work due to early component failure. The work was to be done at the Stamford Shop, which had never done the work. A *Kawasaki* Truck Engineer, a couple of *Kawasaki* field service employees, and I visited for the day. I took copies of all the procedures that would be needed. The Procedures were written in such a manner that one task was presented in each procedure. In this case, measurements had to be taken at each of four bearing locations on the truck (1). The problem location(s) were determined and the springs at the offending axle had to be compressed and the shocks disconnected (2), wheel set at the problem location dropped (3), blocks on the swing arms had to be changed (4), the proper shims had to be applied at the spring seats (5), then the process reversed to reassemble the truck. Railroad Union Rules required not that employees had to perform the work; but they had to be present as if they were doing the work! The oldest, most experienced machinist was sent and happily pitched in. We took some additional time to look at other things. At the end of the day, I sought out our machinist who had worked with us…first to thank him for his help and second, to ask if he had a copy of the instructions…No, he did not! I asked if he would like a copy? "Yes!" I handed him the print-outs I had brought with me, and you would have thought that I had given him a pot of gold! Too often the workers are left in the dark and they truly appreciate being included and having their own reference sources!

Right to the end…

Twice a day I walked through Grand Central Terminal. Particularly in the mornings, I would see the same mechanics prepared to receive and turn trains during the morning rush. If I knew of defects on the train I had just arrived on, I would brief them. Having worked there, ultimately 41 years, many of these people had worked with me at other facilities and we became a fairly close community of Mechanical folk! They would tell me of their difficulties. Since I rode the diesel trains, that was mostly what I saw. Metro-North had purchased *Shoreliner* coaches in four batches over a 20 year period. I had been the Mechanical Department representative for the first two and well into the third before heading to Capital. We sent the earlier cars back to *Bombardier* for rebuild when they were about 25 years old. Changes were made, in some cases to make them the same as newer cars and other cases to improve them further. That meant there were now at least five versions of the car and the electricians were perplexed by the variances. As the Senior Engineer in the Car Equipment Group, I helped everyone in our group at one time or another and had knowledge of what they had done. I went to Brian O'Keeffe who was just finishing the overhaul project and asked him to identify the most recent schematics for the cars. He gave me the file and I printed out a couple of copies. Again, there were happy campers; they now had the documentation they needed to properly do their jobs!

GTW depot Battle Creek, MI (Geletzke collection)

I Just Could Not Believe It!

By: C. H. Geletzke, Jr.

The date was Tuesday, December 14, 1976 and I was on my way to report for my first day as Assistant Trainmaster-Agent for the Grand Trunk Western Railroad at Kalamazoo, Michigan. I had been instructed to drive from my home in St. Clair and while in route, to stop by the office of Transportation Superintendent, Robert C. Gould in the depot at Battle Creek. I left my apartment and my new wife of only two months at about 3 o'clock P.M. and arrived in the Battle Creek depot about two hours later. I immediately entered the Assistant Chief Dispatcher's Office and met with Assistant Chief Dispatcher, Pete Smith. Pete was a great guy, an excellent dispatcher, and I always had a great deal of respect for him!

Shortly, after I entered his office, Transportation Superintendent, Robert C. "Bob" Gould came down from his office up on the second floor and began conversing with Pete and me. No sooner had they begun talking when Pete received a telephone call from one of the South Bend

Subdivision Track Supervisors who informed Mr. Gould about a situation that I will never forget! You see at that time, the South \Bend Subdivision was still double-tracked with an Automatic Block Signal System (ABS) extending virtually all the way from the former Dearborn Station (M.P. 0.00) to the east end of Battle Creek Yard (M.P. 182)...that is with the exception of a C.T.C. single track section known as "Valpo Hill," stretching from Sedley, Indiana (M.P. 50.5 to Valparaiso (M.P. 55.6). Let me state right now that in those days on that entire piece of railroad they could really move some freight! Well, during the previous several weeks the GTW had begun replacing a stretch of "jointed rail" with "welded rail" on the Westward Main Track and I am sorry to state that I no longer recall the precise location; but it was somewhere out there on the "West End." Now Dispatcher Smith and Mr. Gould were talking with the Track Supervisor over the speaker phone and at the end of the conversation the track man said, "You can put all of the Westbound Main Track back in service. It's all finished!"

Pete Smith confirmed the transmission and then the two of them called upstairs to inform Superintendent, Ed Rose. I'll never forget what came next...Bob Gould said. "Ed, we can have all of the double-track back on the South Bend Sub. All of the welded rail is in."

All at once it sounded like Mr. Rose was going to jump out of his seat! He yelled, "Don't you dare put that track back in service yet! The lease on it does not go into effect until 8:00 A.M. NEXT MONDAY! IT'S NOT OUR TRACK YET! Then Mr. Rose went on to explain...apparently the GTW owned the jointed rail; but once the new welded rail was installed, the new welded rail was now owned by a leasing company and the lease would not go into effect until a specific date and time, and even though our Track Department completed the work ahead of schedule, it would not be ours to use until NEXT MONDAY at 8:00 A.M.! None of us could believe it!

That meant that for the next 5-1/2 days, our train dispatchers would have to continue issuing train orders and operating trains over that portion of the railroad as if it was

"Soak It!!!"… and Other Railroad Stories

single track! It was at that point that I realized that running a business today was based on tax advantages and other financial considerations and that running trains was secondary…not necessarily at the top of the list…and that welded rail would just sit there unused for almost another week…NO EXCEPTIONS!

Try that on your model railroad!

View looking south from the GTW Freight Office on Michigan Ave. in Kalamazoo, MI on March 13, 1979. Conrail tracks are on left and out of sight to the right. Firm on right was *Sportel Lumber Co.*

Kalamazoo Slide Show

By: C. H. Geletzke, Jr.

Most of you readers at one time or another probably attended or at least heard about one of the acts in the *Ringling Brothers & Barnum Bailey Circus* in which an extremely small automobile would come driving into the center ring and after completing several circles come to an abrupt halt! All at once, the clown driving the car would exit the vehicle, open the hood and inspect the motor. Shortly an extremely large number of other clowns would come pouring out of the car...so many in fact, that to this day, I still wonder how they got them all in there!?!

On August 3,1978 I had a similar circumstance in Kalamazoo!

If you are interested you can read in my previous books about how the GTW happened to send me to Kalamazoo in December 1976 (just prior to Christmas) to take over the position of Assistant Trainmaster-Agent following the promotion of my predecessor, K. W. "Keith" Charles. On my first day on the job, I was introduced to and met the late legendary GTW Engineer, Jack Ozanich, and remained best of friends until his passing in 2020. Through Jack and attending operating sessions on his original Atlantic & Great Eastern (AGE) model railroad, I eventually came to know many model railroaders and railfans in the Kalamazoo/Battle Creek, Michigan area.

At some point during the fall of 1977 we formed a monthly slide group similar to the one in which I was a member in the Detroit area. Initially, we had about six participants; but primarily through the acquaintances of "Johnny O," our group grew, and pretty soon we had too many members to include in most of our homes for the rotating monthly meetings! It was time to secure a new monthly meeting place.

It was at this juncture that I suggested that we meet monthly in my office...the Grand Trunk Western Railroad Kalamazoo Freight Office. At that time, GTW's Kalamazoo operation involved seven or eight clerks on the day shift (depending whether we were handling the operation at Kilgore Yard and switching the adjacent Fisher Body Plant...the arrangement alternated every year on August 1st between us and Conrail (formerly NYC or PC), one clerk on afternoons, and one on midnights. So, if we began our slide shows at say 7:30 P.M., at most we might only interfere with the work of one clerical employee...and that was F. O. "Frank" Smith, who began his railroad career during the early 1940's as a fireman, was promoted to engineer, and later disqualified due to vision problems in 1969, and immediately transferred to the clerical craft where he spent

"Soak It!!!"… and Other Railroad Stories

the remainder of his career…oh yes, I might add that he too was a railfan! So, I guess it was probably in the spring of 1978 we began holding our meetings at 427 E. Michigan Ave., Kalamazoo, Michigan. Let me mention one more detail regarding the use of this location. I never bothered to ask any of my superiors for permission to use this facility. You see for me, running the Kalamazoo operation was just like managing my own shortline and for the most part, as long as the railroad ran smoothly and the customers were kept happy, I had little interference from any of the chiefs.

Fast forward to our meeting on Thursday, August 3, 1978…I arrived early to get everything set-up. Shortly the others began to arrive: There was GTW Brakeman, L. R. "Larry" Bolton; the late GTW Engineer, Jack Ozanich; the late GTW Mechanical Department man, J. P. "John" Baukus, Jr.; Tom Weaver from the GTW Track Department; the late L. G. Isaac; Tom Bowers; Robert Oom; and probably at least eight others. Now before we began actually showing our slides, Engineer Ozanich suggested, " Why don't you give BO tower a call and just see what he might have coming our way?" (BO was a former NYC interlocking tower a block to our north, which basically coordinated all of the train movements of both CR and GTW within much of the city.) (You see the GTW Freight Office was completely surrounded by tracks at that time with the Conrail's former GR&I-PRR to our west, the GTW running on Conrail's former CK&S-NYC to our east, and the former Michigan Central Mainline to our north on which Amtrak also operated…there were constantly trains occupying the crossings and naturally this frustrated many of the local residents!)

Well, as luck would have it the tower man stated that he did in fact have a train coming north on the GR&I, which would cross onto the CK&S at Gibson Street, and then head around into Conrail's Botsford Yard located along the MC Main on the east side of town. The operator also added that the train was pulling a string of former NYC, PRR, NH, and PC cars, which had been stored out in the woods on the former GR&I Main Track, south of Vicksburg, for months! I thanked the operator and informed my friends. They were all ecstatic…after all, because it was August, the days were long, AND how many night time slide shows have you attended where the participants also brought their cameras!?! This was indeed the perfect venue!

Shortly, we began showing slides; but it seemed like no time at all that we heard a Conrail train in the vicinity of the Gibson Street diamond, blowing for the crossings and headed in our direction. Naturally one of our members stationed himself at the front door watching for the headlight as we all continued to look at slides. Shortly he hollered out, "That Conrail's getting close!"

With that, someone shut off the projector's bulb allowing the fan to continue to run, we all grabbed our cameras and ran out the front door as the crossing gates were just coming down on Michigan Avenue…traffic was already starting to backup. Now I'm not positive; but I believe I was the last one out of the building…and as I ran through the stopped traffic there on Michigan Avenue, I happened to look in one of the cars and there sat John Yeager, the GTW's senior Trainmaster in Battle Creek! To this day, I have no idea why he happened to be there and I just waved and shouted, "Hi John!" as I darted across the street. I then ran south about 50 yards or so to the Michigan Avenue Team Track and began taking photos…the collection of old cars and fast-disappearing paint schemes were unbelievable! Following the train's passing we returned to the freight office and resumed our show…still talking about the cars that we knew we would never see again.

I also recall thinking to myself, I know John Yeager is going to mention the explosion of people out of my office that evening and probably tell my bosses. Yes, I was a bit nervous! But guess what, John was a good guy and a fellow Marine, and to this day the incident was never mentioned to me…not even by John himself!

p.s.
Now you might be inclined to ask whether I learned a lesson!?! Well, in 1994 when I was the GTW's Supervisor of

"Soak It!!!"… and Other Railroad Stories
Locomotive Engineers at Flat Rock, Michigan, I invited the entire *Pennsylvania Railroad Technical & Historical Society-Red Arrow Chapter* membership to my office on a Sunday afternoon to show slides and gave each person a chance to run our Locomotive Simulator! I am guessing this would NEVER happen today; but that is another story!?!

View looking north on the GTW toward the Kalamazoo, MI Freight Office on March 13, 1979. On the extreme left is the former PRR (GR&I) passenger depot. To the left of the GTW trackage is the *Sportel Lumber Co.*, and to the right is the GTW track scale and the LS&MS Freight House.

Contrasting Managers or, I Thought I Was Getting a Raise!?!

By: C. H. Geletzke, Jr.

In the first volume of this series, *When Deadhead Counted As Rest and Other Railroad Stories* I mentioned the first time that I met Grand Trunk Western Railroad Detroit Division Superintendent, Ed Rose in 1968. In December of 1976 I was transferred to Kalamazoo, Michigan as Assistant Trainmaster/Agent and worked for Mr. Rose, who was then

Charles H. Geletzke, Jr.

Superintendent of the more prestigious Chicago Division or "Mainline."

One day in mid-1977 I was sitting in my office in the GTW Freight Office at 427 E. Michigan Avenue (which is now a Sushi restaurant) and my telephone rang. It turned out to be Superintendent Rose (whose daughter, Myrna Wallace was my secretary). When I answered, Mr. Rose said, "How are your doing Chuck?"

I then responded that I was doing well and basically waiting for "the shoe to drop!?!"

As it turned out, we made "small talk" for several minutes and then I finally inquired, "What can I do for you, Mr. Rose?"

His response blew me away and to this day I have never forgotten it! He said, "Oh nothing, I just hadn't talked with you in a while and I just wondered how you were doing!?!" That was it...just a friendly conversation!

Mr. Rose retired in early 1978 and was replaced by a new Superintendent who began his railroad career as a GTW Switchman in Flint, Michigan. (Oh yes, Mr. Rose started as a South Bend Subdivision Road Brakeman in the late 1930's.)

Now let me "blow my own horn" a little bit. With a tremendous amount of help from GTW Sales Representative, Gary Redmond; his boss, Phil Wolcott; and Customer Service Representative, Tom Burke, GTW carload business in Kalamazoo had increased easily by 30 to 40% in the past year! The reason was...we were paying attention to our customers, giving them ALL personal attention and because Conrail (the other carrier in town) was not, we were taking a huge amount of business away from them! In most cases this meant that we were acquiring the road haul on much of this traffic and due to reciprocal switching agreements, Conrail was just delivering and pulling the cars from the firms themselves. This meant that we were now bringing the coal and other products in and out of town for *Upjohn, Georgia Pacific, Bryant Paper, The Brown Company*, and even *Western Michigan University*. I loved it!

What I did not know at that time was that the GTW, Conrail, and the City of Kalamazoo were involved in initial

214

"Soak It!!!"... and Other Railroad Stories

talks about a "Track Consolidation," which if approved would eliminate much of the local trackage where the carriers had parallel routes. What was never mentioned were the number of smaller firms who would LOSE SERVICE ALTOGETHER!

One day in late 1978 I received a letter from Mr. John H. Burdakin, President of the railroad, requesting information on the *Sportel Lumber Company*. *Sportel* was an interesting little operation. It was located directly across the street from my office and normally only received one or two loads of lumber each month on their own spur, the majority of which were generally "stop-off" cars, meaning that they only received a portion of the load after which the car would be forwarded to another lumber distributor where the remainder of the car's contents would be unloaded. This was very common in the railroad industry at that time and pertained to the handling of many various commodities. Also of interest was the fact that *Sportel's* building was originally a banana warehouse. Constructed in the 1920's (I believe) the structure was still equipped with storage lockers and gas lines, which had been used to pump a type of gas into rooms of bananas to hasten their ripening. I don't believe the building had handled any tropical fruit since at least the mid-1950's.

I checked through our local records, found *Sportel* to be a good customer, who always paid their bills on time, and one which never created any problems. I then wrote a letter of reply to Mr. Burdakin giving him all of the pertinent details, and I carbon copied everyone that had been cc'd on the original document.

The letters were mailed and two mornings later, bright and early, I received a telephone call from the new Superintendent. In his blustery and abrupt manner he said, "Chuck, I don't care what you are doing, cancel it, and come on over here...right now!"

I replied. "Yes sir. I will be right over."

I then told my office staff where I was going (I never had a railroad radio while working there) and headed for Battle Creek, which was about a thirty minute drive. While driving I pondered why my boss requested my immediate presence!?! Interestingly, I could not think of anything that I had done wrong; so in conclusion I figured, "either he is going to give me a pay increase, or he is going to tell me that I am being promoted???"

The Superintendent's office was located on the second floor of the GTW Battle Creek Passenger Depot and I climbed the stairs to his outer office, which was occupied by five or six clerks. I approached the Chief Clerk and announced that I was there to see the head of the Chicago Division. She replied. "He is expecting you" and ushered me into his office.

Like all of us managers during that era, the Division Superintendent was dressed in a suit (his was a three piece) and tie and had a massive gold watch chain displayed across the front of his vest. He was seated at his large hardwood desk and interestingly, did not rise to greet me. His first words to me were, "Close the door!"

Now I began to fret…what had I done wrong???

Well, I didn't have to wait long to find out! The imposing Superintendent held up a **copy** of the letter, which I had just sent to Mr. Burdakin and said rather loudly, **"YOU DON'T EVER WRITE A LETTER TO THE PRESIDENT OF THE RAILROAD!"**

Believe me, I was stunned! I am sure that I displayed a "deer in the headlights" expression on my face…never expecting this to have been an issue. I immediately responded, "All I did was reply to Mr. Burdakin's letter, **which was addressed to me**, and carbon copied all of the same people on his list."

With that, the head of the division jumped-up out of his chair and once again hollered, **"YOU DON'T EVER WRITE TO THE PRESIDENT! If you have something you want to say to him, you write to me and I will reply to him!"**

Again I replied, "I just answered Mr. Burdakin's personal letter, which was addressed to me."

With that the well dressed Superintendent walked over to a large white oak four drawer filing cabinet and pulled out a large sheet of paper. It turned out to be a large

216

flow chart demonstrating the Chain of Command for all of the managers on the entire railroad. The Superintendent then stated emphatically, "Look at this!" And he pointed to a point on the bottom of the chart and said, "See this! This is **YOU**, Assistant Trainmaster/Agent-Kalamazoo!" He then pointed to the single person at the top of the chart and stated, **"That is Mr. Burdakin, President of the railroad!** Now if you follow the lines of the Chain of Command, you will see **that YOU report to ME, Superintendent-Chicago Division** and (dropping his voice) also to Division Agent, Angus MacEachin. So once again I say, **YOU** are **NEVER** to write to the President of the railroad!"

It then occurred to me why it seemed that the people at the top often did not appear to know what was going on…in any business! I also pondered, what if I reply to my superior and he or she does not reply to the officer that wrote the letter…how does that make me look!?! I felt as if I was in a no-win situation.

The Division Superintendent then said to me. "That's it, you can go back to Kalamazoo now; but don't you ever write to the President!"

I then dejectedly left the top floor office and returned to Kalamazoo. I never felt the same about being a manager after that!

Looking back, perhaps I was too "thin-skinned!?!"

View looking north at the GTW's little four track Mill Street Yard in Kalamazoo, MI on September 16, 1978. This was where interchange between the GTW and CR (former NYC) took place. The track to the right of the pole line was the Conrail's former CK&S line to Pavilion.

Kalamazoo Track Consolidation

By: Charles H. Geletzke, Jr.

The following statement was posted several years ago on social media after I placed a photo of the Grand Trunk Western Railroad's former Mill Street Yard in Kalamazoo, Michigan taken in January 1979…

"If only that yard was still there…..it would be a game changer for Kalamazoo & a very busy place."
Mike Hnatiuk*
Regional Account Manager CN

* Today Mike Hnatiuk is the Director Business Development, Lake State Railway

As I have stated previously, from December 1976 through May 1979 I was the Assistant Trainmaster/Agent for the Grand Trunk Western Railroad in Kalamazoo, Michigan. During that time I became the youngest member of the *Kalamazoo Chamber of Commerce-Transportation Committee*. That outstanding group generally met monthly and in addition to myself was made-up of the traffic managers of a number of major Kalamazoo industries, truck-line supervisors, and Don Dwyer, Conrail's local Trainmaster. As a member of this organization we all worked together to assist one another in the movement of freight within and in and out of the region.

At one of the meetings in the last half of 1978 we were informed that we were to have a guest speaker at our monthly meeting. It turned out that this woman was the Administrative Assistant to Kalamazoo's City Manager. It also turned out that the topic of her presentation was Kalamazoo's Upcoming Railroad Track Consolidation. Let me confess that this was the first time that I had heard any information or discussion about this upcoming project! When she began her presentation, I listened intently to her every word...all the while thinking to myself, "you've got to be kidding!" When she completed her information session she asked, "Are there any questions or problems that any of you foresee with the implementation of this important regional improvement?"

I immediately raised my hand and was the first member of our committee called-on. I then stood-up and probably went a little too far when I stated, "I only see one problem...**It won't work!**"

I could instantly see the color go out of the lady's face and she then asked me to elaborate.

The two major issues that I addressed were, Number One, they wanted to eliminate and remove all GTW trackage north of Lake Street (including Mill Street Yard where we interchanged with Conrail) and the Conrail trackage (which we used jointly) on the "South Side" running all the way to the Portage Street Team Track! Point Number Two, which I

Charles H. Geletzke, Jr.

will agree had been a major problem for the City of
Kalamazoo since the New York Central (NYC) and
Pennsylvania (PRR) Railroads merged to form Penn Central
in 1968, was the way that many Conrail trains blocked many
of the street crossings for huge amounts of time as they
entered and departed the community. The issue here was that
many of the northbound trains coming up from Elkhart and
going to Grand Rapids had to diverge at Gibson Street and
head into Conrail's (former NYC) Botsford Yard using the
interlocking at BO Tower. Then after setting-off and picking-
up, they would shove all the way back through town, south of
the Gibson Street diamond (approximately a two mile shove
depending upon the length of the train), and then head north
using the former Pennsylvania Railroad's former Grand
Rapids & Indiana (GR&I) line all the way through town,
once again toward the former "furniture city." Southbound
trains were required to perform the same scenario only in
reverse! For these reasons, most of the local citizens detested
the railroad! Over the years I actually witnessed automobile
drivers falling asleep right in front of my office waiting for a
train to clear the Michigan Avenue crossing!

According to the new plan, a new wye would be
constructed west of the local Amtrak depot in the northeast
quadrant of the former GR&I (PRR)-NYC diamond allowing
trains moving both directions to head directly into or out of
Botsford Yard. With this proposal, once a train entered the
yard, after setting-off and picking-up, a yard crew would
have to handle the train's caboose from one end of the train
to the other while the locomotives ran around the train...then,
the entire train would once again require another complete
Initial Terminal Air Test! That would eat-up a tremendous
amount of time!

Well words travel fast and only two days later I received
a telephone call from our Chicago Division Superintendent,
at about 3 o'clock in the afternoon and he gave me the
following instructions. He stated, "I want you to compile
ALL of the material that you have pertaining to the possible
affects and changes in the operation at Kalamazoo if the
Track Consolidation is implemented. And, YOU are to have

"Soak It!!!"… and Other Railroad Stories

all of your material ready to present by 5:30 A.M. tomorrow…then you are to drive over here to Battle Creek where you will pick-up Bill Dempsey (the Transportation Superintendent), Cliff Rose (the Assistant Transportation Superintendent) and Angus McEachin (the Division Agent). The four of you will drive to Detroit (the General Office at 131 W. Lafayette) and meet with the railroad's relatively new President and you will make your presentation to him promptly at 8:00 A.M. explaining your findings and details of the changes in operation!

Now this was a Friday afternoon; so I immediately called my wife and stated that I would not be home for supper that evening and explained the circumstances! Several hours later, she brought dinner to me.

I worked until 3 A.M. putting together as much material as I possibly could supporting my perspective. Not knowing the minute details of the plan, I included the names of the industries that would no longer receive service by rail and the number of loads in and out that the railroad would no longer handle in an average year. I had drawings of the track that would be eliminated and new operating problems that their removal would incur. I noted that the second railroad scale that we had available in town (which served as a replacement for the electronic computerized motion one at Kilgore Yard, which it seemed was out of service on an almost bi or tri-weekly basis) would be removed…meaning that cars requiring weighing (generally about 25 per day) would have to be weighed in Battle Creek! Doing my best I compiled an entire folder of material for my presentation during the allotted 12-hour period. At three in the morning I drove home, showered, changed into another suit and tie, consumed a quick breakfast, and headed over to Battle Creek…about forty minutes to the east.

I found it interesting that my boss instructed me to use my car (as I was the only company officer in the group that did not have a company vehicle) to haul three of my superiors to Detroit…especially considering I had now been awake for over 24 hours!?!

Charles H. Geletzke, Jr.

On Saturday, September 2nd, I drove over to the GTW depot in Battle Creek and picked-up my superiors as instructed by the Division Superintendent. Together we then drove the 125 miles to our General Office in Detroit. Upon arrival I parked my car and together the four of us entered the building, climbed on the elevator, and rode to the upper floor and the office of the railroad's new president. The four of us then entered the outer office and waited to see the corporate president. I guess we waited about ten or fifteen minutes and then were called into his office. The chief executive told us to "have a seat" and then looked us all over…up and down. I recall sitting their nervously holding my bundle of file folders and compiled information. All at once the corporate head started to speak. He said, "I don't care what you think or how this will affect YOUR operation, I want you to comply with any and all requests of the City of Kalamazoo! In the meantime I do not want you talking to anyone about this plan and I WANT YOU TO KEEP YOUR OPINIONS TO YOURSELF! Thank you for coming in gentlemen and have a nice day."

That was it! He never even had the courtesy to ask to see any of the information that I had compiled…that was 12 hours of my life that I would never get back! The four of us then filed out of the office and back to my car.

It was a quiet trip back to the Chicago Division Headquarters…I think perhaps all of us were in a semi-state of shock. We never even stopped to eat or to have a cup of coffee. At the depot I dropped my three bosses off and headed back to Kalamazoo…totally disillusioned. It was not long after that that I began sending out resumes and I am guessing that word got out as to how truly disheartened I was as the next spring I was transferred to Toledo as Trainmaster on GTW's subsidiary the Detroit & Toledo Shore Line Railroad…and that too is another story!

I guess this was my scratch pad…

By: C. H. Geletzke, Jr.

Last evening my wife was out on our patio grilling a steak for each of us and I was inside performing one of "my chores"…setting the table. Since we were having steak, I made the command decision to look in our wash stand and locate the steak knives.

Now the steak knives…we have two boxes of them, which we received as a wedding gift almost 47 years ago…are still stored in their original boxes. As I removed one box from the drawer in the dimly lit dining room, I noticed that there was very small writing in pencil on the top of the box. Curiosity got the better of me and I carried the case into the kitchen, which has far superior illumination for my tired old eyes. As I squinted to see what was written on the almost half-century old item, I could not believe my eyes…I could just barely make out…

Hold	7
CO	9
BD	0
BS	5
NW	1
CR	4
Rip	1

I thought back and realized that apparently one evening in 1979 or 1980, while I was Trainmaster on the Detroit & Toledo Shore Line in Toledo, Ohio, I must have had a discussion with the Yardmaster at Lang Yard and recorded the above information…on whatever happened to be handy at that moment...in this case, the box of steak knives! That little note from over 40-years ago told me that at that moment, on the "Heavy Side" of the yard we had 7-Holds, 9 cars for the C&O, None for the B&O Dixie, 5-for the B&O at Cincinnati, 1 N&W going to Homestead Yard, 4

Charles H. Geletzke, Jr.

for the Conrail at Stanley Yard, and one car for the rip. Incidentally, the B&O was the only foreign railroad for which we pre-blocked southbound traffic. Northbound, we switched cars into five separate classifications for the GTW.

I knew that I had recorded numerous notes throughout my 45-year railroad career; but believe me, I had no idea that I had scribbled notes on my wife's box of cutlery! You just never know!

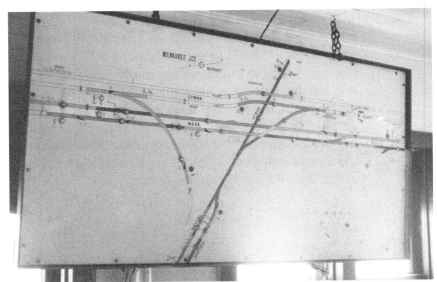

NYC-GTW model board in the CR (former NYC-PC) Milwaukee Jct. tower in Detroit, MI on December 27, 1985.

Spring Switches can be Vicious!

By: retired PC, RI, CR, and NS Operator, James H. Harlow

This caper took place in the early 1980's.

One Saturday afternoon, being forever on the tower operator's "extra board" in Conrail's Detroit District, I was assigned to work second shift at Milwaukee Jct. tower. On arrival and taking over operations, I noticed there was a motionless GTW train stretched across the "Dinky Line" connection to the Holly Subdivision on the Mt. Clemens Subdivision track nearest the tower.

This was nothing unusual; sometimes a train from Toledo running via the Shore Line Sub. would stop at GTW's East Yard, about a mile east of Milwaukee Jct., to wait for a new crew to take it on to Port Huron, or to wait for a switching crew to yard it at East Yard. Whatever the case, this standing train did not concern me, as it was not interfering with any Conrail trains…and being a Saturday, it would not interfere with any SEMTA commuter trains, should this train still be standing there during the late afternoon hours.

When seated at the desk inside the tower, the operator was facing towards Pontiac (geographical north) on the Holly Sub., with his or her back facing most of the interlocking-i.e. Conrail's North Yard Branch and GTW's Mt. Clemens Sub. When this train finally moved, I would not have to be involved with taking any action for it with the interlocking machine. So, I was not concerned about it at all.

I've noted, over the years as an operator on Conrail and having worked on the Rock Island in Chicago as a towerman/train director, that the GTW was terribly fond of spring switches as compared to those other two railroads. There were spring switches just outside of the interlocking plant at Milwaukee Jct.-one on the Holly Sub. at the "Sugarhouse Wye" track connection, and one just west of the plant on the Mt. Clemens Sub., where the Eastward Main Track of the Mt. Clemens Sub's Westward Main Track split into two tracks…what they called the "Main" track and the "Tunnel" track. Those two tracks extended southwest from Milwaukee Jct. past Beaubien St. tower toward West Detroit. (Today this spring switch, I just described, is within a CN dispatcher-controlled interlocking named "CN Murray," with the spring switch now being a power switch.) There were other spring switches on the GTW's main tracks almost within sight of the tower at Milwaukee Jct.

I had never seen a spring switch in use on Conrail, nor had I ever seen a spring switch in use on the Rock Island in Chicago.

Charles H. Geletzke, Jr.

Spring switches could be a problem, IF a train stopped on them, and IF such a train then *backed up* over them without a trainman first inspecting which way the switch was sprung; if not inspected, and the switch was sprung or aligned for the other route, it could derail a train when the truck on one car was on the route the train had arrived on, and the truck on the other end of the car was then being diverted to the other track-IF the switch was sprung for that route. All railroaders are aware of this danger with spring switches.

So this was the case that Saturday afternoon, with this standing train stretched across the plant; This train had trailed through the spring switch on the Main Track, and was standing upon it, with the switch aligned for the Tunnel Track.

I was seated at the desk with my back facing the standing train…when for no reason at all, I whirled around to see it moving very, very slowly…almost imperceptibly…toward the Beaubien St. tower. Realizing in a split second, that it had probably come east from West Detroit on the Main Track and stopped at East Yard, it now had another crew on board, and was *backing up over the spring switch*…probably to back up to a track at East Yard it had originally passed when it first arrived there. In the next split second, I was standing up at the intercom on a shelf we used to communicate with GTW's General Yardmaster (GYM), chopping away at the toggle switch with my hand. The only way to get the trains stopped was to inform the GYM to stop the movement of this train, since there was no GTW radio in the tower.

When I "broke in" (trained as a new employee) at Milwaukee Jct., I briefly toured the GYM's office inside the GTW's office building located diagonally across the plant from the tower. I observed that when the toggle switch on the intercom was depressed in the tower, it would actuate a muted bell at the GYM's desk as an indication the operator wanted to communicate with him. So I knew that by rapidly depressing the toggle switch, the bell in the GYM's communication console was going, "ding-ding-ding-ding-ding-ding, etc."

The GYM answered over the intercom almost immediately, angrily saying, "Stop that! Why are you doing that?"

I screamed at him saying, "Get that train stopped!!! It's backing-up over the spring switch!!!"

I knew he could look out of a window near his desk to observe trains going through the interlocking. Sure enough, a flat car had been caught in the spring switch, which had been aligned for the Tunnel Track under it…and by this time, was looking more like a humongous-size potato chip. It was twisting itself off of the track, with it being coupled to cars on each end of it-the west end coupled to the cars on the Main Track, and the east end truck going down the Tunnel Track, with the other cars on the east end of it trying to follow it. The wheels of the east end truck on the tower side were high in the air when the movement finally stopped; but both ends of the flatcar were still coupled to the cars on each end of it.

Sometime later, I observed that the cars on the east end of the twisted flatcar had been removed…and now a switcher from East Yard had come down on the flat car and tied on to it. I thought to myself, "Oh this should be fun to watch!" The crew very gingerly moved the east end of the flatcar eastward…and believe it or not, the flatcar eased itself, with all of its wheels back on the rail! With that accomplished, the switcher took the rest of the train toward East Yard.

I have to say that this entire incident was one of the screwiest things I ever saw! But what had made me turn around in my chair to see that train backing-up, when it started to happen? There was no noise of any kind when that train started to move. I can only ascribe it to my guardian angels, which have been saving my butt…now and then…over my entire life!!!

Charles H. Geletzke, Jr.

GTW Engineer, Chuck Geletzke in Detroit, Michigan on June 30, 2006.

Interview Profile: Chuck Geletzke

By: Personal Injury Attorney, Stephen A. Kaslik

(Editor's comment: Let me state that this was actually written by Councilor Kaslik when he was a sophomore in high school as an assignment in his English class. Upon completion he gave me a copy, which I have proudly retained all of these years.)

Stephen A. Kaslik, Esq. high school graduation photo.

On October 24, 1998, I interviewed Chuck Geletzke, Jr. Chuck is an engineer for the Grand Trunk Western Railroad and has 31 years of service behind him. He often worries about not getting enough rest, as his job requires him to travel away from his home in Temperance, Michigan often. He sacrifices sleep so he can be a father, a husband, and a provider for his family. Chuck's profile as an engineer

Charles H. Geletzke, Jr.

is classic as he wears bib overalls, a hat, and can sure tell a good story about the past. I met him by going out for his train every other day while it went through Richmond (Michigan). The interview took place in the *Fairfield Hotel* in Port Huron while he was resting between trains.

I began "If you could change one thing in life, what would it be?" Chuck repeated the question as he though hard. I expected a response geared toward the railroads; but this was not to be. "The most devastating thing in my life would have to be...I had a daughter that was born in 1981 that died...and that...that would be it for me," Chuck stated. Knowing that this was very personal, I felt that I was intruding on his family life. Nevertheless, Chuck and I continued the interview with the next question. How would this event be changed? Chuck began "The cause of death was never really 100 percent known; but my wife has a condition called Gestational Diabetic." He went on to say that if they had known about it, greater care would have been taken to monitor the progress of the child. Chuck's daughter, Jill, could have survived had more tests been run and more examinations taken place. This event took place at *Toledo Hospital* (Ohio) in 1981.

I began another question "If you could go back to that day, would you?" Chuck replied strongly "Oh absolutely I would. I definitely would go back; but I can't play God, it's...all in God's hands." Chuck was in his early thirties at this time. What future events would be altered if this was changed? "There would be another mouth to feed, another set of expenses, and probably more activities to do. Or, if I could only have had one daughter and be happy with her, none of my other children could have come along. But, if the other children still did come...my two daughters would maybe share a room, it would change our house for sure. I would just be getting my ducks in a row for college payments for her and a lot of other expenses." Chuck only had his wife, his parents, and other family at this time (no other children). I then asked if he was employed by the railroad at this time. Chuck began with a serious tone "Yes, I worked for Grand Trunk. They were treating me the worst they ever had before." Chuck's wife was due on a Tuesday, his promotion classes to be an engineer began the day before. He made the first part of his class; but he notified the secretary of his absence for the next class. Chuck did not get promoted until 1982, a whole year later because of this event.

I asked if Chuck had learned something from this, and he did. "I've learned that you should never take life and health for granted. Also, family comes first. I always feel guilty when I have to go to work; but I know, and they know that it's what I have to do. Her death...has given me a greater appreciation of life and how important family is to me. That's what I've learned.

In conclusion, I have also thought a little more about life in general after this. It was a quiet day for me after the interview, and I did nothing but think. I thought of how lucky I was to be where I am today. I hope more people think about their situations also after reading this paper.

My Daughter, Jill...what would you have done?

As told by: C. H. Geletzke, Jr.

After including Stephen A. Kaslik's interview as the previous story, I thought that perhaps you might like to hear my side of the story. While I learned a great deal from this event, in all honesty, I have never gotten over it!

When I resigned from my position as Trainmaster on the Detroit & Toledo Shore Line Railroad (D&TSL) a 50% owned subsidiary of the GTW on November 3, 1980 I exercised my seniority as a Locomotive Fireman at Milwaukee Jct. in Detroit, Michigan. Let me state that at that time earning a promotion to Locomotive Engineer was still a three year process...a First Year Exam...a Second Year exam and promotion to Yard Engineer...and finally the Third Year Exam and promotion to work in all classes of Engine Service.

Charles H. Geletzke, Jr.

In my case, I took and passed my First Year Exam in 1974. In mid-1974 the economy took a huge hit and I was furloughed in January 1975…in fact, I was only called 17 times throughout the entire year to work hostling jobs! In December of 75 the railroad contacted me and beginning in January 1976 I accepted a managerial position…wouldn't you know, on that very same day the Crew Dispatcher called and stated that I was "recalled" as a Fireman! Naturally, I stayed in management!

So, after several different positions and promotions followed by my "managerial" resignation I was "marked-up" as a Fireman…now the oldest Fireman in Detroit! By this time and through the improving economy quite a number of new enginemen had been hired and promoted ahead of me. That said, I was still the oldest Fireman and once promoted, I would return to my original standing on the seniority list.

Being the oldest Fireman I was naturally able to hold what in my opinion were the "best" jobs! Upon first marking-up I held the DT&I Puller from Milwaukee Jct. to Flat Rock and return, and later one end of Trains 215/214 the hot piggy-back run from Detroit to Battle Creek and return, which because of the mileage, only worked three round-trips a week. All of these jobs required that I had to drive from my home in Toledo, Ohio to the roundhouse at Milwaukee Jct., which was a 1'15" (one hour fifteen minutes) drive (65 miles each way). This took some "getting used to!"

On Wednesday, December 10th we found out that my wife, Leslie, was pregnant…definitely a major change! The "Due Date" was to be July 18th, 1981.

On Friday, December 12th, I drove up to Tawas City, Michigan and interviewed with C. J. MacPhail the Vice President of the Detroit & Mackinac Railroad and the road's President, C. A. Pinkerton for the job of Superintendent. I was offered the position; but ultimately declined the offer.

Afterward I just continued working as Fireman on Trains 215 and 214 three days a week until June 3, 1981 when I was reassigned as an Engineer Trainee. The company had me working various yard jobs on all three shifts in Detroit through June 20th.

"Soak It!!!"… and Other Railroad Stories

Knowing that my wife's Due Date was getting close, I elected to bid on a regular daylight yard job the 0730 East Line Job with engineer, Leo Roberts, so that in the event of any medical issues I could get to my car at the roundhouse reasonably quickly and race home to Toledo.

On Friday, June 5th I called the office of Road Foreman of Engines, Dennis Dowell and spoke with his secretary. I explained my predicament and explained that my wife's "Due Date" to have the baby was July 18th, and stated that I did not need any conflicts. I also knew that Detroit Fireman, Danny Martin and I were the ONLY two firemen on the entire system that were due for Second Year Exams and Promotion to Yard Engineers. Mr. Dowell's secretary stated, "We will NOT be holding any Mechanical and Rules Classes until the last week of July or the first week of August."

Well, guess what…on Wednesday, July 1st, 1981 I received a call from Mr. Dowell's secretary informing me that I was "notified that Engineer Trainee, Danny Martin and I were to attend a Mechanical Class in Battle Creek during the week of July 20th through the 24th and a Rules Class in Durand, Michigan during the week July 27th through the 31st."

I then explained that if my wife delivered the baby prior to the 20th and there were not any problems, I would be there.

Then the secretary stated…"I think you should try to come anyway!"

I couldn't believe it! I told her that I lived close to three hours away and "if there is any kind of a problem or something happens, I will NEVER FORGIVE MYSELF!"

She then replied, "If you choose not to come, there will be no penalty; but there will not be another class for a long, long time!" (With only two Trainees scheduled for the class, would the carrier really be this inflexible!?!) The lady then said, "Please send a letter to Mr. Dowell confirming our discussion."

I stated, "I will." I felt like I was under a tremendous amount of pressure and that perhaps I had a target on my back; but in my mind, my family came first! I had no idea why they could not wait one more week or so!?!

I continued working the 0730 East Line Job and on Monday, July 20th, two days after our daughter's due date, we went to see her OBGYN. Unbelievably, the doctor and his staff could not find the baby's heartbeat! They sent Leslie for an Echogram…later they pronounced our daughter, "DEAD!" Leslie and I spent the night in the hospital and they delivered our daughter the next morning. We named her Jill Frieda Geletzke. She was baptized by our minister. Despite the fact that all of the staff was fantastic, this was without a doubt the worst day of our lives!

On Wednesday, July 22nd I called Mr. Dowell's office and once again spoke with his secretary. I stated, "I will be attending the Rules Classes in Durand during the following week." The secretary then asked me if my wife had the baby. I replied, "Yes she did; but the baby died!" I am still sorry…I just could not help myself. The secretary could not get off the phone fast enough!

I brought Leslie home from the hospital on Thursday the 23rd and we had Jill's funeral on Saturday, July 25th.

The next week I was in attendance at the Rules Classes in Durand with Danny Martin. Because Durand did not have any motels at that time, we stayed in a motel over at Owosso. I completed the Second Year Rules Exam on July 31st. Additionally, I also received the Fireman position on Trains 215/214 on bid working Wednesday, Friday, and Sunday. I began working that job on Sunday, August 2nd and held that position through December 23rd, when the job was abolished for the Christmas Holiday.

Wondering when I would be able to complete the 2nd Year Mechanical Class I contacted Road Foreman Dowell on January 3, 1982 and asked when the class might be held?

He responded, "Early February."

On February 2nd I called and spoke with Mr. Dowell's secretary and asked the same question.

She replied, "Last week of April or first week of May."

"Soak It!!!"... and Other Railroad Stories

On March 9th I called the secretary and asked again. This time she said, "Sometime in April."

On April Fool's Day once again I asked, Mr. Dowell. He responded, "I'm working on it!"

On April 7th, the secretary's reply was, "Second week of May."

I called back on May 4th for further direction. The secretary said, "Dennis Dowell is on vacation...possibly the last week of May."

Back from vacation, I spoke with Mr. Dowell on May 11th. This time he said, "It depends who will conduct the Rules Classes???"

On May 17th I was called by Mr. Dowell at 8:00 P.M. and notified, "The Mechanical Class will be the week of June 7th in Battle Creek.

During the scheduled week I attended all of the classes completing the session on June 11th at 12 o'clock Noon. I drove back home and marked-up as Fireman on my regular yard job the 0700 East Yard Job and began work on June 12th.

On June 16th I received a call from the Milwaukee Jct. Crew Dispatcher stating that at 12:05 P.M. I was promoted to a qualified Yard Engineer and I "bumped" onto the Engineer's Extra Board. I worked my first job as a Yard Engineer that evening on the 2330 East Yard Job with engine GTW 4900 (GP-9) and Yard Foreman, Jerry "Wohlfiel; and Helpers, John Boczkay and Archie Anderson.

Hard to believe that it took me from November 9, 1973 (my Engine Service Seniority Date) until June 16, 1982...almost nine years... to be promoted to Yard Engineer...I must be a slow learner!?!

Eight months after being promoted to Yard Engineer I was assigned as an Engineer Trainee on February 14, 1983 on road trains and was instructed to accumulate 6,000 miles in road service. Now looking back at my timebooks it became quite apparent that the U. S. Economy must have taken another hit! You see during my period of instruction, not only was I working with "old head" Engineers who were being paid an additional two hours pay each trip for training me; but most of these jobs additionally had a Fireman on them, some of which hired in on the railroad back in the mid-1960's! As you might guess, thus, there were now four of us on the headend on each of these trips…that meant that someone, usually the Fireman, had to ride the second unit!

I also discovered, actually recalled, one other interesting bit of information. I was initially assigned to Trains 454/455, which was ordered for 0530 and operated as a "turn" every day from Detroit to Port Huron and back with Engineer, Jerry Caron. Now here's the funny part…one of the most senior Engineers, "Tennessee" Ernie Stiles bumped Jerry off the job, so he could collect the extra two hours pay every day! Naturally, we all get it monetarily; but Ernie Stiles was one of those guys who would NEVER LET A FIREMAN RUN HIS ENGINE! Believe me, I became a legend because under the working agreement, Ernie had to let me run! Thus, I was probably the ONLY Fireman that ever ran for Ernie!

April 22 was my final day as an Engineer Trainee and four days later our second daughter, Abby was born! Praise the Lord she was born alive and healthy and to this day is doing very well!

Our Third Year Rule Exam and Classes were conducted in the GTW Rules Car at Battle Creek, MI. Here we see author, Chuck Geletzke; Rule Instructor Don Butler; and L. R. Bolton on June 10, 1983. Interestingly, both Larry Bolton and I would later be promoted and work together as Supervisor's of Locomotive Engineers. (L. R. Bolton photo)

On June 6, 1983 my good friend and fellow model railroader, Flint Fireman, Larry Bolton and I attended a week of Third Year Mechanical Classes in Battle Creek with Road Foreman, Dennis Dowell. This was followed the next week with five days of Rules Classes conducted by the late Rules Instructor, Donald Butler, which concluded on June 17th. On June 23rd Road Foreman, Dennis Dowell had me report to the West Tower in Pontiac, Michigan where I took my Third Year and Final Exam. After grading it and telling me that I passed, we drove to a nearby pub where a small celebration was in order. So how about that, nine years and seven months after being hired as a Locomotive Fireman, I was finally a

Charles H. Geletzke, Jr.

promoted Road Qualified Locomotive Engineer…that has to be a record!?!

On Saturday, June 25, 1983 I was called to work my first Road Train, 454/455 from Detroit to Port Huron and return as Locomotive Engineer. We had three GTW GP-9's, the 4921-4907-4901 and I worked with Fireman, John Karakian (who is now the *Bof LE* General Chairman); Conductor, John Szlapa; Flagman, Jim Butcher; and Head Brakeman, Benjamin H. Planck. At the end of the trip Ben presented me with a complete set of the train orders signed by the entire crew!

Last Trip as a Fireman

I thought that I would add a little postscript to the preceding story, thinking perhaps from an historical perspective, you might like to know when I worked my final trip as a fireman.

On May 26, 1987 I "showed" at our regular starting time of 1400 for my "regular" assignment, Trains 439/438 #1, at Flat Rock, Michigan. It turned out that I was working with Engineer Gene Clark, who was called off the Milwaukee Jct. Engineer's Extra Board. The rest of the crew was made up of Conductor, Jim Berry; Flagman, Rich Fraley; and Head Brakeman, Bob Fuller. We had engines GTW 5820 (GP38-2)-MILW 2019 (GP40)-GTW 5849 (GP38-2). In addition to the crew a railfan friend of mine, Bob Wise who wrote the *Morning Sun* book on the SOO LINE, and was a Sales Representative for the Southern Pacific (SP) at that time had me arrange to obtain a Release of Liability Form and arrange for him to ride with us. The trip was uneventful and we tied-up at Battle Creek at 2345. We then went to the motel for our layover.

For whatever reason, we were not ordered out on Train 438 until 0100 on May 28th (A 25 hour and 15 minute layover!) with the GTW 5824 (GP38-2) & 6420 (GP40). I completed my last trip as a Fireman at 1130. And I believe Bob Wise enjoyed the trip and took lots of photos!

"Soak It!!!"... and Other Railroad Stories

Now here was the best part...a few days later, Flat Rock Superintendent, Lawrence T. Wizauer inquired of me..."I saw from the Release of Liability Form that you had a 'passenger' riding with you the other day."

"Yes I did. He said he was a Sales Rep. for the Southern Pacific."

"SOUTHERN PACIFIC!" Mr. Wizauer blurted out. "What the hell did he want!?!"

I just shrugged my shoulders and walked away.

AT&SF westbound west of Devore, CA on November 9, 1990. (J. G. Tyson photo)

California Dreamin'
by Dan Lawecki

In May 1985, my employer, a northern Indiana architectural and engineering firm, sent me to Los Angeles for a two-day seminar on *Electrical Grounding Systems and Practices*. It was my first trip to southern California and not knowing if and when I would have another opportunity to visit the Los Angeles area, I decided to extend my stay for a few days so I could take in some of the local sites and scenery.

239

Charles H. Geletzke, Jr.

I participated in the usual tourist activities such as visiting Beverly Hills and Hollywood; but the real lure for my extended visit was the West Coast railroad scene. I had stacks of railroad magazines at home that featured photos and information about the railroads in and around Los Angeles; but I knew that I would have to compress my lofty plans into a practical visit to a couple of places, so that I would not have to be driving for hours upon hours. There simply was not sufficient time available for all that I wanted to see.

The seminar had been held on Thursday and Friday. Following the conclusion of the seminar on Friday, I went back to my hotel room, changed clothes, and navigated my rented car to *Dodger Stadium* to take in a game between my beloved Dodgers and the Pittsburgh Pirates. In a classic pitchers' duel, Jerry Reuss of the Dodgers outgunned Rick Rhoden of the Pirates as the Dodgers prevailed in a 1-0 victory.

On Saturday and Sunday I visited the tourist spots; but I also made time to visit the Santa Fe Surf line, where a steady stream of Amtrak Surfliners made their way between Los Angeles and San Diego. With the backdrop of the beautiful Pacific Ocean and the rugged California coast line scenery, it was a great way to pass the time.

Resting in my hotel room on Sunday evening, I planned my next excursion. I wanted to visit Cajon Pass and in preparation for that adventure, I had packed a dog-eared copy of the September 1974 issue of *Trains* magazine in my suitcase. Featured in that issue was a Cajon Pass photo essay by the late Richard Steinheimer, the dean of West Coast railroad photography. His piece included maps of the area around Cajon, perfect for a first-time Midwest rail enthusiast visiting the area!

AT&SF 140-120-___-___ at San Bernardino, CA on November 9, 1990.   (J. G. Tyson photo)

I got an early jump on traffic on Monday morning, and my first stop was San Bernardino, where the Santa Fe operated an intermodal yard. There, a beautiful structure that housed the Santa Fe depot and division offices was a visual treat. Then it was time to head to Barstow.

Barstow is located in the Mojave Desert. The Santa Fe operated a large classification yard in Barstow and I recall stopping at a McDonald's restaurant near the yard to grab some food that I ate while watching the AT&SF hard at work. Refreshed by the food and energized by the rail activity, I got back in the car and drove to Cajon Pass.

Following the maps found in the magazine article, I was able to drive into the area known as Sullivan's Curve. A rancher named Herb Sullivan had visited this location frequently during the 1930s and 1940s, taking numerous photos in the process. Both the Santa Fe and the Southern Pacific had laid tracks through this area, and the rock formations in the background were a real treat for a "Flatlander" like me used to seeing acres upon acres of corn and soybean fields! Soon, a Union Pacific train, exercising

Charles H. Geletzke, Jr.

trackage rights on the AT&SF, eased through the curve, and I can still recall how the sounds from the motive power echoed off the rocky backdrop as the train progressed through the area. Aside from the tracks of the Santa Fe and Espee, the area looked like a scene from some 1950s shoot-em-up Western movie. Sullivan's Curve has been well documented by photographers from near and far; but until one experiences it in person, you cannot fully appreciate the beauty of it. I pinched myself just to confirm that I wasn't dreaming!

Later that day I drove to Cajon Summit, where I parked my car on the berm of the road and was able to look down onto the tracks below my vantage point. Trains climbing the Summit slowed to a snail's pace as they crested the hill .

Soon evening was approaching and with a flight back to the Hoosier State scheduled for the early morning hours on Tuesday, I decided to head back to the hotel. It had been an informative (the seminar) and entertaining trip, and I felt fortunate that the weather had cooperated. It had been a great trip!

Railroad Memories

By: Chris Howe

While I am not nor ever have been an actual professional railroader, I have been interested in trains my entire life. I am pretty much the only person in my family who caught the train bug, and I think it all goes back to my Grandfather, Waveland W. Howe. He was a career railroader nearly his entire adult life working for the Pennsylvania Railroad (PRR), Penn Central (PC), and finally Conrail (CR). While I was raised knowing that my grandfather worked for the railroad, I never knew the extent until finding some stuff after my grandma died that filled in some background details.

242

"Soak It!!!"… and Other Railroad Stories

My Grandfather hired on with the PRR in Fort Wayne, Indiana as a steam locomotive fireman in 1938 and held that job until being drafted into the Navy during World War II. I have seen some correspondence from during the war that basically said that the PRR was not planning on holding his job for him. (Editor's note. I wonder if this was because of the fact that as a locomotive fireman at the time he was drafted he may have been entitled to a job deferment?) So, when the War ended in 1945 my grandfather got a job as a taxi driver in Fort Wayne. I did notice that on one of his discharge papers he stated that he wanted a railroad job; so, he definitely wanted to be back on the railroad!

Grandpa held that job until November 4, 1947 when he was re-hired by the PRR again, this time as a Car Inspector and re-established his seniority date. This would be the job he would hold all the way until the end of his career working out of Piqua (pronounced PIC-way) yard in Fort Wayne. By 1975, the year I was born, my grandfather had enough seniority that every night he drove over to Baker Street Station (the Fort Wayne depot) to inspect the arrival and departure of Amtrak's *Broadway Limited.*

1975 was also the year my Dad and his siblings got my Grandfather featured in a newspaper column that was published regularly titled, '*Meet your Neighbor.*' This was where I learned that my Grandfather's nickname on the railroad was "W.W." Then about ten years ago, I met a retired railroader who worked with my Grandfather back then at a local railroad history event in Ft. Wayne, who said he always called him "Howie."

Outside of work, my Grandfather loved fishing, to the point where he bought a camper trailer and a Ford pickup to take with him as he planned to travel around to fishing spots all over the Midwest once he retired. Sadly though, my Grandfather never got to retire as he died from a heart attack in February 1979. I do have a photocopy of his last ever paycheck he got from Conrail…a whopping $1100 in 1979 dollars!

Charles H. Geletzke, Jr.

Since I was three and a half years old when he died, I have very few memories of him from when he was alive. There are two railroad related ones that will stick in my mind forever though! The first was probably in 1977 or 78 as I rode with my Grandmother to pick Grampa up from work one night. There used to be a small shanty at the east end of Piqua yard that my grandfather worked out of sometimes referred to as "Linker." What I recall seeing was the large four track signal bridge and all the PRR position signals lit up, which seemed to this two or three year old boy, like a fire breathing dragon! It is just a vivid memory and one that I am glad that I can hang onto!

The second memory is one that I too have never forgotten and no one in my family has yet let me live it down! In this same time period, 1977 or 78, my grandfather took me over to the Winder Street roundhouse, which was the PRR's engine servicing facility in Fort Wayne. There we met one of his friends who let us up into the cab of an EMD switcher, most likely an NW2, as they had quite a few of them around there for yard power back then. Everything was going great until the guy in the cab blew the whistle! I got scared and started screaming and crying as my Grandfather held me and tried to get me to settle down; but all I wanted at that moment was to get off that engine! (Editor's comment: I'll bet many of our readers experienced the same sensation at an early age being near a locomotive or a steamboat!?!) In the end, we got back down and drove away; but I still recall looking back, and while I cannot recall the number, I do know the switcher was still lettered for the Penn Central!

I think because of my grandfather and the fact that I loved the color blue, I developed an early interest in Conrail; but I noticed as I grew-up in the 80's, that the Conrail trains didn't come through Fort Wayne like they used to do. I would later learn about the rail rationalization of the 80's and how the Ft. Wayne main received the chopping block, being reduced to a single track railroad and eventually losing its signals after Amtrak left in late 1990.

The other railroad in my area where I grew-up was the Norfolk & Western (N&W) [formerly the Wabash

"Soak It!!!"... and Other Railroad Stories
(WAB) and the Nickel Plate (NKP)] in my hometown of New Haven, Indiana. I recall riding behind steam engine NKP 765 back around 1983 from New Haven down to Muncie and back (rare mileage!). What I really remember from it though was while we were waiting for them to service the locomotive and for the train to depart, my Mom and I walked through the middle of the 1951 built NKP enginehouse, which at that time still had a track running through it. I recall the big hole in the floor (a drop pit), and being careful to stay away from it and how no one was there and nobody said a word to us about walking through it! Today this is no longer possible because N&W successor, Norfolk Southern (NS), closed it off and remodeled the space into expanded offices for the dispatchers and other division officials.

Two other things I recall from the N&W side was how the building used to have a large sign on the side of it, which you could see from the road that said, "*Norfolk & Western Railway.*" This was eventually changed to say "*Norfolk Southern.*" The other was, that up until 1989 or 90, you could always see several high-hood GP30's over at the yard's diesel pit until they were sold-off or retired.

Back in the 80's there was (and still is) a large soybean processing pant in Decatur, Indiana called *Central Soya* (now *Bunge*). It was at the end of the old Grand Rapids & Indiana (GR&I) line that ran from Adams interlocking on the Ft. Wayne line to Decatur and all the way to Richmond, IN back in the day. The PRR referred to it as the Fort Wayne Branch and by the time I was born, the portion from Adams to Decatur had become the Ft. Wayne Secondary. Conrail would later change the name to the Decatur Secondary.

They were shipping out many unit trains back then and I recall seeing a lot of different foreign power, with names I only knew through the pages of *Trains* and *Model Railroader*. Additionally, Conrail was running a great deal of six-axle power of their own down there. Because I had a cousin who lived right there in town in a home literally facing *Central Soya's* yard, I was down there a lot visiting!

Charles H. Geletzke, Jr.

Some of the memories that stick out in my mind include one night coming back from Decatur and pacing the line along US 27, which follows the tracks north out of town for a couple miles and seeing a pair of Santa Fe yellow bonnet SD40-2's on a train. On another day I recall seeing a Chicago & Northwestern (C&NW) EMD SD50 or SD 60 pulling one of these trains. And, my favorite sighting of all was seeing a pair of Southern Pacific (SP) units, including one in the Kodachrome "Shouldn't **P**aint **S**o **F**ast (SPSF) scheme. On another occasion, my cousin's wife mentioned to me about seeing a train with a yellow caboose she had seen. Turns out it was lettered C&NW. On another trip I was lucky to see a train on the trip home trailing a former PRR N5C caboose…the only one I ever saw in service!

During the 1980's I was also fortunate to see several Conrail trains on lines that are now abandoned. The first was coming back from visiting an aunt and uncle who lived out in the country close to Churubusco, IN. Upon returning back to Ft. Wayne I recall having to wait for a Conrail train on the old GR&I branch, which at that time ran only from Ft. Wayne to Kendallville. A few years later I recalled seeing the tracks torn-up and then gone forever. Today that former crossing is next to the 4-H county fairgrounds and part of it is used as a road for exhibitors to get into the fairgrounds.

Another time I was up in Michigan on the old New York Central (NYC) Air Line route that ran from Jackson, Michigan to Three Rivers and by the time of Conrail it was called the Elkhart Branch. Well, right where the interchange for Interstate 69 and M-60 exists, west of Tekonsha, the interstate used to go over the line and I remember seeing a Conrail train down there one time. It must have been the rail rip-up train, as it was the only train I ever saw there, and the tracks disappeared shortly thereafter. If you drove past that spot today, you'd never even know a rail line ever ran through that spot!

I graduated high school in 1994 and finally obtained my first camera in 1995. From then on I was able to record my railroad memories on film instead of just in my head! That was also the same time I met fellow railfan, Jason Hall, who today is still a good friend. We would end up traveling all over the Midwest, mainly in Indiana, Ohio, and Illinois shooting trains, and seeing a great deal of railroading that you cannot recreate today sadly.

One of our favorite spots to hang out back in the late 90's, during Conrail days, was at Bryan, Ohio, which was the home of *Spangler Candy* (you probably are familiar with their *Dum Dum Suckers*) and *Ohio Art* (the manufacturers of *Etch-a-Sketch*). At that time Conrail based several locals out of Bryan and given that this took place over 20-years ago, I can now admit that sometimes at night, I would climb into the cabs of the locomotives that were stored there and take their old Bulletin Orders that had been left there. I still love collecting railroad paperwork! I remember one night, probably around 1998, when Train BUEL (Buffalo to Elkhart) stopped right in front of us and the friendly crew invited us up into the cab of a brand new BNSF GE dash 9 that was leading. The engineer gave us a quick overview and I recall looking all around trying to take it all in. Shortly he received the signal to go; so we climbed down and they continued on their way.

Another story from Bryan involving Conrail took place in 1999. I had a friend who shall remain nameless who had briefly worked for the Canadian Pacific (CP) and NS before realizing he wasn't cut-out for it and quit. Well, this friend still had a couple of red fusees and he decided he wanted to stop a train on the Chicago Line that night at Bryan. He put down one fusee for an eastbound; but since the train was on Track 2, the crew never said anything about it over the radio, as it was beyond the nearest rail of an adjacent track and did not affect them. (Editor's note: That was really a stupid thing to do!) Shortly, he saw another headlight heading down Track 1 (You could literally see a headlight from a train coming out of Archbold as that track was so straight at that location!) and placed his remaining fusee. To set this up, Train TOEL was working the siding at Archbold, Control Point (CP) 329, making a pick-up and was passed by Train TV99, which was a hot *United Parcel Service (UPS)* train. Mind you, this was also only a few months after the deadly Conrail wreck at Stryker, Ohio in January 1999, which killed two people; so it was still fresh in everyone's minds.

So we were sitting in my friend's car in the Amtrak parking lot in Bryan when we heard, over the scanner, "TV99 to TOEL. Are you guys working ahead there at Bryan?"

"No, we're still back here at CP 329 in Archbold."

"Okay, well we encountered a fusee here at CP 340 and thought maybe it was you." Then TV99 reported the incident to the Toledo West Dispatcher who advised them to run 30 mph from CP 340 to CP 342 looking out for anything in the way.

My friend, at this point, realized he had screwed-up by "fuseeing" the hottest train on the railroad and felt bad. (Editor's note: He's lucky he didn't get caught and go to jail!) We watched as Trail Van 99 crept by us and noticed the crew looking around for anything and everything until they reached the next clear signal at CP 342 and could start highballing again. After the train had passed, my friend admitted that had he known that it was TV99, he never would have done it! (Ed: It was a stupid thing to do regardless!) Until now, I have never told a soul about what happened that night, and again, since its over 20-years later, I feel safe telling the story. (Ed: Well don't ever do it again!!!)

Switching gears, another interesting story involved my friend Jason and me when we were out on the old Santa Fe main at Mazon, Illinois in 1997. Eastbound traffic was backed-up getting into Chicago and the dispatcher was holding trains out on the mainline on this particular day. We were sitting at the old depot in Mazon and east of town was a Union Pacific (UP) trackage rights train parked with SP power on it that we had viewed earlier in the morning on the way over there. Shortly, a BNSF eastbound came up to a stop in Mazon with a brand new BNSF Heritage1 painted dash 9 GE widecab. The crew got off to visit the nearby convenience store and jokingly told us we could "take the train for a spin." Jason and I took several photos of the lead unit before the crew returned and Jason joked that he tried to take the train for a spin; but the SP train was in the way. The crew climbed back aboard and when they finally received permission to go, gave us two toots on the horn as they took off and completed their journey to Chicago. On a completely unrelated note, we caught a westbound that day passing through Mazon with a matched set of seven or eight Santa Fe yellow bonnets including a 1970's era yellow and blue paint job EMD SD40 or SD45 B-unit!

Another cool memory is from October 1997 along the Santa Fe mainline at Toluca, Illinois. There was a westbound freight chasing Jason and I as we worked our way west along the line. We finally stopped in Toluca to shoot it and the leader turned out to be a Santa Fe yellow bonnet GP30. No sooner had it passed when we heard the whistle of an eastbound train; so we set-up for it and low and behold it had a BN GP30 in the lead! That was two consecutive trains with GP30 leaders in 1997! I remember noting to myself how historic and rare that event was that day!

One of my favorite spots to sit and watch Conrail was the Amtrak platform at Waterloo, Indiana, which was about 40-minutes north of where I lived in New Haven. One night in 1997 I was up there and I spotted an eastbound off in the distance and as it got closer I realized it was not only short but it was "hauling the mail" as well! As it blew past me I quickly realized that it was an eastbound OCS (Own Company Service) business train with a pair of E8's pulling it! That turned out to be the second and last time I ever saw that train (The previous time was in 1996…also in Waterloo.).

Another location where I loved to hang out was Garrett, Indiana on the CSX former Baltimore & Ohio (B&O) mainline to Chicago. Well in 1996 it was announced that the steam locomotive Milwaukee 261, a 4-8-4, would be running an excursion across the B&O. I was so nervous that they would leave in the middle of the night, I ended up driving to Garrett after work, and sleeping in my car to ensure I'd be there if it left under the cover of darkness! It turned-out that it didn't depart until the next morning and I was able to get a few shots of it passing the old two-story

Charles H. Geletzke, Jr.

Garrett depot before it was torn-down a few months afterward.

In the fall of 2001, Jason and I began following the CSX former B&O mainline from St. Joe, Indiana east toward Deshler one morning and we started noticing train after train parked on the eastbound main track as we drove eastward. When we got to Defiance, Ohio we spotted Train Q387 sitting there with a pair of brand new BNSF Heritage 2 paint dash 9 GE widecabs. As we were taking our photos of the engines, one of the crew members came out and asked if we would like to climb up and sit in the cab. The only caveat was that we had to drive him over to the nearby *McDonald's*, so he could get some breakfast. The friendly crew member turned out to be the train's conductor. When the engineer came back inside, the conductor told him that we were going to take him over to get breakfast and asked if he wanted anything. When we returned, the crew was amazed when we told them about all of the parked trains lined-up in front of them! They ended up getting a signal shortly; so we watched them head out of town before continuing on our way to Deshler.

Recollections of the Blizzard of 1978

By: Chris Howe

I read your memories of the Blizzard of January 1978 in your book *Don't Flush in the Station and Other Railroad Stories* and wanted to share with you a couple of stories. The first was triggered by the story of your Track Department guys who were basically on duty, stuck at Kilgore Yard, during the entire storm.

This was from Rick Williams, a former Conrail employee who was working in Ft. Wayne in January 1978 and here is his story...

Best memories of my Conrail years was the Blizzard of '78...went to work at Fort Wayne Piqua yards at 11:45

250

P.M. on 3rd trick shop engine…no snow. By 2:00 A.M. it was snowing so hard, they sent the other three yard jobs home early. By 3:00 A.M. snow was so bad our cut of 13 or 14 cars got stuck in the snow coming down off the hump! Trainmaster then shut the yard down, no mainline trains were arriving or departing on account of the snow and drifts. Superintendent ordered us to take two geeps and a caboose, get on the Westbound Main, and run back and forth between Adams tower and Junction tower every 30-minutes. He gave us a written order to violate the Hours of Service. We did this from approximately 3:00 A.M. on Wednesday morning until 4:00 P.M. on Friday afternoon. At 4:00 P.M. on Friday, they had us try to start clearing the hump…took us 12-hours just to move the 13 or 14 cars from Wednesday morning! They finally put us up in a hotel on Saturday for 8-hours rest. We made overtime from 7:45 A.M. on Wednesday until 4:00 A.M. on Saturday, continuous time, plus they had to pay our regular day's pay, because we were ready to work every night! Made more money in four days then I ever made in one pay period in my entire railroad career. Let it snow!

Now while I was only 2-1/2 years old and have no actual memories of the storm, the following is a story from my family. My Grandfather was either not at work that night, or was possibly sent home? The entire neighborhood came out and shoveled our street. My Mom and a neighbor heard that one of the grocery stores was open; so they walked right down US 30 in New Haven…a four lane, normally busy highway, to the grocery store! Those were some crazy days for sure!

GTW Milwaukee Jct. yard office in Detroit, MI as seen on June 2, 1987. The window where the injury was sustained was on the first floor, just beyond the doorway. The building was permanently closed on July 7, 1987.

Injured at a Safety Meeting!?!

As told by: C. H. Geletzke, Jr.

One of the engineers that I worked with a great deal during the first 19 years of my railroad career was Jack Riddle. Jack was a Korean War Veteran, a Purple Heart recipient, and a former steam man that I had a great deal of respect for! In addition to being a fine Locomotive Engineer, until the mid-1980's Jack had been the Local Chairman for Division 812 of the *Brotherhood of Locomotive Engineers* and the Engineer's Representative on the Grand Trunk Western Railroad, Milwaukee Jct. Safety Committee. As I recall, near the end of 1985, Jack decided that it was time for him to step-down from the Safety Committee position and handed the job over to a younger individual. Now I do not recall if this was accomplished through an election or by appointment; but beginning in February 1986, I became the Engineer's Safety Man.

"Soak It!!!"… and Other Railroad Stories

I soon found out, the Committee generally met one day a month, and all of us various members would take the day off from our regular jobs and attend the Safety Meeting. If there were any "major issues" we would get together on the side on another day.

On February 6, 1986 I drove in and joined the Safety Committee at 9:00 A.M. for the first time. It was held in the old Milwaukee Jct. Yard Office in Detroit, Michigan. Only minutes after I entered the Conference Room and sat down at the large table, someone came running in, yelling that one of our employees had been injured right down the hall!

The injured party turned out to be Crew Dispatcher, Jim Anderson. Apparently he walked out into the Crew Room, raised the old double-hung window, which no longer had a latch to secure it in a closed position…because of the weight of the counter weights, the window would rise on its own if there were not additional weights holding it down. Well, the "other weights" were actually lantern batteries…six of them! Jim's purpose for raising the lower window pane was his intention to holler out to an employee/member of the Safety Committee (who was out in the parking lot) and ask him if he was going to attend the Safety Meeting? So, Mr. Anderson lifted the window and a battery lost its balance and fell from a height of about nine or ten feet, striking Jim in the head! It split his head wide open and he had to be taken to the hospital for stitches!

For me, that was the first and last time that I ever heard of any employee being injured at a Safety meeting! Can you believe it?

He made the wrong person mad!

As told by: C. H. Geletzke, Jr.

I believe that it was in 1986 (I did not go back through the records) that I was called to work the GTW 1530 All Purpose with Yard Conductor, Joe Fruciano. Before I go any further, let me tell you a little about Joe. On the side, Joe

Charles H. Geletzke, Jr.

had a carpet cleaning business; and if you needed or wanted
to know anything at all about "the ponies," Joe was your "go
to" guy! But if Joe happened to be ordered as your conductor,
you'd better be prepared to watch him like a proverbial
hawk!

On the afternoon of our story we doubled-up our drag
at East Yard in Hamtramck, Michigan with cars for D&M
(Detroit & Milwaukee) Yard (primarily for the *Chevy Gear
& Axle* and *Forge Plants*) on the headend, D&TSL cars for
Toledo in the middle, and Westbound's for Ferndale Yard on
the rear ahead of our caboose. We then completed an Initial
Terminal Air Test and departed.

We headed west and then rounded the Sugar House
Wye to the Holly Subdivision. Only about a mile away, we
stopped and set-off the D&M cars. After completing the set-
off we tied back on our train, got permission from the Train
Dispatcher, and crossed-over to the Eastward Main Track.
Once we were through the crossovers, the tailend crew lined
them back to normal position and we headed for Chrysler
located in the City of Highland Park, Michigan.

Now let me digress and tell you a little about
Chrysler. At one time this was a huge manufacturing
complex, assembly plant, and World Headquarters for the
Chrysler Corporation. Most of the railroad work there was
handled by the Detroit Terminal Railroad. The factory
originally opened in 1910; but by the time I started my
railroad career, the portion adjacent to and serviced by the
GTW was reduced primarily to heat treating and forge work.
In the early 1970's *Chrysler* expanded their Engineering
Department there and its facilities as World Headquarters. By
the mid-1970's our work there disappeared completely...in
fact, it was reduced to one stub track, which would only
accommodate two tri-levels (which were spotted only
occasionally for testing purposes). Beginning in 1996 the
complex was virtually shut-down and all offices were moved
to Auburn Hills.

Now let's get back to the 1530 Tramp (excuse me, in
1969 in Detroit, the GTW changed the name of all of the
"Tramp Jobs," to "All Purpose's," because the name was

254

"Soak It!!!"… and Other Railroad Stories

considered demeaning! Interestingly, the GTW still had "Tramp Jobs" working in Battle Creek when I retired in 2011…I don't get it!?) We headed west to Chrysler, running against the current of traffic on the Eastward Main Track and stopped at the double-ended siding located on the south side adjacent to the Eastward Main and along the outside of the *Chrysler Corporation's* fence. This track was named the Chrysler Lead. Normally and specifically on this trip, we were going to head into this track, which was close to a mile long, with southbound cars for the D&TSL (these cars would be picked-up later in the evening by Train 422 running from Flint to Toledo). On this day we had about forty cars; so we headed in. Now as I previously stated we still had three or four cars and our caboose on the rear end and Conductor Fruciano stopped the movement with these cars on the Main and made a cut. What he failed to consider was that the head Westbound car was sitting on a street crossing…Commor Avenue…and Commor was the main entrance and exit to the *Chrysler Plant* on the east side! Oh yes, and it was now about 6:00 P.M. and RUSH HOUR! We pulled the Shoreline's into the clear in the Chrysler Lead, tied the cars down, cut-away, and returned with our light unit to the balance of our train.

When we arrived, who was sitting there…first-out at the crossing…trying to leave the plant, none other than *Lehigh University* graduate, Lee Iacocca (I had to throw that in as my daughter graduated from *Lehigh*!)…naturally we all knew of him at that time, as he was the individual who literally saved *Chrysler*! Let me say this, you could see the steam coming off Mr. Iacocca's forehead! I have to believe that he was furious…and there stands Conductor Fruciano without a care in the world! If only he had cut the cars off two car-lengths further to the east! But, I can tell you from personal experience…that thought never crossed his mind! I felt bad.

You can only imagine, the next day ALL Four of us on the crew received a talking to…that this was NEVER to happen again!

Charles H. Geletzke, Jr.

Danny Keenan's Ladder

As told by: Charles H. Geletzke, Jr.

The date was November 24, 1986 and I was called off the Grand Trunk Western Railroad's Milwaukee Jct. Engineer's Extra Board to work the 1600 (4 o'clock P.M.) Chevrolet Job with Foreman, George Hicks; and his two helpers, Bill Carter and Danny Keenan. This assignment went to work at D&M (Detroit & Milwaukee) Yard in Hamtramck, Michigan and spent its entire shift within the confines of the *Chevrolet Gear & Axle* and *Forge Plants*. On this day we had the GTW 4903, a passenger GP9, for power.

Now let me state that this was a job that I always enjoyed working and if it were still on, I probably never would have retired! The reason that I liked it was because it worked Monday through Friday and, because the crew "ran their asses off," it was an "Early Quit Job!" On most days the crew was on their way home by 7:30 P.M. or so! Once started, they never took any breaks, and never stopped running! Interestingly, the two switchmen on the job, each had day jobs too. Bill Carter worked doing telephone repair for the *Michigan Bell Telephone Company* and Danny Keenan, who was the same age as me, was a pharmacist at one of the Detroit area hospitals. Thus because this was such a good job, both of them continued working on the railroad to supplement their incomes.

At the time of our story things were very different on the railroad…that is to say that rules compliance was not nearly as strict, corners were cut, and because of the allowed early quits, the men had a definite incentive to hustle. Naturally, because the crews did not waste any time, this made firms like *General Motors* extremely happy and they certainly gave the railroads' a tremendous share of their business!

One item that was entirely different during that era was the temporary placement of cars in a track. At that time if you were going to shove a car into a track and cut away from it, it was not necessary to always apply a handbrake. Instead, all a switchman or a brakeman had to do was find a block of wood referred to as a "chock" and shove it under the wheel of the car, which would retard it from rolling. This was commonly done on all of the railroads that I worked for prior to the late 1990's. Today, a trainman would no doubt be disciplined for this activity; but you can easily see that it took much less time compared to climbing up on the car, applying the brake, and then climbing down off the car…not to mention repeating the process when you next wanted to move the car…oh yes, and don't forget the need to include the use of a "Brake Stick" to secure and release the handbrake on some railroads! Yes, the difference in time involved is today hard to imagine!

Anyway, on November 24th we were hurrying to get done and I noticed that apparently *Chevrolet* had implemented a recent grounds clean-up campaign as I did not see any chunks of wood lying around the plants to be utilized by our switchmen. Well, it was at about this time that Pharmacist Keenan had me shove an empty 50-foot boxcar into a track that he was going to insert into the middle of a cut of cars in an adjacent track in a few minutes. He signaled me to shove ahead with the car, stopped me when we were clear of the adjacent track and then I saw him foraging around for a block of wood. Naturally, he was in a hurry; but there were no wooden blocks anywhere! Well, let me state that the pharmacist was no dummy…in a matter of seconds he spotted a section of a relatively new wooden extension ladder lying up against a nearby fence. He walked over, picked-up the ladder and immediately stuck one end of one of the ladder's stiles under a wheel of the car. With that, he reached over, pulled the pin, and signaled me to backup! What's that that they say about the "mother of all invention?"

I loved working with those guys!

257

Charles H. Geletzke, Jr.

Fellow GTW (CN) Locomotive Engineers, Chuck Geletzke and Jack N. Ozanich operating the Sandy River & Clear Lake Ry. on November 22, 2004.

"Railfan Acres"

By: C. H. Geletzke, Jr.

No doubt many of you as railfans and modelers were familiar with the late John N. "Jack" Ozanich. Jack had not only been an Army veteran, a telegraph operator and later a Locomotive Engineer for the Grand Trunk Western Railroad (GTW); but he was well known by modelers everywhere for his fabulous HO scale model railroad, the *Atlantic & Great Eastern (AGE)*, a fictitious New England passenger and freight carrier.

Now, I first me Jack in December of 1976, on the very first day that I was transferred, by the GTW, from Port Huron to Kalamazoo, Michigan as Assistant Trainmaster-Agent. Jack was working the daylight #1 yard job at Kilgore Yard and after being introduced to one another, we became best of friends. At that time, Jack was still unmarried and lived with his Mom in Paw Paw, Michigan where he had the "original AGE. My wife, Leslie and I had only been married for a little over two months at the time of the transfer; so let me state that her first trip over to Paw Paw for a "mini" operating session was a true eye opener to say the least! Up to this point in her life, she had met very few of my railfan friends and had never attended an actual operating session. Even today, she still talks about how Jack would call on the spur of the moment and announce that he was having an "Emergency Operating Session" and that he would like me to drop whatever it was that I was doing and drive IMMEDIATELY over to Paw Paw!

In May of 1979 we (Leslie and I) were transferred to Toledo, Ohio when I was promoted to Trainmaster on GTW's subsidiary, the Detroit & Toledo Shore Line Railroad (D&TSL). During the time that we were there, Jack was married and he and his wife purchased (I believe) 28 acres on the east side of Battle Creek, Michigan and on the north side of the GTW Flint Subdivision Mainline. Together they built a beautiful home, which was not only perfect for Jack's wife to run and train her sled dogs, horses and other farm animals; but was architecturally designed to house the "NEW" Atlantic & Great Eastern!

For those of you who knew Jack and witnessed all of his amazing accomplishments, we soon found out that this GTW Locomotive Engineer had additional and greater plans for those 28 acres, which included the highest point in Calhoun County. In no time at all he began grading the right of way for an outdoor 7-1/2" gauge live steam railroad, which would acquire the name Sandy River & Clear Lake. Now please allow me to state that this was not your "normal" inch and a half scale railroad; no, Jack and his friends scaled down the Maine two-footers to a gauge of 7-1/2 inches, which permitted friends and family to ride within the railroad's coaches and caboose! Over the next several years the railroad accumulated a roster of four steam locomotives, a diesel, and a motor car. The railroad covered his entire plot of land having over an actual mile of track with two wyes, a turntable, and roundhouse. It truly was an amazing accomplishment!

Well, one day, probably in the later part of the 1980's, our telephone rang and Leslie answered the phone.

She said, "Jack wants to talk with you and he sounds all excited!" (By this time I had resigned from railroad management and was back working as a GTW Locomotive Engineer out of Milwaukee Jct. in Detroit, Michigan.)

Leslie handed me the phone and I responded, "What's going on, Mr. Ozanich?"

Jack replied, "You are not going to believe what just happened! The property right across the road from me (between the road and the GTW Mainline) was just put on the market and is up for sale! There are 40 acres there and they only want $500 per acre (truly a tremendous price)...that's only $20,000! I was thinking that you and Larry Bolton (a fellow GTW Engineer and fellow modeler who was living in Grand Blanc, Michigan at the time and working out of Durand and Flint.) could buy it together...each of you could build new homes there...AND, **WE** CAN CALL IT RAILFAN ACRES!!!" Before I could even respond, Jack went on to say, "Maybe we could even get permission from the Highway Department to tunnel under the road and run the live steam railroad over there!?!"

I couldn't believe it! You talk about enthusiasm!

I then responded to Jack, "Well I'll have to talk to Leslie."

The ever impulsive Jack replied, "I understand...let me know right away and in the meantime, I'll talk with Larry! You can't wait too long...it's really a nice piece f property!"

When I had finished talking with Jack, I turned toward Leslie and told her of Jack's plan. Just as soon as I mentioned that Jack wanted to name the property, RAILFAN ACRES! Leslie responded, "Over my dead body!"

Later I spoke with Larry and he too stated that his wife, Jan, had a very similar reaction.

Looking back, I am certain that the property itself would have been an outstanding value; but I also know that as good of a friend as Jack was, we never could have been neighbors!

Management Benefit Tales

By: Retired GTW Manager of Personnel Administration,
James Krikau

I've drafted some "anecdotal" comments re: management –
typically headquarters ("puzzle palace") type issues...

The Grand Trunk Western Railroad management ("non-
schedule") employees health care plans were top-notch back
in the late 1970's as it was with many companies back then.
The words "co-pay" or "in network providers" were unheard
of terms. But with exceptional coverage's, there were
certainly some exceptional issues that arose...which in
retrospect were quite humorous.

FALSE TEETH DILEMMA – I received an irate phone
call from a Transportation Department manager complaining
that our dental plan was terrible because it wouldn't
reimburse him for his set of false teeth. Upon checking the
claim, it turned out that he had been reimbursed for a new set
of them just a couple of years ago. The plan covered one new
set of dentures every five years. So, when I called him back
with the information, I got chewed out and called a lot of
names along with a threat to sue me and the dental plan.
After the tirade, I asked him why he needed a new set so
soon after the last ones. His reply was, "I've lost a lot of
weight over the past two years and the old ones don't fit
anymore!" I assume he paid for his new set because he came
across quite loud and clear over the phone that day!

EXPENSIVE TEETH CLEANING – On another occasion,
I received a call from a senior operations executive
complaining that his claim for teeth cleaning was denied. It
didn't seem to make sense to me. So I asked him for more
info. He told me his first visit was paid for; but his second
visit wasn't. I asked why he had two different appointments
for a teeth cleaning. His response was that the dentist told

261

him that he couldn't finish in time on the first day as he had other scheduled patients. So, he made another appointment to finish the job. That seemed strange to me to have two separate appointments for a routine teeth cleaning. So I asked if there was a specific issue or problem. The response was it took a lot longer for the dentist, because as he put it, "I haven't been to the dentist in quite a long time!" I recall asking if the dentist was "steam cleaning his teeth?" That didn't go over too well...

By: Retired GTW Director of Personnel, James Krikau

COMPANY PHYSICALS – The GTW had its own Chief Medical Officer (an M.D.) who conducted return to work physicals, new employee physicals, and annual exams for certain management employees (considered a perk). And as most males will recall, the very last step of the physical exam was the prostate check. Typically, it's the most unpleasant as the routine for conducting it was universal ("bend over and spread 'em"). As I was experiencing this last phase of the physical, I couldn't help but ask the Chief Medical Officer (Dr. Gallant, at the time) why he only used one finger for the exam. He was taken aback by the question and he asked me, "What prompted that question?" I couldn't help but blur out, "If you use two, you'll get an immediate second opinion!" Dr. Gallant laughed so hard and I found out later he relayed that story to many other males at this specific step during their "management physicals".

VASECTOMIES – I received a company phone call from an Assistant Trainmaster inquiring if our health care plan covered vasectomies. He looked through the booklet on eligible coverage's; but couldn't find anything on vasectomies. I told him it was covered the same as another procedure (dilation & curettage, as a matter of fact); but hadn't yet been listed in the summary booklet. He was relieved to hear that and then went on to say further that he had been working on getting up the courage to have one for the past year. I told him it was no big deal in my experience.

He then asked me if I had had any side effects and my
response **(in a falsetto voice)** was "Just one!" After a long
pause – and him cussing me out – the ATM said it would
probably take him another year to build up the courage to
have one.

By: Retired GTW Manager of Quality, James Krikau

POSTSCRIPT "A CLASSIC MANAGEMENT PRANK"
– Back in the early 90's, I had my knees scoped and couldn't
drive for a while. A GTW colleague of mine would pick me
up each morning and drive to work downtown at the Detroit
Brewery Park Headquarters. He himself was wearing one of
those heart monitors that hung around your neck back then.
One morning, I decided to pull a prank on him. As he waited
in my driveway, I came out of the front door and got into the
car. I had hidden my garage door opener in my coat pocket.
Just as we were backing out of the driveway, I depressed the
door opener in the pocket. We both saw the door go up. I
expressed surprise and asked my friend if he happened to
bump his heart monitor thereby sending a frequency that was
the same as my garage door opener. I asked him to jostle his
monitor again – and I pressed the garage door opener in my
pocket – and the door went down. He was amazed! We went
through this drill a couple of times. Then as we headed off
for downtown Detroit, I asked him if he thought he might
have opened many garage doors accidentally in his
neighborhood. He said he didn't know. I then suggested that
when we get into work, he should call his doctor's office and
check this out with them.

When we arrived at H.Q., I rounded up a couple of other
managers from the Engineering Department (signals) and we
proceeded to my friend's office. I told him that the engineer's
with me were extremely interested to find out if a heart
monitor could send out frequency signals. I asked him to call
his doctor's office over the speaker phone, so we could all
hear. He dialed up the number. A nurse answered the call.

Charles H. Geletzke, Jr.

Here's exactly what happened: My friend, "Can my heart monitor open a garage door?" (Silence for a moment on the other end followed with a "WHAT? From the nurse). He then repeated the question – at which time the three of us quietly got up and left his office leaving him to try and explain why he called his doctor or if his doctor may refer him to some "other kind" of specialist!!!

The D&TSL's 17-stall roundhouse at Lang Yard in North Toledo, Ohio as seen on March 22, 1980. The Boiler House and its whistle were located directly behind the GP7.

I always wanted a whistle!

By: C. H. Geletzke, Jr.

From the time I was in high school and visited an antique shop in northern Michigan, which had a huge selection of steam whistles for sale, I always wanted to have one! The shop probably had at least twenty of them, some with brass barrels and others that were nickel plated...all were way too expensive for me as a young teenager!

As I have stated previously, I officially began my railroad career in 1967 working as a Fire Builder in the

"Soak It!!!"... and Other Railroad Stories

Grand Trunk Western's (GTW) roundhouse in Pontiac, Michigan. At that time the 10-stall roundhouse still had two fully operational stationary steam boilers that were only used during the colder months of the year. Each boiler was connected to a 2-1/2" pipe that was connected to a steam whistle on the roof. A long steel cable ran down the south side of the building from the whistle to a big steel loop on the west side of the main doorway. Additionally, there were two smaller whistles in the interior rafters of the structure that were connected to the compressed air lines running throughout the building and between each stall. I did blow the larger of the two whistles one time; but was hollered at by Bob Slaght, the Roundhouse Foreman! He screamed, "Mr. Geletzke, that is not a toy!" I never touched it again! Sadly the roundhouse was closed on November 5, 1988; yet the boiler house was retained as a storage center for the Signal Department beginning April 5, 1991. The roundhouse was finally demolished on December 2, 1999; but I have no idea of what ever became of those three brass whistles.

Beginning in 1973 I would often work the Grand Trunk Western (GTW) Hostler job at the Milwaukee Jct. roundhouse in Detroit, Michigan. Occasionally I would climb the permanently installed steel ladder to the roof of the former Machine Shop portion of the former 26-stall roundhouse and take photos from there. Because the structure too had a small stationary boiler, it also had a brass whistle on its extreme eastern corner. Once again, that building was closed on January 11, 1987 and torn down on February 15, 1999...but here again, I believe the steam whistle disappeared long before the demise of the building.

Where there's a will there is a way...I also knew that the former Detroit & Toledo Shore Line Railroad (D&TSL) roundhouse at Lang Yard in North Toledo, Ohio still had its whistle on the roof of the boiler house there. With a little research I determined that the original boiler room structure was built in 1906 and that it was expanded in 1929. The facility was shutdown in 1982 after the GTW acquired partner, Norfolk & Western's (N&W) 50% interest in the carrier; but the components of the steam facility remained

265

Charles H. Geletzke, Jr.

intact. In early December 1992 I received word from my late friend, John P. Baukus, Jr., who worked in the Mechanical Department and additionally handled environmental issues for the GTW in Battle Creek, that a contract had been signed to demolish the Lang roundhouse before the end of the year. He also told me that he was sending me a letter granting me permission to acquire the whistle from the boiler house roof there; but suggesting that I'd better move rapidly!

During the next several days I contacted a friend and member of my church, Don MacDermid, who owned a local Toledo plumbing business. I explained the mission that I was about to undertake and asked if he might have a couple of large pipe wrenches that I might borrow. Don said to come by his shop and that he would fix me right up, which I did.

I thought that even though I had written permission for the project, that it would be better to attempt to acquire the item during a weekend when there would be fewer employees and less officials around. On Saturday morning December 5, 1992 I returned to Hamtramck after working a trip on Train 2438, and tied-up at 12:45 A.M. While eating breakfast I called the crew dispatcher and was informed that I was second out and would probably work again on Saturday afternoon. I threw all of Don's tools in the trunk of my car and headed over to Lang Yard and parked on the far south side of the roundhouse. I then walked through the interior of the 17-stall building over to the boiler house on the far north end and tried to determine a way to get to the whistle, which was located on the roof above the second story. After climbing to the second floor I found a hole where a skylight had formerly been located. My next project was to find a ladder. The roundhouse was still full of big heavy tools, many from the steam era, which were scattered everywhere. I finally found one section of a wooden extension ladder that had two broken rungs. I carried it to the second floor and found that it just barely reached to the top of the skylight. I then climbed up through the opening and found the whistle, which was different from most that I had ever seen. Instead of having a brass or nickel-plated barrel, it was made from a piece of six-inch steel pipe...it may have been nickel-plated

266

at one time; but believe me the plating must have disappeared during the Second World War!

Now that I had a route to the roof, I thought that I'd better return to my vehicle and get my tools. Now remember this was in 1992 and still before I owned a cell phone! So before walking to my car, I walked over to the yard office and told the yardmaster, Skip Ullum, that I would like to use the phone to call the crew dispatcher. Skip and I were good friends; but I never explained exactly what I was up to. The crew dispatcher informed me that I was "now First Out and that there was nothing yet in the picture; but I might be ordered any time."

I told the crew caller that I would "call him back in one hour and that if anything came open to just mark me up."

I then hurried back to my car and claimed the two massive wrenches, a pipe cutter, and a four-foot pipe extension…together all of the tools must have weighed 25-pounds! I then carried them back through the roundhouse, up the stairs, and made three individual trips, up to the roof. Without wasting any time I adjusted the jaws on one of the pipe wrenches and applied it to the brass whistle valve fitting on the bottom of the assembly. Then, as I began to exert pressure, the 2-1/2" pipe connected to the valve snapped with a "CRACK," catching me by surprise and it was a miracle that I was not thrown off the roof! The whistle itself went crashing down four feet and landed on the roof itself. After examining the ancient relic I guessed that it probably weighed about 30-pounds and struggled to safely carry it down the rickety ladder…then once again I made three more reverse trips carrying Don's tools back to the relative safety of the second floor.

It was probably more that 100-yards back to my car and I carried the whistle first and immediately put it inside of my trunk. I then made another trip back and retrieved the four plumbing tools. With everything tucked away safely, I returned to the Yardmaster's Office and called the crew dispatcher for a second time. It turned out that I had just been ordered for an afternoon yard job, the 1500 All Purpose at

Charles H. Geletzke, Jr.

Hamtramck, and would go on duty at 3:00 P.M. I then drove to Detroit and worked until 1:00 A.M.

The next morning I awoke and went to church with my family. Before leaving I brought the whistle into my home and put it down in the basement. It turned out that I was not called to work again until 8:30 P.M. on Pearl Harbor Day for Train 201. When I returned home at about 7:30 A.M. on December 8th, my wife was furious! It just so happened that there was a small hornet's nest inside of the whistle and as far as she was concerned, "they were taking over the basement!!!"

Over the next several years I learned a little more about the history of that whistle. Several of the older members of my church and several of the older Shore Line employees told me that the Shore Line used to blow it precisely every day, seven days a week, at 8:00 A.M., and again at 5:00 P.M. They seemed to recall that that stopped sometime in the mid-1970's. Oh yes, the roundhouse at Lang was actually dismantled between December 22nd and 29th, 1992.

Well, I have now reached the age where I have to begin relinquishing my collection of railroad memorabilia and sadly, for the most part my children are not interested. So, the other day I called a young railfan friend, Alex Bogart, and asked if I might drop something off at the shop where he works. When I opened the rear door on my truck and removed the heavy item from the back, I don't think he could believe it!

Now I hope that he gets as much enjoyment out of this piece of history as I did, and I really hope that he can arrange someday to attend a regional "Whistle Blow" that they have or used to have up near Port Huron and perhaps hear the sound that daily began and closed out the lives of so many Point Place, Ohio and North Toledo residents!

GTW Conductor, Ben Gibson's (Center) Last Trip! Engineer Mark Sopoliga (left) and Brakeman, Donald G. "Mr. Safety" Swarbrick on right in Detroit, MI on November 20, 2003.

You're Not Going to Believe It!

By: Charles H. Geletzke, Jr.

Don't worry; we ALL know the rule…newspapers and anything except reading material furnished by the company is not supposed to be read while on duty!

On the other hand, do you know how many hours in a forty-five year railroad career I have spent looking at red signals…sometimes for hours? Or would you like to hazard a guess as to how much time I have spent waiting for my train to be made-up, or how many hours I have waited to get into or out of a yard. Or if there is a problem with the train itself, do you know how long it might take a conductor or brakeman to walk that train and return to the headend? Don't tell me that I cannot read a newspaper or book while I am waiting as long as I am attentive and able to listen to what is said over the radio! This is generally all non-productive time.

Charles H. Geletzke, Jr.

This reminds me; my old neighbor in Toledo, Bernie Wolfram, worked for a short period of time on the assembly line at Whirlpool in Clyde, Ohio and said that during the course of working an eight hour shift, management would change their job on the assembly line four times just to alleviate boredom and repetitive motion injuries. Now I have never worked on an assembly line; but Bernie said that on his particular line a washing machine would begin its journey every seventeen seconds! Do you know how many conductors and brakemen I have told this story over the years? It used to be fun to tell the story and then say to the guy across the cab. "Let's see, we have now been sitting here at this red signal for two hours and fifty minutes. How many washers have gone down the line in that length of time? Yes, railroaders can get bored and railroading can very easily ruin a person from working anyplace else…that is as long as you did not mind working seven days a week at all kinds of odd hours, possibly being away from home for a week at a time, working on holidays, or in bad weather, in bad neighborhoods, and at a job that can be extremely dangerous!

In all my years on the railroad I only recall one man getting in trouble for reading a newspaper. That was my good friend Ben Gibson. Let me tell you about Mr. Gibson. Ben grew-up as the son of a coal miner in Kentucky. He was a Viet Nam veteran and an expert paratrooper and Army Ranger who went on to retire from the Army Reserve after being activated for Dessert Storm. I know that Ben had over thirty years service as a switchman, brakeman, and conductor on the railroad when he retired. Ben and his late brother John were both good railroaders and good guys to work with. Enough accolades, let's get back to the story. One month before Ben was to retire an Assistant Superintendent, whose name I will not mention, spotted him riding in the conductor's seat on a yard engine running light from Milwaukee Jct. to East Yard…a distance of about one mile. Their speed was maybe 15 mph. This over-zealous manager spotted Ben reading the newspaper! He called on the radio and had the engineer stop the movement and return to the B.O.C. yard office. The Assistant Superintendent could have

"Soak It!!!"… and Other Railroad Stories

quoted the rule and chewed Ben out; but no instead he "pulled Ben out of service!" That little event did wonders for all of our morale. Ben served his time, came back for a few days and then retired on November 20, 2003. What was the point!?!

Dispatching on the Norfolk Southern

By: retired NYC, PC, CR, and NS Clerk and Train Dispatcher, Eugene Gray

I hired out on the New York Central Railroad (NYC) in the Spring of 1967 at Airline Jct. in Toledo, Ohio in the Clerical Department. Over the ensuing years and through the following mergers, I went on to work for the Penn Central (PC), Conrail (CR), and lastly the Norfolk Southern (NS).

When the Norfolk Southern took control of Conrail's Dearborn Division, I had become a Train Dispatcher and was working the Chicago East Desk from CP-421 to CP-482.

On Conrail, at Christmas time, all of the trains were run to the next crew change points, or as close as possible. They stationed *Greyhound* busses in Chicago, Elkhart, Toledo, Cleveland, and Pittsburgh to bring the crews back to their home terminals.

The Norfolk Southern had a different mindset and just stopped trains on the mainline, not blocking road crossings, and tied them down. Then they got the crews off and taxied them to their destination or originating terminals. Once the trains were stopped, the Track Department had to go out and put derails ahead of and behind the trains parked on the mainline.

Our new Division Superintendent was from a coal hauling division of the NS. Following the Christmas Break, he put out orders that "all coal trains would get the first rested crews!" This was not a decision that the former Conrail people were accustomed to!

One day I was holding a coal train at CP-462 in Rolling Prairie, Indiana. Unfortunately, that "Control Point" was only a diamond and there were no crossovers there; but it was a great place to store trains…almost four miles long with no grade crossings! The next crossover, ahead of the train, was at LaPorte, Indiana. Unfortunately, there was a merchandise train stopped at that interlocking also! But, according to our orders, a crew was called first for the coal train!

After sitting there for several hours, the Superintendent came down and asked if there was a crew on the coal train and he demanded to know why I was not moving it??? I am guessing that even though there was a crew on the coal train, and there was not a crew on the merchandise train stopped ahead of it, with no place to cross-over, was beyond his grasp!?! For me there was no possible way to move it!

I was really surprised that I wasn't pulled out of service; but since the Assistant Superintendent was a former Conrail person and familiar with the territory, I was only threatened…

The Dumper at the *Detroit Edison Company's* Monroe (MI) Power Plant as seen on January 23, 2011. (Geletzke collection)

An Impeccable Impression!

By: GTW Division Engineer,
.Bob Cerri

Detroit Edison's Coal Business Unit hired a new Account Manager and our (Canadian National's) marketing folks set-up a tour at the Monroe Power Plant to show him around and I tagged along, since I had the highrail (truck). Everyone but him dressed in dark clothes; but he wanted to set a good impression and wore a sparkling white dress shirt. At the end of the tour, he looked just like the rest of us!

Being Well Prepared!

As told by: GTW Car Inspector, Bob Dell to his son, David Dell

For about 18-years, my dad, Bob Dell, inspected cars at the Port Huron (Michigan) Car Shops for the Grand Trunk Western Railroad (GTW). He bid this job after working more than 20-years inside as a welder. Later, he would retire after 42-years of credited service.

When he walked the yards with over 30 sets of tracks inspecting everything on the cars, he hand carried a plethora of tools and gear. He always had two clipboards with notepads of paper, pens and pencils, and a couple of baggies to put the notepads in when it was raining or snowing. Of course when it was snowing or if there was any noticeable accumulation, he carried a small shovel. He always said, "It's much easier to shovel snow out from underneath a car than dig with your hands!" In one pocket he carried a gauge for checking coupler knuckles and a gauge for inspecting wheel flanges.

Next to his pens and pencils was a yellow lumber crayon, which he used to mark loose or missing rivets. He had a little pouch the railroad had sewed up for him in the

273

Coach Shops, in which he carried a handful of bolts and nuts. These were used to secure the doors shut after he was finished inside.

In his hands he carried what he called a "single-jack," or in layman's terms a 2 lb. one-handed sledge hammer. This he used to bend over the end of bolts, so the nuts couldn't be easily unscrewed. In the other hand he carried a brake shoe bar that he used for opening the brake beam, so he could change-out brake pads or brake shoes. There were 5 gallon buckets full of shoes scattered throughout the yard, for just this endeavor.

During the summer months, he carried a Tupperware container with him as well. All of the briars and brush along the yard boundary were full of wild strawberries, blueberries, and raspberries. It was my dad's mission to collect as many as he could before the rabbits got to them. Sometimes this container, that was full by the time he got to the west end limits, was empty when he walked back through his office door!

What's in YOUR pocket!?!

Micro-Economics

By: Charles H. Geletzke, Jr.

As I stated in an earlier saga, in 1994 Bill B. transitioned from his position as a Grand Trunk Western Railroad brakeman and conductor and entered the GTW Locomotive Engineer Training Program. Following the completion of the program, he was promoted to Locomotive Engineer. I was one of three Supervisors of Locomotive Engineers at that time and participated in his instruction.

Several years later, I was "back in the ranks" working as an engineer myself and very early one morning I walked into the Locker Room of the B.O.C. (Buick-Oldsmobile-Cadillac) yard office in Hamtramck, Michigan and changed into my bib-overalls. Once I was dressed, I walked down the hallway and into the Crew Room. As I entered the room, I noted that Engineer, Bill, was sitting in there on one of the wooden benches at a table all by himself. I then said. "Good morning, Bill," and asked, "What job are you working this morning?"

Bill then informed me that he wasn't going to work; that he had "tied-up" about twenty minutes earlier, and that he was waiting to drive home.

I had forgotten that Bill had told all of us before and made no secret of the fact, that his wife did not permit him to come home and possibly wake her up, prior to a certain time each and every morning! From what many of us could tell, this even applied when we were "working on our rest" (being called back to work in eight hours)! And if that was not difficult enough, Bill lived in Port Huron, Michigan and had a good fifty mile drive each way, to and from work!

I then told Bill that similarly, I had a 63 mile drive each way, and that it took me about and hour and fifteen minutes to drive each way. I said. "When the board is really turning, I am only home for about five and one-half hours! You know, we HAVE TO GET OUR PROPER REST!"

Bill then stated the he would head home in about ten minutes.

Next Bill started complaining about his wife's Cadillac breaking-down. He stated. "I told her to have her car towed to the dealership…after all, she has the *AAA (American Automobile Association)* Gold Card, which will tow HER car, for free, up to 90 miles!" Then, without me even asking him, he continued, "Me, I only have the regular Triple-A membership card, that will ONLY tow my car up to a maximum of three miles."

At that point, I could not stand it anymore! I said to Bill, "You mean to tell me that your wife drives a brand-new Cadillac…just around town, and she has virtually UNLIMITED towing…and you drive that old Ford Escort over 50 miles each way…in all kinds of weather, and YOUR membership will only pay to tow your car up to three miles!?! It seems to me, you need to exchange cards with your wife!"

Charles H. Geletzke, Jr.

Engineer Billy B. looked me right in the eye and stated, "Oh no, I couldn't do that!

I guess I'll never understand!?!

BNSF in Mr. Batanian's part of the world on April 2, 2013. (Jeff Mast photo)

Early Quit

By: retired AT&SF Engineer; Road foreman of Engines, Amtrak; BN and BNSF Engineer, L. E. Batanian

I was working as Engineer on the afternoon 3:59 P.M. Hump Job in the new Barstow, California Santa Fe Hump Yard. The yard was brand-new and crews were still getting the drift on how things worked.

We were having a pretty good day; but ran out of trains to hump. It was just after dark...around 9:30 or so when the Humpmaster told our Foreman, Tom, to go grab a cab off the Cab Track and set it on an eastbound train in the Departure Yard and tie up. As had been the custom for moves like this, one Switchman took me down the Lead onto the Balloon Track and then to the Cab Track where we grabbed a cab...Easy move!

We set the train then headed back west on the Balloon toward the Lead in the Receiving Yard. There was a road crossing at grade where the engines came out of the Diesel Service Area with a STOP sign.

My locomotive was an old "Gater" that had been converted to a hump engine with a slave unit…#1300 if I remember correctly? The slave was on the west end and the 1300 was on the east end headed east. I was backing up.

The Switchman was sitting in the Fireman's seat looking back. All of a sudden…BAMM!!! And our engine turned up onto the Engineer's side at a little less than 45-degrees. It really knocked us for a loop!

Now if you ever walked through the *Haunted House at Calico Ghost Town*, that is what it was like trying to get out of the locomotive.

Shoemaker (the Switchman) was with me and I managed to get out the door and down the steps; but had to jump from the last step down to the ballast. Once down, we looked back and saw what had tipped us over! An outbound Engineer came out of Diesel Service with several units and nobody on the point! He ran through the STOP sign at the road crossing at grade striking us in the fuel tank with the drawbar of his rear (leading unit).

Diesel fuel was everywhere…also, it had ignited! Flames were shooting up 50 feet in the air!

I told Shoemaker to jump-up and hand me the fire extinguisher. He replied, "F___ You!" Probably a smart assessment.

I climbed back up into the cab and grabbed the extinguisher and tossed it down on the ground. Then I climbed back out and once again jumped off the bottom step onto the ballast; but this time it was right into the diesel fuel, which was spilling out onto the ground. I tried spraying toward where the two engines met in a T-bone. It was no use!

Help arrived from the Diesel Service and they too tried to put the fire out. They had about as much luck as I did. It was time to let somebody who knew what they were doing, to take over! That would be the *Barstow Fire Department*. Once they arrived it was all over!

I felt Shoemaker and I were pretty lucky that night while going for a quit! They could have hit us right where

Shoemaker was sitting. The worst that I got out of it was...I ruined a pair of *Chucka-Boots*.

It took two 100 ton cranes, brought down from Bakersfield, California, to untangle the mess. Charges were brought against both crews and an investigation was held.

The crew, that hit us, was found at fault for not stopping and not protecting the point of their movement.

(Note: Shoemaker's brother was killed shortly before or after this incident. He was deadheading between San Bernardino and Barstow, California, riding on the rear unit of a train. Heavy rains had washed out the Mainline. The lead units went over the washout. Shoemaker's engine went down the mountain. The engines that went over the washout came back down on top of the unit Shoemaker was on...pounding it into the ground! I do not think they ever found him, RIP Shoemaker.)

You cannot make this stuff up!

It's Railroading!

The Closest I Came To Dying and Getting Fired in the Same Day

By: retired AT&SF Engineer; Road Foreman of Engines, Amtrak; BN and BNSF Engineer, L. E. Batanian

In 1994 Amtrak powers that be made the decision to cut management Nationwide by 600 managers! In the first round they were offering 6 months salary for you to pack your bags and leave. The next round would be forced...

My old boss, Assistant Superintendent, D. L. Ridgeway, had retired a couple of years after we set up the Operating Department in Salt Lake City, Utah. Dave was not the easiest man to work for; but he was a good Railroad Man that came off the Illinois Central gulf (ICG) in Illinois. He had been a road Foreman of Engines (RFE) back there and knew Passenger Service like the back of his hand! He taught me a lot.

"Soak It!!!"... and Other Railroad Stories

Soon after we set up Salt Lake City, we got a new Superintendent in Los Angeles, California. The Rocky Mountain Division (our division) came under his jurisdiction. His name was Lonny Stearns. Lonny was also off the ICG.

To give you an idea about why we were there was this...Amtrak from the beginning paid whatever railroad they were operating over, for them to provide crews to operate Amtrak trains.

Slowly, over a period of time, Amtrak negotiated its own labor agreement with the *BLE (Brotherhood of Locomotive Engineers)* and the *UTU (United Transportation Union)*, which allowed them to hire their own crews at an hourly rate instead of a universal mileage agreement.

In the agreement, the men working for the railroads over which Amtrak operated were given the chance to bid on the jobs that would now be controlled by Amtrak. It was a mess to say the least!

Some "pencil pusher" laid out the runs, which were so long, that some even crossed over from railroad to railroad! This maneuver caused the Rocky Mountain Division to have men bidding on the operating jobs from four different railroads! How they blended the seniority fairly, is still a mystery to me!

My job, was to just hire the men...not to question!?! And hire I did! I went through hundreds of men to fill all the slots created by this new contract.

You see, the contract allowed the crews to flow back to their home road for up to six months, if they did not like the Amtrak job. And flow they did! Many came for a VACATION!

Two of our westbound trains had layovers in Sparks, Nevada and Las Vegas. Crews would bid in those jobs and take advantage of the layovers for as long as their wives would allow them...or they got a Rule G...whichever came first!

I had so many Rule G violations the first year, I lost count!

Charles H. Geletzke, Jr.

I am sure many paychecks were left in Nevada until their wife gave them the Hereafter! If you don't know what that means, I am not going to tell you in this story!

It took about two years for the hiring process to settle down and we finally got a good selection of men who liked their jobs and wanted to stay in Salt Lake City, Denver, and Albuquerque.

Years slowly moved on with Ridgeway retiring, me having to temporarily fill his job, me not getting his job, and me having to train my new boss from Philly. Now that came with some interesting moments.

One happened to involve my Father-In-Law, "Wild Bill" Gust... (If you have not read Chuck's previous book...*unit Trains and Other Railroad Stories*, buy it and read it. You will learn about "Wild" Bill.) and it happened at Deer Camp.

My new boss was an East Coast deer hunter and asked if he could go on a Mule Deer Hunt with Gus and me..."Ahhhhhh...Sure!?!" I said.

Gus and I hunted with a side wall tent and a wood stove and a 1963 Jeep CJ-5.

My new boss rented an RV. We were invited in to have a look around and as THE BOSS was opening this cabinet, in that cabinet there was all BRAND NEW hunting clothes hanging in the closet...every shirt lined-up facing the same direction...neat as a pin!

After the tour, we went outside to stand around the campfire and shoot the breeze. THE BOSS had a little table set up with a bottle of *Chivas Regal*, a bucket of ice, and some tumblers. As we were talking, THE BOSS fixed himself a drink, not thinking to offer one to the two people whom he was going to be hunting with.

Now I do not have a taste for it; but I knew that Gus would enjoy one, so I leaned over and quietly told THE BOSS that he "might ask Gus if he would like a drink."

With that, he asked Gus if he would like a cocktail and handed the bottle of *Chivas Regal* to him. He then turned around to get a tumbler and some ice. At this point I knew things were getting interesting!

"Soak It!!!"… and Other Railroad Stories

As THE BOSS turned back toward us to hand Gus his glass, I thought I saw his knees bend when he saw the bottle upside down and Gus taking an EXTRA long pull!

"Well, I guess you won't be needing the Tumbler," was all he could say as Gus was wiping his lips with his shirt sleeve. It was a priceless moment that I will forever remember!

THE BOSS soon left Salt lake City returning back to the East Coast. His ticket punched…on to the Northeast Corridor he went.

I was back to the same old grind.

Lonny Stearns soon retired in Los Angeles and was replaced by T. H. who was 180 degrees out from Mr. Stearns! It seemed that nobody could do anything correctly for this man. The morning conference calls turned into the morning Beatings! The beatings would continue until the moral improved! It just depended on who was at bat on any given morning…we ALL took our turn!

When 1994 rolled around, Amtrak decided it was top heavy in Management. They came up with a plan to get rid of 600 managers. They were offering 6 months salary for you to pack up and leave. If they did not get the magic number of 600, they would start carving!

For some reason I felt I could not survive. The daily beatings had made me uneasy despite the fact I was the one who set up Salt lake City as a crew base. I went home and told my wife what was about to happen at Amtrak.

That Sunday, in the paper, there was a quarter page ad taken out by the Burlington Northern Railroad (BN). They were looking for Locomotive Engineers to work in the Pacific Northwest. They were offering a $25,000 signing bonus…"Huh?"

I managed to slip down to L.A. where the BN was holding job interviews for Engineers at a hotel next to LAX (Los Angeles Airport). I interviewed with them and left with a job offer…then back to Salt Lake City…all in the same day! I then called L.A. and talked with the Director of Amtrak Personnel, Hank Engle. We had become friends over the years and I told him "I was leaving the company."

Charles H. Geletzke, Jr.

Hank was a little surprised that I was going to take a buyout and leave my RFE job in Salt Lake City!

I told him my reason and that "I was just burned out!" He understood.

I explained to Hank that the BN only had one glitch. Candidates had to go back to Overland Park, Kansas and go through a crash course at their Locomotive Engineer Training Facility. If you passed...you got the job! If you failed...you were out the door! Now what?

I learned long ago, the hard way, not to burn your bridges down behind you! Learning this lesson could be costly!

I knew that I would not have a problem at Overland Park, in fact the outcome was a bit of a surprise!

I explained to Hank about the glitch. He told me to put one of my Engineers in Salt Lake City on "Special Duty" to watch the place and go back to Overland Park and do my thing. He said that he would cover for me with Amtrak; but not to send in the buyout papers. He told me to wait until I finished my course.

I felt very honored the he thought enough of me to do this. I went back to Kansas and completed the course as well as the Simulator. I had never been in a simulator before...that thing was so realistic that if you chewed, you would be looking for a place to spit!

While back there I ran into some old Santa Fe friends...Jerry Pollett and Randy Jenkins. When Jerry spotted me, he jumped over a row of chairs to get to me. I wish that we had been able to be in the same class; but he was assigned to another. Randy was the B of LE Local Chairman up in Bakersfield, California. We were assigned to the same class. The surprise came when the class ended. Each class awarded the "Top Gun" Award for well...The Top Gun. I was taken aback when my name was called for this honor! In fact, I was the only one! Another student came over to my desk and snatched-up my tests and scores to look at them...thinking he should have won...oh well!?! Sore loser, I guess!?!

When I checked out of the hotel, I dropped my Buyout Papers into the *FedEx* box outside the door and sent them to Hank in L.A. I would soon be leaving for Vancouver, Washington…Wham-Bamm!!!

A few years after I got to Vancouver things started slowing down and I was about to get cut-back to the ground. I was hired as an Engineer; but due to new labor agreements each man hired was also given a Brakeman's seniority date.

I had heard that the Utah Railway was offering a $10,000 signing bonus to Locomotive Engineers. I sent my resume to them and got hired over the phone! Huh?

Now what?

I was working for two railroads!

I went to see the BNSF Superintendent in Vancouver and asked for a Leave of Absence. To my surprise, he gave it to me! (Yes, I was back where I started! The BN had merged with the Santa Fe.)

Half the bonus money was in my bank account before I got down to Provo and the Utah Railway.

They put me on the Extra Board. You have to remember this was my old Amtrak RFE Territory. So, I was busy working locals and going up and down the mountain with a pilot. It had been three years since I was last over the division. I was soon ok'd to the Utah Railway Yard in Helper and up to some of the mines.

One day I was called to go past Helper all the way out to Wellington, Utah. They gave me a Conductor Pilot and off we went to Wellington to get a coal train. I had a yellow block coming into Helper with the first notch set…and I'm thinking "the next signal is Springdale." WRONG!!!

My Pilot was over across the cab bullshitting with the Conductor. As I saw the depot ahead, God told me, "No you idiot! There is a pot (dwarf) signal where you used to spot #6!" I no sooner had that thought in my head and I DUMPED THE AIR! The Pilot stopped talking to the Conductor. "Huh?" And he jumped up!

I started applying the Independent Brakes (on the locomotives) to keep the slack bunched up.

As we came around the corner I saw the FRED (Federal Rear End Device or Marker) on the rear end of an eastbound train, just past the pot signal! We were screaming past the depot!

The Conductor and Pilot were headed out the door!

I could feel the empties squat down and I told them. "We're gonna stop! Calm down." Funny, I am telling them to calm down and I am squeezing the seat.

Sure enough, that empty coal train sat right down and made a perfect spot! I looked out the side window and there was the pot signal. I looked out the front window and there was FRED! Phew!!!

Looking back in the mirror I could see a pick-up truck speeding up the side of the train. The Conductor and Pilot were white as ghosts...I'm still stuck in the seat! The Rio Grande Road Foreman got out of the truck, with a big ole cowboy hat on his head, looked up at me and said, "What was the Pucker Factor on that one, Leon?"

"Pretty high," was all I could say.

The Pilot and the Conductor had no idea what had just transpired, nor how the train felt as it squatted down. They were too busy Bullshitting and going out the door...LOL!

Now let me say, that was the ONLY TIME that I almost died and got fired in the same day!

You can't make this stuff up.
It's RAILROADING!

Trespassers!

By: retired AT&SF Engineer; Road Foreman of Engines, Amtrak; BN and BNSF Engineer, L. E. Batanian

After reading what happened to you in your book, *Unit Trains and Other Railroad Stories*, about the man who lost his legs in a suicide attempt, it got me thinking about an event that happened to me on the BNSF.

When I was Amtrak's Road Foreman of Engines on the Rocky Mountain District, I spent several days in Grand

Jct., Colorado with the Amtrak Claims Department lawyer.
We were at an unmarked crossing leading to the *Coors Beer*
Ceramics plant. A short time earlier, Number 5 had hit and
killed a woman going to work. The family was suing Amtrak.
The lawyer was timing how long it took from the time the
Engineer started to whistle until he hit the crossing. I
remember he had us put out pie plates at a couple of spots
besides at the whistle board for the Engineer to whistle at.
Hence, I had to be there several days, as Amtrak only ran one
train a day…

Later, on the BNSF, I got called out of Pasco,
Washington on a westbound grain train…a 12,000-tonner!
These trains were not too bad to catch out of Pasco, even
though they only had a couple of units…sometimes more;
but most of the time two. The division had a "river grade"; so
there was no reason to waste power! When the grain was
running, the trains got over the road pretty good!

So there we were, coming around the curve heading
into Camas. Our good trip was almost over and soon it
would be sundown. Now we just needed to get into
Vancouver! We were in "power" even though the track was
"down river;" however, the terrain was not. I remember
looking down the right-of –way seeing a guy on the tracks.
That was not uncommon, as there was a protected crossing in
Camas and pedestrians often walked across it.

I started to whistle as soon as I spotted him. This was
well in advance of the whistle board for the crossing. The
conductor said, "Leon he is walking west between the rails!"

I was really laying on the whistle! I set the first notch
on the 26L automatic brake valve and thought to myself,
"maybe he cannot hear me;" so I throttled off and kept up the
whistle. There was no response from him.

The train started to slow down a bit; but we were still
doing 42 mph…we were a "45-miler." As we got past the
point of no return, I yelled at the Conductor, "I'm going to
plug them!" To be honest, I also told him, "If we kill this
guy, I do not want to end up in court telling a jury in a civil
suit that I did nothing wrong…"

Charles H. Geletzke, Jr.

Sure enough, we hit him! The sound his body made hitting the front of the locomotive was a sound I will never forget! Nobody would, or could!

We were halfway through town when we got stopped. I immediately picked-up the radio after we it him and shouted, "Mayday, Mayday, Mayday...come in Vancouver Yardmaster. This is westbound Train ____ at Camas. We have just struck a trespasser!" The term trespasser was used on the D&RGW (Denver & Rio Grande Western Railroad) down in Utah to describe anyone on the property that was not authorized to be there. I then told the Yardmaster to, "Call the Police and an Ambulance as soon as possible!" The young Conductor, at this point, had not yet made an attempt to get-up and go back to see what the situation was. He was a bit shook-up! As was I! I said, "Look, one of us has got to go back and it's not me! It's time to earn your pay! I know it is not a pleasant thing to do; but it is your job! The authorities will need you back there, so they have a location and personnel to respond to. The sun is setting...take a couple of fusees with you, so they can see you when they arrive." With that he got up and headed back toward the rear of our train.

I soon saw a fusee light-up and it wasn't long before the police and an ambulance arrived. Sadly it was a fatality!

It did not take long before the locomotive cab was full of people! The Terminal Superintendent, a Trainmaster, Road Foreman of Engines (RFE), and the BLE (Brotherhood of Locomotive Engineers) Local Chairman, all were present. (The Local Chairman later became the RFE...Hmmmm?) He was a member of the *Crisis Response Team.*

I assured everyone I was fine, as did the Conductor when he was interviewed. I told them how I handled the train...and about the events leading up to striking this person.

We were then told that a yard crew would be out to relieve us. With that, the *Crisis Response Team* was out the door! As he exited the cab, the Terminal Superintendent said, "I'll be back to give you a ride into town."

"Sounds good to me," I responded. I just wanted to go home. I knew that I had no control over what had just happened. I knew in my heart that I had done everything that I could possibly do!

The next thing I knew, a Police Officer climbed up the steps of the locomotive and walked in the front door uninvited! I had heard of this happening before...it had happened to Amtrak crews while I was RFE in Salt Lake City. We had a policy, developed with the help of the BLE, I believe, that the Engineer of a train was under no obligation to give a Police Officer his/her Drivers License...even if they were told it "was for Identification Purposes ONLY!"

I have the upmost respect for Police Officers...always have and always will! It is sad to say, something that is lacking today in a lot of people! This was taught to me by my parents beginning from an early age!

Well wouldn't you know it, those were the first words out of this Officer's mouth..."I will need to see your Drivers License!?!"

Huh???

No introduction. No, are you all right? No may I come in? Just, "Can I have your Drivers License?"

I politely told the officer that he, "did not have the right to ask me for my Drivers License nor to even be on the locomotive without permission, and would he please turn around, go out the door he just came through, face the steps and safely climb back down to the ground and wait." I stated, "I will call the BNSF Supervisors on the scene and they will come to talk with you...the BNSF Railway will give you all the information that you need."

Had the Officer approached me in a different manner, I may not have been so quick to ask him to wait on the ground...But he didn't, and I did! There was no turning the clocks back now!

I called the Terminal Superintendent back to the head end to speak with the Police Officer. Shortly he returned; but they never climbed back on the locomotive; so I cannot tell you what exactly was said.

The relief crew soon arrived and we got our grips and climbed off the engine.

Charles H. Geletzke, Jr.

The Crew Wagon was parked on the right-of-way next to our train. It was a Company vehicle. The Terminal Superintendent said to get in with him and he would give us a ride back to town.

I said, "That's fine with me. I just do not want to be driven back by the scene of the accident!" The Coroner had been called and they were working to get the Deceased out from under the train. Well, wouldn't you know it! He (the Terminal Superintendent), headed right down the right-of-way, and passed the site where they were dragging the guy's body out from under a covered hopper!

I said, "What the heck are you doing!?! I told you I did not want to go back there!" There was another road leading off of the right-of-way to the left; but that idiot just kept going! To say I was pissed was an understatement...!

The company had a policy that gave us up to two weeks off with pay, after being involved in an accident like this.

I took the full two weeks!

After I returned to work, I found out that the guy had committed suicide. They found a note in his home. It is sad to think that this man's life was at this low of a point. Life is a gift! I only wish that he had the foresight to seek help. I do not think people who do these sort of things are thinking about how it will affect the people **they choose**, to do it for them.

Pretty sad...

As Always,

Leon

Markers

By: C. H. Geletzke, Jr.

I am going to make the assumption that most of you readers are familiar with the changes that have occurred with

"Soak It!!!"… and Other Railroad Stories
railroad marker lights over the past sixty years or so. Prior to around 1965 or even 1970 most railroads had kerosene marker lamps applied to the rear ends of their trains…both freight and passenger. Beginning sometime in the early 1960's many carriers electrified the markers; or in several cases even decided to utilize reflectorized markers in the same manner. During the early 1980's many railroads began eliminating cabooses on their freight trains and began hanging a red flashing light on the tailend of their trains…the problem with this was that without a crew member riding in the rear car, the engine crew had no idea if their entire train was intact or if they even had the proper required air brake pressure in the rear of their train! The major problem with this feature was the fact that anytime a train stopped unintentionally, someone would have to walk all the way back to the rear car and ascertain that the entire train was intact!

I am guessing that it was in the late 1980's that the two major air brake manufacturers, *WABCO (Westinghouse Air Brake Company)* and *New York Air Brake Company* developed what would eventually become to be known as either an EOT (End of Train Device) or on some railroads a Federal Rear End Device or "FRED" for short. The advantage of using the EOT or FRED was that in addition to displaying a flashing red light to the rear of the train, it also electronically monitored the air brake pressure on the end of the train and sent and electronic signal to the Receiver Display Unit (RDU) located on the leading locomotive's control stand where the engineer could monitor conditions of the train's air brake system. Additionally, these EOT's or FRED's would also give the engineer an indication of whether the rear car of the train was moving or stopped. In only a short amount of time the *Federal Railroad Administration (FRA)* declared the use of the EOT's to be mandatory and used on all over the road trains and in other special conditions. Lastly, the train could additionally be put into Emergency, if the engineer elected to trigger an electronic radio transmitted signal to the rear of the train when equipped with one of these new devices.

Charles H. Geletzke, Jr.

I am going to guess that it was probably around the year 2000 or so and the former Illinois Central Management was brought in to teach us on the former Grand Trunk Western Railroad how to move trains over the road and to "properly" serve our customers, that they assigned a new Assistant Superintendent at our terminal in Flat Rock, Michigan. In this instance I have no intention of revealing his name as he was actually one of the few "good guys," and was generally well respected by the majority of the workers. When I tell this story, it is not because the gentleman lacked experience...he definitely did not...no, in this case the trouble was that he was not yet totally familiar with the territory he was supervising!

Now let me also state that I was not involved in this incident...what I am telling you is strictly hearsay.

One day we had a freight train moving either north or south between Lang Yard in North Toledo, Ohio and Sarnia, Ontario...this was over the former Detroit & Toledo Shore Line Railroad (D&TSL). When the train was in the vicinity of the former New York Central (PC-CR-NS) FN tower in Trenton, Michigan (located about two miles east of Flat Rock Yard) the train developed problems with its EOT. The crew immediately notified the train dispatcher, who in turn called Flat Rock Yard and arranged for a new marker to be brought out and replace the one that was defective.

Instead of having someone from the Car Department jump in a truck and take the train a new marker, the job was given to the relatively new Assistant Supe.

Now the junction at FN tower was a rather intricate interlocking! Looking at it from south to north the North and Southbound Mainlines ran parallel to one another in those directions. The former D&TSL came north paralleling the Northward Conrail Main on the east side and then crossed all the way over to the west side of the Southward Main at FN tower. Then to add to the confusion here, the former Detroit, Toledo & Ironton (DT&I) Railroad's River Subdivision came east out of Flat Rock, curved to the north paralleling the Southward Conrail Main Track and then crossed all the was to the east side at FN tower.

"Soak It!!!"... and Other Railroad Stories

As the railroad officer approached FN tower, he immediately spotted the tailend of a northbound freight train and drove to the rear car. He then contacted the train's locomotive engineer and secured permission to exchange markers. Once permission was granted, he closed the angle cock on the rear of the last car and swapped the defective EOT for its new replacement. Once the exchange was completed, he opened the angle cock and cut the air back in and then called the engineer giving him the I.D. Number of the new marker. The CN engineman then punched the new number into the RDU on his control stand...and waited! The company manager punched the button on the new marker and still nothing!

Shortly, the tower operator at FN tower contacted the CN train to see if they were by chance having marker problems!?! The conductor replied that yes they were. Well, would you believe that the new Assistant Superintendent unwillingly actually changed out the marker of an adjacent Conrail train!?!

Twenty minutes later both trains were on the move and sadly for the new official word of his dilemma spread across the system like wildfire!

We all have to learn the territory!

Who arranges this?

By C. H. Geletzke, Jr.

In my early days on the Grand Trunk Western Railroad (GTW), when we were called to deadhead, we generally went by train...passenger or freight. Once our passenger trains disappeared, if the railroad wanted to transport us somewhere, it was generally in a company van, normally driven by a clerk or occasionally by a Trainmaster in his company vehicle.

By the mid 1970's the railroad was contracting with several on-line livery services to transport us where and when we were needed.

Charles H. Geletzke, Jr.

By 2001 the carrier generally was using one of three limousine companies, in Chicago-*Howard Cab*, out of the Flint area it was *ABC Livery Service*, and in and around Flat Rock and Detroit they contracted with *Milepost Livery Service*. I have no idea who arranged the calling or how they generally determined which outfit to call!?! But here was a day that really mystified me...!

On August 27, 2001 the crew dispatcher called me to "Pilot" Pontiac Engineer, Mike Bennett working Train 455 With Conductor, Larry Williams over the Conrail Shared Assets from Coolidge located in River Rouge, Michigan to Vinewood in Detroit...a distance of only a little over five miles. Mike's train had engines GTW 5930 & 5912 a pair of SD40's with only 12 loads and 16 empties, 1,913 gross tons, and was 1,739 feet in length. I was called to report for duty at Flat Rock at 12 o'clock Noon and we departed at 1:55 P.M. **As it turned out, we were routed "The Old Way" over the former N&W Old Main Line and onto the GTW at West Detroit. Thus, we did not even run via the Shared Assets and all of the territory was parallel trackage that Mr. Bennett was already qualified on. You might say I was just along for the ride and served no real purpose!**

I got off the train at Milwaukee Jct. at 3:45 P.M. and walked to the B.O.C. (Buick-Oldsmobile-Cadillac) yard office in Hamtramck to wait for my ride back to Flat Rock. Fortunately, I did not have to wait very long as an *ABC Livery Service* Chevy Suburban arrived only 25-minutes later, having driven 75-miles from Flint to take me 24-miles south to Flat Rock. We arrived at Flat Rock Yard at 4:50 P.M. and I tied-up and went off duty only nine minutes later at 4:59 P.M.

Now here was the best part and the point of the story...do you know that when we arrived at Flat Rock there were six *Milepost Livery Service* vans there waiting with nothing to do! Yes, only 24 miles from Hamtramck and yet the railroad called a van for me all the way from Flint to drive me 24-miles in the opposite direction 24-miles...I'm sorry; but I didn't get it then, and I still don't today!?!

On March 19, 1985, sixteen years prior to the date of our story we find the GTW 4904 working at Avery Ave. in Detroit, MI switching the "Corn Sweetener." Between every pair of tracks was a brick driveway, which permitted vehicles to access each railroad car.

And then it stopped!

By: C. H. Geletzke, Jr.

Interestingly, my employer, the Grand Trunk Western Railroad converted the former team track at Avery Avenue in Detroit, Michigan into a facility designed and set-up strictly to handle inbound covered hoppers and tank cars carrying granulated sugar and liquid sugar to the various bakeries, soft drink bottlers, food processors, and breweries throughout southeastern Michigan in the late 1970's. It was known as the *Corn Sweetener* or Food Term and by 1976 was the highest revenue producer on a "per car basis" on the entire railroad! Six days a week railroad cars would be spotted there and their contents transloaded to trucks for regional distribution. Now I have never learned why; but around 1999 or so, this business just stopped and the facility was abandoned. For several years, I never noticed any activity around the former team track in any manner.

293

Charles H. Geletzke, Jr.

Let me state that initially as a team track it was designed as a stub-ended facility with 20-tracks and an operating freight house handling LCL (Less Than Carload) freight. It was constructed with driveways laid with heavy paving brick between each pair of tracks, so that horse and wagons and later trucks could be driven directly to each car spotted there for loading and unloading.

I guess it was in July or August of 2001 that I first noticed several people working there almost daily removing the paving brick and stacking them in neat piles. I recall wondering if the railroad knew what they were up to?

On September 27, 2001 I was working my regular assignment, Train 384 from Flat Rock to Sarnia, Ontario and riding with us was GTW Police Detective Willingham. We were ordered for 5:30 A.M. and had units CN 5298 (SD40-2W) & 2520 (C44-9WL) with 39 loads, and 49 empties, 5879 gross tons, and we were 5,376 feet in length. As we neared Avery Avenue at about 9:15 A.M., I mentioned the activity that I had noticed at the former "Sweetener." Detective Willingham seemed to be immediately interested and stated that he would do a little investigating.

It apparently did not take long for him to "rock the boat," because the very next day when we passed that area returning on Train 383 at about 10:30 A.M. I did not spot any activity in the area at all! In fact, those brick piles remained there for over two more years...untouched, and finally one day the railroad contracted with a brickyard to have them removed. Oh yes, by that time those paving bricks were selling for about $4 each at local building supply companies. And, as you might imagine, I never heard any mention of the theft that we had prevented.

Changes in the wind…from one extreme to another!

By: C. H. Geletzke, Jr.

On September 22, 2001 I worked Train 383 from Port Huron, Michigan to Lang Yard in North Toledo, Ohio, was "bussed" to Flat Rock, and tied-up at 3:17 P.M.

By supper time I was feeling sick! I called the crew dispatcher and booked-off sick at 7:05 P.M. with a cold. I was told by the Crew Dispatcher, that per Superintendent, Wayne Johnson, that "if you are off in excess of 24-hours, you will have to have a note from a doctor to return to work!" (Looking back, it almost makes me wish that my daughter had already completed med school by then, and she could have written the note!)

On October 13, 2001 Regional Manager, Ty Gibson offered me a choice of jobs as Trainmaster or Road Foreman of Engines. I said, "Thanks; but I am not interested."*

- Regular readers will recall that I had previously been a GTW Trainmaster from January 1976 through November 1980 and Supervisor of Locomotive Engineers from 1993 through 1995.

I couldn't believe it! On October 23, 2001, Regional Manager, Ty Gibson gave me a monogrammed "CN" golf putter and said, "For the good job that you have done!"

I was overwhelmed!

During December 2001 I was a regularly assigned Engineer working Train 384 north from Flat Rock to Sarnia, Ontario one day and would return the next on Train 383…seven days a week. On December 21, 2001 I returned home from a roundtrip, tying-up at 6:18 P.M.

I was scheduled to have one week vacation beginning December 23rd. I asked the crew dispatcher if I worked my regular northward trip on December 22nd, would they deadhead me back home to begin my vacation.

Charles H. Geletzke, Jr.

The crew dispatcher stated, per S.T.O. (Supervisor of Train Operations), Wayne Johnson, "they will not allow you to work one way and deadhead home. You will have to book-off and lose a trip!"

I was actually surprised that they did not make me work the next trip and lose a day of my vacation!

Uncertainties like these would be the reason that many railroads today are having trouble retaining young employees and this was "just the tip of the proverbial iceberg!"

Things Can Change in an Instant!

As told by: C. H. Geletzke, Jr.

Isn't it unbelievable how one minute your life is going great and only a fraction of a second later your whole world can disintegrate…thankfully, sometimes God steps in and it only falls apart partially!?!

March 29, 2003 turned into one of those days. I was the regularly assigned Engineer on Canadian National (former GTW) Trains 384 and 383. We would run from Flat Rock, Michigan northeast to Sarnia, Ontario, taxi back across the St. Clair River to Port Huron, lay-over, and take a train back to Toledo, Ohio and a taxi back north to Flat Rock…then wash, rinse, and repeat…seven days a week! I was ordered for 0730 at Flat Rock working with a Flat Rock Conductor, Jerry Mihm, who was called off the Extra board…by this time we were "Conductor Only"…working without any brakemen. For motive power we had the CN 5256 (SD40-2W)-5550 (SD60F)-2589 (C44-9W)-9410 (GP40-2LW)-5410 (SD50F), which we had to wait for as it was coming in on an Extra 385. We finally got off the Fuel Dock at 1050, ran out to the north end of the yard and doubled Track #11 to #10. We had 46 loads and 63 empties, 6,014 gross tons, and were 7,732 feet in length. After meeting Train 242 and Yard Job #109 we finally departed at 1155.

"Soak It!!!"… and Other Railroad Stories

We pulled north 6.1 miles to FN tower (Milepost 37.3 on the Shore Line Sub.) in Trenton and sat at a red target from 1220 until 1240. (Incidentally, FN tower was closed permanently two days later at 0900.)

Once we received a clear signal we continued north to Coolidge (M.P. 46.2) an interlocking at the north end of the former D&TSL Dearoad Yard and stopped at 1300. Twenty-five minutes later we received a Restricting Signal and entered the Conrail Shared Assets and ran north to West Detroit (M.P. 50.2), approximately four miles and stopped for a red signal at 1345. After a westbound Conrail freight cleared, we got on the move again at 1400. Five minutes later we passed the controlled switch at Vinewood (M.P. 50.8 on the Shore Line Sub.) and reentered former GTW track.

Yes, this could be a real stretch of "Stop and Go" railroad…to make a non-stop trip across this portion of the city only happened on a very rare occasion! At Beaubien (M.P. 54.0) we had to stop again at 1420 and meet an Amtrak Extra #517…a relative rarity! Ten minutes later, we were headed north.

We pulled up to East Yard (M.P. 6.7 on the Mt. Clemens Sub.) (the GTW's major yard in Detroit) arriving at 1450 where we were blocked by Train 383. Once they were out of our way, we picked-up 3 loads and 14 empties. We now had 49 loads and 77 empties, 6789 gross tons, and were 8,962 feet in length. We left town at 1550.

Now here was where things got interesting! We were approaching 8 Mile Road (the northern border of the City of Detroit and M.P. 10 on the Mt. Clemens Sub.) at the maximum allowed speed of 30 mph. The crossing gates went down in plenty of time, I had the bell ringing, the headlight was on bright, and I was whistling signal 14L (two longs-a short-and a long) in the proper manner. I saw a white Chevy, headed east (compass direction) pull-up to the crossing and stop. All at once, in the blink of an eye, some idiot came flying up behind this poor lady…crashed into the rear of her car, which was properly and safely stopped…and literally drove her car through the horizontal crossing gate and right out in front of our train! It happened so fast! I immediately put the train's brakes in EMERGENCY! The white Chevy stopped right on our track! Then, in only a fraction of a second that woman, opened her door, jumped out and ran toward the rear of her car clearing the left rear quarter-panel, JUST AS WE TOTALLY DEMOLISHED HER CAR!

I had never witnessed anything like that before! If she had been even a fraction of a second slower, she would have been under that car in front of our locomotive! I immediately thanked God for saving her life!

We came to a stop at 1605 and we immediately called our Dispatcher who notified both the City of Detroit Police and Fire Departments. Additionally, they called the emergency personnel of the City of East Pointe (formerly East Detroit) as 8 Mile Road actually bisected the two town's borders.

The weather was partly cloudy at 36 degrees. When we came to a stop the third car behind the units was occupying the crossing and there was no damage to the front of the unit.

I was so thankful that the driver of the white Chevy was okay! I believe the Police arrested the man driving the White Caprice, which plowed into her!?! Neither Conductor Mihm nor I ever had to go to a deposition or to court regarding this incident.

When the car and everyone were clear, we departed at 1655.

We then ran railroad direction East to the bridge over the Pine River (M.P. 51.46) where we were "staged" (new CN and IC terminology for being held by the Dispatcher #3 who controlled traffic on the Flint Subdivision) from 1815 until 1840. Finally after being released, we once again got underway, passed Tappan (M.P. 55.6 an interlocking at the west end of Tunnel Yard in Port Huron) at 1855. Having "cleared Customs," we rolled through the St. Clair Tunnel into Canada and stopped at the extreme east end of Sarnia Yard at Blackwell at 1925. We were relieved by a CN crew, climbed into a taxi, and returned to Port Huron where we went off duty at 2015.

"Soak It!!!"… and Other Railroad Stories

We were then driven to our hotel where we got something to eat, went to bed, and awaited a call ordering us for the return trip on Train 383 the next morning at 0615.

It just goes to show, you might be doing everything right; but in a fraction of a second…everything can change!

After years of visits I was finally selected as the "Guest of the Day" at the *Fairfield Inn* in Port Huron, MI. I once "roughly" calculated that over the last thirty years of my career, I averaged staying approximately 130 nights/days a year in motels! (Geletzke collection)

Charles H. Geletzke, Jr.

GUEST OF THE DAY!

By: C. H. Geletzke, Jr.

Here is another piece of real trivia. When the *Fairfield Inn* opened in Port Huron, Michigan in the late 1980's the GTW signed a contract with them and our train crews began staying there. By the time of my last visit, I had attained more "stays" than any of their other patrons…by far!

Reap What You Sow

By: Retired GTW Locomotive Engineer and Supervisor of Locomotive Engineers, Lawrence R. Bolton

For the last 20 years my wife and I have escaped part of Michigan winters by vacationing in Florida. As most of you know, Florida in winter months is choked with "snowbirds" (residents of cold states and Canadian provinces that flock to the warmer climes in the south). With all the extra people inhabiting the area, almost every activity involves waiting…waiting in traffic, waiting for a table at a restaurant, or waiting in long lines at the grocery store, for example.

While waiting to begin a round of golf at the first tee, meeting other snowbirds is a common way to pass the time. Conversation typically begins with, "Where are you from?" since at that time of year, it seems that snowbirds outnumber Floridians. The answer is usually a cold climate location. Once, while waiting to tee off, when queried with that question, I answered, "the Cereal City." The gentleman initiating the conversation replied, "I'm from Vicksburg (Michigan)." After some additional small talk the man from Vicksburg asked, "What did you do for a living?"

"Locomotive Engineer" I answered.

To which he immediately replied, "I hope it wasn't for that CN!"

300

"Why, what did they do to you?" I replied.

He then told me the following story.

While a resident of Vicksburg, the man made his living farming land closer to Marcellus, MI. He owned two parcels of farmland that was divided by the right-of-way of the former Grand Trunk Western (GTW) mainline. In the summer of either 2003 or 2004, he needed to run an electrical line under the now CN track. In the past, when needing to make improvements to his land that involved the railroad right-of-way, the GTW would charge a nominal fee to draw up a legal contract for the project. This time, after contacting CN, he was told his request to run the electrical line would cost $5400! He was shocked at this huge charge; but desperately needing to get electrical service to the other field, he paid what the CN asked. In the fall of the same year CN suffered a derailment on the track between the farmer's two fields. He was asked by the railroad if they could use an area of his land near a county road to stage equipment needed to rerail railcars and repair track. The railroad also wanted to build a temporary road on his land from the county road back to the derailment site. The farmer told the railroad he would allow their request; but it would cost them. His fee for the use of his land would be $5400. When the railroad's attorney phoned to ask how he had arrived at that amount for the use of his land, the farmer related as to how he was treated the previous summer. The attorney was taken aback and stated that he had previously counseled railroad management not to treat people in such a heavy-handed manner. The farmer did receive compensation for the use of his land.

"Just what do you guys do?"

As told by: C. H. Geletzke, Jr.

I guess it was on a beautiful sun-shiny day in the spring of 2004 that my next door neighbor, Lew Barthalis, approached my wife and I as we were out working in the yard and enquired, "May I ask you a question? Just what the hell do you guys do?"

I am certain that we both turned toward him with that "deer in the headlights look" and my wife responded, "What do you mean, Lew!?!"

With that, Lew cleared his throat and said, "Well, you guys have been living here for quite a while now (we moved there in 1992)...and you give Brenda (his wife) and I the impression that you are just normal neighbors; but why then does the Federal Government keep checking-up on you!?!"

In unison we responded, "What do you mean?" and that we had no idea what it was that he was talking about!

Lew said. "Well, I guess it was back in the late 1990's, someone from the *Secret Service* appeared at our door and started asking questions about a Gerald Geletzke. They said he was your brother, Chuck." I said that "I never met him. Then they asked a few more questions and then left."

Both Leslie and I said that we had no idea; but that like me, my brother began his truck driving career and also worked for the railroad through the mid to late 1970's. Following college graduation he joined the U. S. Navy where he was an aviator. When my parents passed away in the late 1990's, my brother and his wife changed their "permanent" mailing address to ours, as he and his family moved frequently as was typical of our military service men and women. Apparently at that time he was being considered for promotion to Wing Commander!

We had no idea that the government was talking with our neighbors...they never spoke with us!

Then in late June or early July of 2000 a representative of the *FBI* (*Federal Bureau of Investigation*) once again appeared at the front door of the Barthalis' family and asked a whole litany of questions again; but this time they were about me!

Again, I had no idea that this interrogation had taken place; but putting the pieces of the puzzle together and after consulting my old timebooks, I realized this was just prior to July 9, 2000 when I was "asked" to work as Engineer on an

"Soak It!!!"... and Other Railroad Stories
Extra 610 North with units NS 9355 & 9337 on a "Trial Run"
for President George W. Bush's Campaign Train from Lang
Yard in Toledo, Ohio up the former D&TSL and GTW to
Pontiac, Michigan. Almost a month later, on August 4, 2000
I did work as the Engineer on the "actual" Campaign Train,
PX 60361 North, with the CSXT 9993 & 9992 again from
Lang Yard to Pontiac.

Neither Leslie nor I, nor any of our children had any
idea that we had all been investigated!

Well, apparently the Federal Government was not
finished with us yet! Sometime in late 2003 or early 2004
representatives of our government made another trip to
Temperance, Michigan and questioned a number of our
neighbors! This was the recent visit that Lew was asking
about. Apparently, he had asked several other neighbors and
they too confirmed that they had been questioned...on ALL
THREE OCCASIONS!

And yes, we had no idea!

This time we figured that it was because one of our
sons had applied for admission to the *United States Naval
Academy* and apparently Uncle Sam wanted to know what
made him tick and did he appear to have any issues that they
should be concerned about!?!

In all three instances we had no idea of what had
transpired; but looking back, we can certainly understand
why our neighbors must have certainly been curious just why
our Federal Government had to look at us at least three times
over a ten year period!?!

Helpful Hints

By: C. H. Geletzke, Jr.

During the first 35-years or so of my railroad career I
generally stuck the train orders or operating bulletins that I
received in one of the upper pockets of my bib overalls.
Occasionally, like many of the other locomotive engineers I

would slide them into some of the upper piping in the locomotive cab where they would be easily accessible.

I guess it was sometime between 2005 and 2010 when one of my best friends and without a doubt one of the most conscientious railroaders I have ever known…got into trouble at Pavilion, Michigan! As he stated he was running between Battle Creek, Michigan and Chicago. The TGBO (Tablature General Bulletin Order) (a modern computerized version of former train orders…you have to admit that has a "real ring to it!?!) had restrictions within restrictions resulting in the one they missed. It was not in mileage order, and was on the page following a work block, which they had already entered. It was not a matter of being tired as it was a westbound daylight run (so they were not even facing into the rising sun). My friend stated, "We weren't distracted as the conductor and I were discussing the upcoming restrictions. We both overlooked the slow order because of the sequence on restrictions. This was still not an excuse and we should have seen and observed the restriction. Following the violation, the track foreman contacted the SLE (Supervisor of Locomotive Engineers) who contacted TD-4 (Train Dispatcher #4) who put us in the siding at Marcellus. There we sat until the Trainmaster from Battle Creek arrived to pull us out of service and transport us back to Battle Creek. I was decertified for 30 days!"

Would you believe that within a year later the same SLE rode a westbound freight out of Battle Creek with my good friend and asked if he could run the train? My buddy called signals and temporary restrictions; but not far into the run the supervisor totally blew through the permanent 40 mph speed restriction at Vicksburg! All my friend said to him was, "See how easy it is to overlook something!?!"

In our discussion following the event this professional railroader confessed. "You know, I don't care who you are or how good you are, we ALL make mistakes! No one can work over forty years in this industry and not commit errors and occasional rule violations…most of which are never seen nor noticed by anyone! In this case I knew that I was wrong, I am embarrassed; but we ALL make occasional errors…even the

OFFICIALS! I figured it was much better to admit what I did and take my licks."

Now unlike my good friend, I also made <u>many</u> errors (none really serious) while performing my duties. I was the accused in a number of investigations, received demerits; but was never given any actual time off.

One day during the last ten years of my career, I too overlooked a slow order on the single-track Mount Clemens Subdivision. It was not a serious or drastic violation, no damage resulted. And it was not even observed by any corporate officers; but nonetheless I violated the rules. In this case I was distracted (I have since learned that as I have gotten older, this occurs more frequently)! I was talking with my conductor and went over the track defect 10 mph too fast. Naturally, I was embarrassed and decided that I had to develop a better system to remind me of all of these details.

That evening I attended a meeting at my kids' high school and observed a teacher drawing with a dry-erase marker on the "chalk-board." I thought to myself, "What a great idea!"

The next day on my way to work, I stopped at a store and purchased a package of markers. When I arrived at work I inserted one into my grip, signed-in, picked-up my operating bulletins, and went out to inspect my locomotives. After completing my examination, I sat in my seat and began reading my bulletins; but this time I did something different! I took that dry-erase marker and wrote a short note pertaining to each item in the bulletins in sequential or mileage order right on the windshield, directly above my face. Naturally my conductor, Craig Joyce, asked what I was doing. I explained the situation and during the remainder of the trip, each time I fulfilled one of the restrictions in the bulletin, I would take a paper towel and remove the writing from the windshield. By the end of the trip I decided that I liked my new idea and continued using that method for the remainder of my career!

If you are a locomotive engineer today, I highly recommend this little technique, perhaps it may keep you too out of trouble!?!

Charles H. Geletzke, Jr.

Personal Record

By: C. H. Geletzke, Jr.

On July 6, 2007 I set a new "Personal Record on CN Train 383. For power we had the CN 5732 and 5764 a pair of SD75I's. After picking-up, we departed at 1505 with 154 loads and 35 empties. We had 17,748 gross tons and were 12,908 feet in length.

We arrived at Lang Yard in Toledo, Ohio at 1745.

I was working with Conductor Bob Fortner and Brakeman, John Jameson.

Old Dogs Can be Hard to Train!

By: C. H. Geletzke, Jr.

By August 8, 2007 I had been the regular assigned engineer on Trains 382 and 383 for a long time! Speaking of a long time, as of July 5th I had been working on the railroad for 40 years and over that period of time, I had experienced a huge number of changes!

One item that I could NEVER get used to was watching a new young engineer work while taking signals and instructions over the radio from a conductor or brakeman, while the man was in plain sight and yet the engineman often was not looking at them! I was taught that you NEVER take your eyes off the nearest crew member to you who was passing signals unless you had a prior understanding! That takes us to our story…

On Wednesday, August 8, 2007 I was called to report for duty to work Canadian National Train 382 at Lang Yard (the former D&TSL yard) in North Toledo, Ohio at 0300. I was working with Conductor, Gary "Lewan" Lewandowski. I immediately went out the door and inspected my two units, the CN 5670 and 5663 a pair of EMD SD75I's. We "doubled" or actually "tripled" Track 63 to 61 to 52 and

"Soak It!!!"... and Other Railroad Stories

completed our Initial Terminal Air Test. We had 6 loads and 138 empties for a total of 7,759 gross tons and we were 11, 787 feet in length...over 1200 feet in excess of two miles! We departed at 0545.

We made a rare non-stop 44 mile run over the Shore Line and entered our trackage rights over the Conrail at Coolidge (M.P. 46.2) in River Rouge, Michigan at 0720.

We pulled up to Conrail's Rouge Bridge (M.P. 47) and stopped for a red signal at 0723. Seven minutes later we were underway once again and in 8/10ths of a mile we had to stop for another Stop signal at Delray. We stopped at 0735 and began pulling at 0740...remember, we had over two miles of train!

We then pulled ahead about four miles crossing the Conrail diamonds at West Detroit, circumnavigated the loop through Bay City Jct., and called out the "Slow Approach" signal that we had at Vinewood (M.P. 51.2) to reenter the former GTW. When we were only two car lengths from the signal moving at less than 10 mph the signal dropped to RED right in our face! Because we were so close to the signal and because we could not see a conflicting movement, I just brought the train to a nice gentle stop.   You don't ever want to put a two mile long train in EMERGENCY, especially on winding track, unless you perceive it to be a true Emergency! We stopped at 0810, received permission from Train Dispatcher, "JRM" John McKinnis, and began pulling again at 0815.

At Milepost 54.0, Beaubien, where were crossed Conrail once again, we encountered another Stop signal and halted our progress at 0830. One hour and 25 minutes later we finally received a Clear Signal and began pulling at 0955.

Gary and I pulled up to B.O.C. (Buick-Oldsmobile-Cadillac Yard) and stopped at 1015. We then swapped trains with the crew on Train 383. 383 was a true contrast having only 62 loads and 20 empties, yet was heavier at 9,024 gross tons, and was only 5,079 feet in length. For power we now had the CN 2246 (GE ES44DC) & 5363 (SD40-2W). We started to head south at 1020.

Charles H. Geletzke, Jr.

As we rolled past the headend of our former train, the new crew noticed that three cars deep, we had a DANGEROUS tank car, a UTLX 202422, which was improperly marshaled. Overhearing our conversation, the B.O.C. Yardmaster, Jerry Wohlfiel instructed us to set the car off in the south end of the Farm Track, which was adjacent to the Southward Main Track (formerly the Westward Main Track until IC management took over!). We could not believe that the previous crew did not notice the improperly marshaled car when they made the pick-up at East Yard in the first place!

Gary and I continued to pull ahead only about five or six cars to the point where he would make the "cut" and set the offending car out. What we did not know was that CN Superintendent Bill A. and Assistant Superintendent, Clarence R. were "hiding in the bushes" performing an Efficiency Test!

Gary gave me car lengths and instructions, "over the radio," as to where to stop. After closing the angle cock and applying a handbrake he stepped out away from the train and gave me a hand signal to pull ahead. I released the Independent Brake, opened the throttle and pulled ahead. Even though I had Gary in sight the entire time, he used his radio to tell me to stop. Gary then lined the switch for the Farm Track, gave me a hand signal to back-up, and guided me back to a single car in the track that we were going to have to tie-on to. All of this was done with hand signals. Once again, Gary closed the angle cock, applied a hand brake on the tank car...while standing on the ground, and then told me to pull ahead, using his radio. He then restored the turnout to the normal position, told me over the radio to back up, and we tied back on our train...THAT'S WHEN THE FIREWORKS COMMENCED!!!

Superintendent A. came on the radio stating, "Conductor on CN Train383 you are being pulled out of service for improperly applying a handbrake!" Then he called, "Engineer on Train 383 you are being relieved from duty because you moved without being given the number of car lengths that you were required to move and your

308

conductor changed from radio to hand signals and did not inform you of the change and you did NOT question it!"

"Oh my God" I thought to myself! "How did I get through the previous 40-years, the first several of which were WITHOUT RADIOS, using only hand, lantern, and fusee signals, and generally without specific car lengths. I guess I had always assumed that if I could visually see the man directing the movement at all times and read his body language too, we were making the movement safely! Oh my God, what had I done!?! And just imagine, I had just completed 40-years on the railroad and up until now, HAD NEVER BEEN RELIEVED FROM DUTY!!!

Gary and I then gathered our belongings, secured the train, left it right where it was, and walked over to the B.O.C. yard office. A cab picked us up at 1250 and drove us back to Lang Yard.

We arrived at Lang at 1405 and tied-up at 1448. I then called and booked-off sick.

The next day, August 9th, Crew Dispatcher, Norm Rendell called and notified me that I was to receive an Investigation Notice for "Improper Radio Procedure," which was to be held on August 17, 2007. The notice was sent to me care of my Local Postmaster and I signed for it and picked it up at my local post office on August 10th. Let me just state that all of this did wonders for my morale!

On August 10th, I took a Personal Day and my wife also had me make an appointment with my personal physician to have my blood pressure checked. Leslie was worried about how the stress was affecting me and said, "Your color looks bad!" Following the doctor appointment, I "marked-up" and worked every day consecutively until my off day on August 21st.

Interestingly, on August 16th Mr. A. and Mr. R., were once again lurking in the weeds and performed another Efficiency Test on my Conductor, Kris Kirkendall and me as we gave a "Roll-by Inspection" to Amtrak Train 350 at Vinewood from 1512 until 1523. Apparently we passed!?!

Additionally on August 16th, I received a letter from Road Foreman of Engines, Brian Balon (who I promoted to

Charles H. Geletzke, Jr.

Engineer) stating that when he rode with me back on June 25th, that I did an "Excellent Job!"

On the day of our scheduled investigation, August 17th, I received a call from the crew dispatcher stating that the Investigation was being postponed until a later date…more stress!

Later that day, my *BofLE* Local Chairman, Dan Harris called and asked if I would agree to sign a "Letter of Reprimand" without any further penalty or punishment. I agreed; but also stated that this entire incident was a "total joke and an embarrassment!"

In conclusion let me state that while I could see the transition of attitude from one day to the next, this was certainly NOT the same railroad that I hired-out on! Back in the day, if a supervisor disapproved of one of your actions, he or she would take you aside and have a discussion with you and as long as you did not repeat the incident, that would be the end of it! We had respect for those managers; but that my friends, IS NOT MODERN RAILROADING!!!

CN Conductor, Bob Reutz is seen using a Brake Stick at CSXT's Stanley Yard in Toledo, OH on July 20, 2008.

"Brake Sticks MUST Be Used in the Proper Manner!"

As told by: C. H. Geletzke, Jr.

Charles H. Geletzke, Jr.

How many of you know what a brake stick is, or better yet, have ever used one?

Now I have to admit, when I began my railroad career in 1967 I did work with several old-time "boomers" who had cut their teeth on other railroads and talked of using "brake clubs." These were a baseball bat-like piece of hardwood (generally ash) that could be inserted into the brake wheel on a handbrake to increase the amount of torque the brakeman or switchman had to aid in increasing or decreasing the pressure of the brakeshoes on an individual car. These were generally used by Hump Riders before the invention of car retarders or by brakemen in mountainous territory. (See attached photo) In an emergency an axe or pick handle could be supplemented in its place.

Trademark on an actual brake club that I acquired from the former NYC hump at Livernois Yard in Detroit, MI in the late 1960's.

But what about a Brake Stick?"

If I can recall correctly, I believe that the CSXT instituted a policy on or about February of 2008 that in order to apply or release a handbrake on a car, the employee "must use an approved 'Brake Stick' to perform this task!" Oh yes, and "before using a brake stick, the employee must have watched the CSXT's video on its proper usage!" (Note: I am paraphrasing in these quotations to the best of my ability.)

I soon learned from fellow railroaders that a "Brake Stick" was actually a telescoping metal device with a type of hook on one end that could be extended to a length of perhaps fifteen feet. Its purpose was to enable a trainman to be able to apply or release a handbrake from a position on the ground, so he or she would not have to climb up upon a car. When extended, the hook was designed to even reach high handbrakes on cars, which had never been lowered.

"Soak It!!!"… and Other Railroad Stories

Now at that time I was working as a Locomotive Engineer for the Canadian National Railroad (CN) out of the former Detroit & Toledo Shore Line Railroad's (D&TSL) Lang Yard in North Toledo, Ohio and I must admit, I had never heard of an item called a "brake stick." Apparently this was a totally new concept instituted by the CSXT and as far as I knew, was not required nor yet used by any other carrier in our area.

As most of you know I have recorded a copious amount of notes over the course of my railroad career; but for some reason never made mention of this specific event…I am making an "educated guess" that it occurred on Saturday, February 9, 2008. On that day I was called to work CN Train 383 from CN's Lang Yard to the CSXT at Stanley Yard on the extreme southeastern side of Toledo, Ohio with Conductor, Mike "Cookie" Shirey. We were ordered for 0415 and on this day had two GP38-2's, the GTW 5823 and GTW 4909. At 0843 (You will notice that on this date I am listing the time **right to the minute!** Throughout my entire career, while in freight service we always rounded off to the nearest increment of five minutes. In earlier days, in passenger service, delays were recorded to the minute; but since I had been recently receiving so much grief from the new "IC-Illinois Central" managers, I began documenting EVERYTHING I did, "to the minute," as a means of "self-protection!). We departed Lang with 68 loads and 36 empties, 9,994 gross tons, and we were 6,203 feet in length.

We then ran non-stop (an extremely rare occurrence) across the former Toledo Terminal Railroad, now owned by the CSXT, semi-circling the east side of Toledo and pulled into #5 Receiving Track at Stanley Yard and stopped at 0935. Now here was where the dilemma occurred! You see, Conductor Shirey knew that once we cut away from our train at the south end of #5 Receiving, he was required by the CSXT Bulletin to apply a handbrake on the head car and possibly several others, if necessary, before we left that track. But remember, this was Cookie's first trip over to Stanley since the bulletin went into effect…what should he do? What would you do, if you were in his shoes?

Well naturally he referred to the "universal" operating rule which clearly stated, "In case of doubt or uncertainty, the safe course must be taken!" So, he called the Yardmaster and stated the fact that there was a brake stick lying on the ground near his location; but he was not yet trained nor qualified in its use.

As you can imagine, the yardmaster went crazy, notified the Trainmaster, and instructed Conductor Shirey to "wait right there!" Oh yes, I neglected to mention that the outdoor temperature was about 2-degrees Fahrenheit and I was just sitting up in the cab of the 5823 looking in the mirror at the "Show" that I knew was about to take place!

I kept looking at my *Ball of Cleveland* gold pocket watch and 22-minutes following Cookie's discussion with the Yardmaster, the Trainmaster came flying down to our location in a proverbial cloud of dust driving a CSXT pick-up truck! He quickly jumped out of the vehicle and from his mannerism and gestures, it appeared to me that he was yelling at Mike and looked as if he might even be on the verge of a stroke!

I have to hand it to Mike, he appeared as cool as the weather he was dressed to work in…shortly with his hands flailing in the air, the CSX official climbed back into the truck and raced off toward what I am assuming was his office! It was at that point that Mike climbed back up on the engine and told me about the recent practically one-sided discussion. The Trainmaster could not stand the fact that Mike was virtually able to quote the bulletin verbatim, and continued to state that he was "required to watch a video on the proper usage of the brake stick."

Well, it was 32-minutes from the Trainmaster's departure until he returned to our location and jumped out of the truck and plopped a video player on the hood of his vehicle. He then fiddled around with it for several minutes and finally got it to work! Meanwhile, Mike was standing right along side of him the entire time. When the presentation finally began, I once again started watching the minutes pass on my watch. The video presentation lasted precisely 15-minutes. At the end of the presentation, I watched as Mike picked-up the brake stick and applied hand brakes to the south three cars. Once the company officer was satisfied that Mike could indeed perform the task safely, he placed the electrical device back in his truck, had Mike sign a form that he had been properly instructed in the use of the brake stick, and headed off to another point in the huge yard. Thinking back, I am amazed that the Trainmaster did not have the foresight to additionally have me too watch the presentation in the event that I also might one day be required to apply a handbrake on a car…apparently, he was not thinking that far ahead!?!

Mike then received permission from the yardmaster and herded our units to the north end of the yard. I changed ends on the units and our outbound Train 382 was finally ready for us to tie on at 1150. Mike tied the units on and released several handbrakes properly using the required brake stick. We departed at 1232 with 23-loads and 87-empties, 6,600 gross tons, and we were 6,722 feet in length.

On the way back we encountered a red signal at Vickers and had to wait for an NS train to pass. I got off the engine and took several photos.

We then got going and arrived back at Lang at 1320, yarded our train in Tracks 61 and 64 and tied-up at 1418…a 10-hour and 3-minute day.

Looking back, I just have to believe that when the CSXT instituted that new Bulletin they certainly could have devised a better plan to educate the employees arriving from foreign railroads, and definitely not have created so much animosity toward a worker who was merely making an effort to comply with their instruction…particularly during that era when all of us had to revert to constantly looking over our shoulders as a form of self-preservation!

Territorial Qualifications

By: C. H. Geletzke, Jr.

Today I finished reading a wonderful railroad book titled: *The Life and Times of a Railroad Engineer* , written by

Charles H. Geletzke, Jr.

Bud Hoekstra. Bud is the older brother of retired GTW Conductor, Chuck Hoekstra, that I worked with at Kalamazoo and out of Battle Creek, Michigan. Bud began his railroad career on the Illinois Central Railroad in Chicago in 1959 at the age of 16, later became a Locomotive Engineer, eventually left the Illinois Central Gulf, hired out on the Soo Line, and retired from the Canadian Pacific following the SOO's acquisition of the Milwaukee Road. One of the book's chapters deals with the tragic wreck on Amtrak that occurred on January 4, 1987 between an Amtrak passenger train and a Conrail train operating on trackage rights. The outcome of this terrible incident in which 16 people were killed, evolved into a program requiring Locomotive Engineer Certification, which became totally effective on December 31, 1991. It mandated the institution of Alcohol and Drug Testing for all Locomotive Engineers, Certification for all Locomotive Engineers every three years (or more frequently based on the plan submitted to and approved by the FRA for each individual railroad), and territorial qualifications to be renewed annually...and eventually, portions of this Federal Law was applied to many other railroad employees in other crafts.

On September 1, 1993 I was appointed to the position of Supervisor of Locomotive Engineers (SLE) on the Grand Trunk Western Railroad at Flat Rock, Michigan. On this job I was involved with not only Engineer Certification; but also the training of new engineers and the operation of our Locomotive Simulator. In one of my previous books, *So, You Think You'd Like to Railroad and Other Railroad Stories*, I included a story titled: <u>Engineer</u> <u>Training</u> <u>Program</u> in which I describe the daily workings of Engineer Certification and the details of what prompted me to resign from that position and return to the craft of Locomotive Engineer myself. After reading Mr. Hoekstra's book, it occurred to me that perhaps I should mention how Territorial Qualification works nationally, for all promoted Locomotive Engineers.

Let me start off by stating that on the day, March 27, 1995 that I bumped back onto the GTW Locomotive Engineers' Spare Board at Hamtramck, Michigan, I WAS

316

"Soak It!!!"… and Other Railroad Stories
QUALIFIED TO RUN A TRAIN OVER
APPROXIMATELY 818 MILES OF THE ENTIRE GTW
RAILROAD INCLUDING THE FORMER DT&I, D&TSL,
in addition to the adjoining foreign connections over which
we had trackage rights!

Now when the new Federal Engineer Certification
Law was put into effect, it clearly stated that to remain
qualified to operate over any and all railroad trackage, an
engineer had to make a trip over that territory ONCE A
YEAR! It even stated that as long as he/she rode over the
territory, in a coach on a passenger train, in a caboose, or
even in a high-rail truck, that would suffice. But, if in fact
that individual exceeded the yearly limit, by even one day, he
or she would be required to have a pilot (another qualified
ENGINEER) ride with them to reestablish qualifications.

Let me state that prior to the institution of this federal
law, generally, if an engineman felt comfortable to run a train
over a piece of railroad in his/her own mind, that was
considered sufficient. Naturally, each individual railroad may
have had their own rules and requirements pertaining to this
issue.

Now for me, primarily working out of Hamtramck (a
Detroit suburb completely surrounded by the City of Detroit),
Michigan, I primarily operated trains between Detroit and
Flat Rock; Detroit and Battle Creek; Detroit and Sarnia,
Ontario; and over the former D&TSL to Toledo, Ohio and to
the foreign connections there.

So allow me to show you how this system worked.
By the following year, March 27, 1996 I was no longer
qualified to operate over the former DT&I south of Flat Rock
to Cincinnati, Ohio. I lost my qualification on the GTW's
former Romeo Subdivision between Pontiac and Richmond. I
could not work the Kalamazoo Subdivision, and lost my
qualification on the Flint Subdivision Mainline between Flint
and Port Huron. On June 4, 1996 I lost the ability to work
west of Battle Creek to Chicago and on September 4, 1996
forfeited my qualification between Durand and Flint.

Let me also explain that on our railroad, we had
"System Seniority." That meant that if an engineman had

enough seniority, he or she could bid-in a job anywhere on the system. Now hypothetically, if I elected to bid on a job working west of Battle Creek, for example, once I received that position on bid, I would have to make at least one trip over the territory with a pilot to become requalified on the territory.

My territorial qualifications remained the same for a number of years. On June 2, 1999 I bid-in the Engineer's Spare Board on the former D&TSL at Lang Yard in Toledo, Ohio. The advantage for me was that I would only have a 7-1/2 mile drive to work, vs. the 62-miles that I had been driving each way to and from Hamtramck. As for the territory that I would be working and due to changes in our *Brotherhood of Locomotive Engineers* Working Agreement, I would basically remain working over the same territory.

On October 8, 2000, due to a reduction in force, I was cut-off the Spare Board at Lang and bumped onto a regular through freight, Train 264/385 working between Flat Rock, Michigan and Sarnia, Ontario with a layover in Port Huron.

A major change occurred to my list of qualifications on March 20, 2001…I was no longer qualified to work between Pontiac and Battle Creek! But wait, only six days later, I encountered a major surprise…the crew dispatcher called and asked if I would like to work a Train B399 from Battle Creek to Griffith, Indiana! I stated that I would accept the call; but that I would require a pilot as I was no longer qualified over that territory on the South Bend Subdivision. So, because the company was in a bind, I was instructed to drive to Battle Creek (from Flat Rock) and informed that Battle Creek Engineer, Stan Sienicki would be my pilot. Stan was probably 20-years my junior and I had actually promoted him to engineer in 1994. Isn't it funny how things sometime work!?! After laying over at the former IC Markham Yard, we returned to Battle Creek the next day on Train 454. I was now once again "qualified" over a portion of the South Bend Sub.! Now let's look at this trip from an economic perspective. At that time, we were still paid by the mile….and 100 miles was still a basic day. I drove my car 163 miles from Flat Rock to Battle Creek, then worked under the tutelage of a pilot for 169 miles from Battle Creek to Markham Yard…a total of 332 miles. The next day I would return via the same route….a total of 664 miles. Engineer Sienicki would be paid 338 miles for his roundtrip. Now here is the really sad portion of the equation…after making this roundtrip and requalifying on this portion of the railroad, during the remaining ten years of my working career, I NEVER EVER was called to work over that territory again!

On August 4, 2001 I lost my qualifications for working the Holly Subdivision between Royal Oak and Pontiac as I had not worked over that territory since I was called for President Bush's Campaign Train from Lang to Pontiac on August 4, 2000. So, now all I was qualified to work was the line from Sarnia, Ontario to Toledo, Ohio and from FN tower in Trenton to Flat Rock as well as a small portion of the Holly Subdivision from Milwaukee Jct. to Royal Oak….oh yes, and from Battle Creek to Markham until March 21, 2002.

On March 27, 2002 I was called "In Emergency without a pilot" to run Train 243 from Flat Rock to Flint. I guess I requalified myself!?! And, on August 12, 2002 I was ordered once again "In Emergency" to taxi from Flat Rock to Hamtramck, pick-up Conductor Zeke Wojnowski, taxi to Battle Creek and return to Flat Rock with Train 752…so now, I once again "self-qualified" from Battle Creek to Durand. Hey, I was just doing "as I was instructed!"

A major change occurred on February 9, 2004 when the Brotherhood of Locomotive Engineers on the GTW ratified a new contract promoted by CN's President, E. Hunter Harrison to go to an hourly working agreement. We would no longer be paid by the mile; but instead by the hour, with a 10-hour Basic Day and overtime after ten hours. With this change, we also lost the "early quit," that is, when our work was completed, we were no longer permitted to go home early…it was mandated that we had to remain on the property for at least 9-1/2 hours…even when working through freights over the road! This ended the incentive to get our work done as quickly as possible. Additionally, under this working agreement, we were all given two days a week off and qualified for a weekly guarantee…as long as we did not "book-off" or "miss call."

Well, let me say that "this changed everything!" It quickly became apparent that most of us would rarely exceed the amount paid in the guarantee or if so, by only a small amount…especially when we could ONLY work five days! In short order, most of the enginemen learned that it was no longer to our advantage to be qualified to work over large portions of the railroad. Thus, if the crew dispatcher called and said, "I want you for such and such job." If you could reply, "I'm not qualified over that territory," they would have to go down the list to the next person and get them to work. Meanwhile, you could just sit home and "collect the guarantee without being penalized!"

On the downside, what this did was to make the earnings of most engineers fairly similar regardless of seniority. The days of taking every call that came along, "working right on your rest," and working seven days a week, was a thing of the past! Looking back, I can recall sometimes working as many as ten times in a seven day week…granted, I was not home much; but it sure was nice on payday! Believe me, this new agreement destroyed all incentive and seniority wise, made us all relatively equal.

In summation, while on March 27, 1995 I WAS authorized to work over 818 miles of railroad, when I retired on December 4, 2011, I was just barely qualified on 120 miles of territory! Things just were not the same! And, who was the winner in this contest???

Accumulating Seniority

By: C. H. Geletzke, Jr.

In his book *The Life and Times of a Railroad Engineer** retired IC, SOO Line, and CP Locomotive Engineer, Bud Hoekstra, makes a profound statement in Chapter 38 when he states, "When a man or a woman goes to work in train or engine service, about all he or she has is seniority. A person is constantly evaluating their position on the board projecting the one day chance of holding a decent job."

Ask any unionized employee working a seniority based occupation and I am certain they will tell you that their lifestyle and generally, their income, improved as they moved up the seniority ladder. This was definitely true for me working as a locomotive engineer on the Grand Trunk Western Railroad…at least until the last several years or so of my career.

Without going into a great deal of detail, when I established my seniority as a fireman on the Grand Trunk Western Railroad on November 9, 1973 a GTW engineman was permitted one week vacation after 1-year of service, two weeks after 2-years, three weeks after 10-years, four weeks after 20-years, and five weeks after 25-years or more.

Every fall a bid-sheet would be posted at each individual terminal and all enginemen were permitted to bid (in seniority order) on the weeks that they would like to have off. In the larger terminals, such as Battle Creek, Durand, Pontiac, and Detroit sometimes as many as five or six openings might be permitted for bid for every week. During times of slowdowns, such as weeks during "automotive changeover," even more openings might become available for bid.

Now when the Vacation List was opened to bidding, naturally, the senior engineman would get ALL of his choices…he could take individual weeks or group them together and take all of them in one block…it was kind of like choosing your seats in a theatre or at a ballgame. Next the Number Two Man would make his choices and so on…all the way down to the youngest employee. With a system like this, I am sure you can see that the youngest people on the list might not necessarily get the weeks of their choosing! If none of their choices were open, they would generally be "assigned" vacation time from the weeks that remained open. Now if for some reason a week opened-up due to a "vacation change," retirement, an individual resigning, or even heaven forbid a death, a younger person could request a vacation change and be "awarded" the week on a "first-come first-serve basis." This was basically how the system worked for years and years and naturally as an individual moved-up in seniority, his or her choices would improve...of course things could also change if the railroad incurred a reduction in business and reduced the number of workers in a particular terminal.

For me, personally, this system worked fairly well...when I was young and single, the week or two of vacation that I received did not really matter too much. After I married and had a family and my children were young, we would often try to take our vacations at times no one else really wanted. The nice thing was knowing that I would not be on the bottom rung of the seniority list forever and that generally, I would gain a "turn" or two on the list every year...Lord willing, eventually reaching the top of the list!

Well, would you believe that only a year or two before I retired in 2011 all of this changed!?! Yes, the railroad began hiring and promoting a large number of new enginemen in the 1990's and by approximately 2009 they were in the majority. As a group they went to the General Chairman of the *Brotherhood of Locomotive Engineers* and complained that it was "unfair that the senior employee on the seniority list should we awarded all five of his five choices!"

Apparently, the General Chairman agreed with their position and negotiated with the railroad's Labor Relations Department and adopted a change. From that day forward, the senior engineman would be awarded his first choice ONLY...if he or she elected to take more than one week in a block; the individual would still receive all of the weeks in that increment. After that, the second "oldest" person would receive their "first choice" and so on, down to the youngest person on the list. Once everyone had been awarded their "first choice," bids would be accepted for everyone's second choice...then third, fourth, and fifth in the same manner.

Now I have to state that personally, I think that this was short sighted on the part of the younger workers. To me, these younger individuals failed to see that they would not be on the bottom of the list forever...so much for what I was

"Soak It!!!"… and Other Railroad Stories
told when I began my railroad career back in 1967…"Son,
you have to pay your dues!"

* *The Life and Times of a Railroad Engineer*, Hoekstra, Bud, copyright 2012, Chapter 38, page 301.

Thankful I was Nearing the End of My Career!

By: C. H. Geletzke, Jr.

March 28, 2011

Personal letter to my *Bof LE* Local Chairman:

On Friday, March 25, 2011 I was called by "the crew dispatcher's computer" to work Train Relief #382. After delivering the train to Sarnia, Conductor, C. D. Joyce and I were transported back to Port Huron to pick-up two additional men for transport back to East Yard (in Detroit). The driver of the *BTS* van had to go to the gas station for gas; so we just waited.

While waiting, Trainmaster, L, came into the "Book-In Room" and asked if he could speak with me.

I replied, "Yes sir."

He then took me back into his office, closed the door, and stated. "I want you to listen to something." He then sat down at his desk and punched a code into his computer and said. "Listen to this." At this point he got out of his chair and told me to "sit down," and motioned to his chair.

As I sat in his chair he said. "You will have to put your ear close to the speaker." Which I did.

At this point I had no idea what I was going to be listening to. I listened very closely and heard a recording of the crew dispatcher's computer saying something like…"This is the CN Crew Dispatching System. We have a call for Gel-a-tek-C-H-Chuck. Are you that person? I heard my voice reply, "Yes." The computer went on to say…"You are ordered for Train Q1446123 in through freight service to Port Huron Tunnel on duty at Flat Rock at 1030 and are to report to East Yard at 0949. (I believe that this is approximately correct…I did not take any exception to the call.) I could hear my voice reply…"Yes." The computer then went on with the rest of its other routine questions and prompts.

Upon listening to the conclusion of the taped recording, Mr. L turned to me, looked me in the eye and emphatically stated. "See, you knew you had to lay-over!"

I immediately became defensive as over the past two years I have had numerous encounters with Mr. L and I feel as if he has singled me out as one of his personal "targets!" I then replied that "I was not called to layover!"

He then said, "Yes you were. That's what the computer said!"

I then replied that "my conductor on that day (Wednesday, March 23, 2011) Christopher Lacey, was called personally by the actual crew dispatcher and WAS told that he would lay-over. I was called by the computer and was NOT told!"

Mr. L then began to explain the call to me. He stated, "When you get a computer call and it states in 'through freight service' to Port Huron, that means that you are going to lay-over! If you are called in 'turnaround service,' that means that you are NOT!"

I then stated that "I did not know this and that NO-ONE had ever explained this to me before." I then went on to say, "Mr. L, I do not have a problem with laying over. I have worked lay-over jobs for years. I would be working one now; but we do not have any regular road jobs at all out of Detroit!" I then said, Mr. L, if they want me to layover, all they have to say is…Bring your toothbrush!...and I will be glad to pack my things and will lay-over without any problem." I then stated, "It seems to me that the computer has in the past told me that I am going to layover." I then inquired stating, "How hard would it be for the computer to just say **'You are going to lay-over!?!'**" Why does everything have to be in a secret code? How hard would it be to clearly state that **'You are going to lay-over!?'**"

Mr. L then went on to say, "If you have a problem with this or a question, you should stay on the line and follow the prompts and talk to the crew dispatcher."

I replied, "Mr. L I have tried this; but sometime you have to wait as much as thirty minutes for a real person to answer…or, often they never answer at all!"

At this point, Mr. L turned to me and said, "I am putting YOU on notice! I have explained this to you. I will tell 'them' about our conversation and in the future, unless the computer says 'in turn-around service' you are to plan on laying-over!"

At that point I began to realize the Mr. L had other managers involved in this issue and I asked, "Who is 'them?'"

He replied, "Crew Management." (I noticed that in these situations, managers always use or give a pronoun or Department Name rather than someone's proper name.) After that reply, Mr. L turned to me and said, "You are dismissed!"

I then returned to the Book-In Room.

Several minutes later, Mr. L walked into the room and handed me an 1-1/16" x 8-7/16" note (See attachment), which said. "I spoke <u>again</u> with Mr. Geletzke he stated that he has in the past had the computer say the words 'Layover' that it wasn't to his understanding that 'through freight service' ment (sp?) that he was in fact called to lay over is there anything that has been put out or can be put out so that I don't have crews saying they were called in Turn when in fact called to layover.(no ? mark)"

At this point, I was becoming very stressed, and I replied to Mr. L stating, "Mr. L, my morale is really getting low…in fact it is down in the toilet!" I then went on to state in front of an audience (which I probably should not have said.) "You know, Mr. L, I was once in management myself? One day my supervisor (Joe Waldecker) said to me…Do you know what your problem is? Your problem is that you care!!!" I told him, "I analyzed that statement and thought to myself…if my **PROBLEM** is that I care, what does that say for the attitude of my boss? Two weeks later, I resigned from management!"

Mr. Local Chairman, I hope that I am not making a huge issue out of this. If the problem is just one of miscommunication, I can deal with it and go on. Being called to lay-over is truly not a problem for me. But why do I have this nagging feeling that Mr. L is taking aim at me and had deemed me (in his own mind) as one of his problem children who needs to be taught a lesson? In July I will have been railroading for 44-years. It is interesting that in all of those years, the ONLY supervisor that I have ever had issues with has been Trainmaster L!

Let's see what happens in the future,

Respectfully submitted,

Chuck Geletzke
Locomotive Engineer Division 812
Hamtramck, Michigan

Half an inch at Speonk, LI

By: Retired Chairman, Adrian & Blissfield Railroad, Art Single

A person familiar with this incident related this story to me

At a rail terminal near a major east coast city a few passenger trains layover each evening. There is a multi-track double-ended yard there. Seven or eight years ago, an engineer was written up for leaving his consist beyond the fouling point of a switch from one of the yard tracks. The next train through wiped the front corner of his engine, which I think is now being scrapped. He was written up for violating the yard track's dwarf signal by parking beyond the fouling point.

"Oh, no," says he. "I stopped without tripping the signal. I did nothing disallowed." And with that, he fought the charges.

When the investigation concluded, they found that the insulated joint feeding the dwarf had been placed too close to the fouling point of the switch, in fact, beyond it! For many years, everybody else had parked far enough back that they were in the clear. But this time, this engineer went right up to the insulated joint. The signal was proven to be good, and he had not violated the signal although he had violated the "clearance envelope." So, the engineer was cleared and the track circuit installation was corrected.

Now the speculation begins…

Was he really the first guy to park that close to the insulated joint? Did the ballast settle and tip the track a little? Did the center bowl or bolster casting on his engine truck wear enough to let the engine tip a little more than it or others had in the past? Did the ground shift? Who knows! But they did move the insulated joint back a ways.

Charles H. Geletzke, Jr.

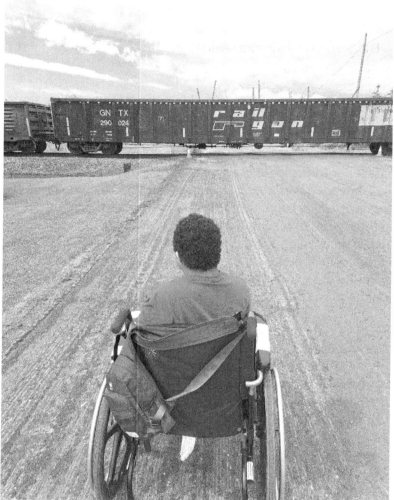

Cierra Dorin watching train on June 28, 2022. (Tom Dorin photo)

Creating Memories with your Children

By: Canadian National Locomotive Engineer, Tom Dorin

After completing a recent trip home from Stevens Point, I wanted to get our daughter, Cierra out for a wheelchair ride and me, a good walk. The weather was great;

so we had an opportunity to spend some quality time with each other. We live close to the Union Pacific (UP) tracks, so no matter which way we go, we encounter the tracks and depending on our route, we will either cross over them or under them twice along the way. We are always hopeful that we will see a train; but that rarely happens on these walks.

We were at the beginning of our journey when we approached and crossed the track for the first time. At this point everything was clear and quiet. We then continued walking our regular route and as we got a few blocks away from the crossing, we heard the whistle, and we knew that the "UP Transfer" was making its way to Superior. We quickly turned around and raced back to the crossing in time to see the train go by. As the engine got to the crossing, the Engineer gave us a friendly wave as he guided the train along it route.

As the train went by, I stepped back a bit as I wanted to take a picture of this moment. Cierra was enjoying the passing train. I snapped the image!

I have looked at this picture a few times since the walk and it brought back good memories of my Dad who took us out often to watch or even ride trains. My Dad was a rail enthusiast, and he enjoyed the hobby very much. He also took time to share his interest wit us, which was something that we could share together.

My Dad was going to school to work on his Doctorate; so we lived in Gary, Indiana; Marquette, Michigan; Duluth, Minnesota; East Lansing, Michigan; North Branch, Minnesota; and Superior, Wisconsin. I was fortunate enough to live in the pre-Amtrak era, so we got to ride trains from the Great Northern, Northern Pacific, Chicago & Northwestern, Chesapeake & Ohio, and the Grand Trunk Western. As a matter of fact, in order to give my Mom a break, my Dad would take my brother and me on trips to Durand on the GTW. We would leave Lansing on the *Maple Leaf* and return that night on the *Mohawk*. We would hang around the depot in Durand and watch the train activity until the *Mohawk* arrived to take us home. We did the same with the C&O, where most of our trips were to Plymouth; but we did take one trip to Grand Rapids. Again, we would hang around the depot until the train was ready to take us back.

These outings with my Dad really enhanced the hobby for me, and eventually it lead to a lifelong career in the railroad industry. My current employer is the CN, and I have handled many trains to and from Superior that have travelled through Durand. As I near retirement, Durand is a place I would like to visit again to rekindle the memories of the time spent with my Dad.

Due to our daughter's physical limitations, she will not be able to experience all that I was able to do. However, for her, just seeing the train is the most important thing. And, just like my Dad, I use these walks to help give the Wife a small break while we go on our adventure. As stated above, we do not usually see a train on the tracks near our home; so to give her the chance to see one, we often jump in the car as a family and drive around until we see one or two. I feel it is important that we include this in her life since she seems to enjoy it very much. And, I enjoy her company!

I do think that it is important that if you have a child that enjoys trains, that you try to get them out to see them. They can be viewed from safe locations, and if you are knowledgeable about the job or hobby, you can pass this knowledge on to your child. This will help you form a bond with them that is very special. It will also give you a chance to spend quality time with your child, and possibly give your spouse the needed break she/he is looking for.

I am truly grateful for the time my Dad spent with me! It has lead to a career that I enjoy very much and I have met and worked with some great people over the years. I now try to share this with our daughter, and hopefully these trips will lead to some good memories for her as well.

It is very sad to me to report that Cierra "CeCe" R. Dorin passed away on October 26, 1922. My condolences to her parents, Tom and Katy (Meys) Dorin. May CeCe rest in peace.

Remember When…

By: C. H. Geletzke, Jr.

Today I attended our monthly Grand Trunk Western Railroad (GTW) Retirees' Breakfast in Detroit, Michigan. One of my friends, Vincente Relf brought in a GTW Yardmen's Seniority List from Hamtramck, Michigan dated February 15, 1995…on the list were the names of 72 working switchmen with an additional 10 men who were still carried on the list, yet were off due to various disabilities. Additionally, there was the name of one more man who years earlier had elected to retain his seniority and go to work for Amtrak as a Trainman.

As we passed the list around the table one of our members recalled, "when I started working here in the late 1960's, there were over 300 names on the list and it was six pages long! (We had 56 yard jobs a day in Detroit at that time! Today, in 2022 there are NONE!)

With that retired Switchman, H. J. "Harry" Gary who was sitting next to me sounded off, "Yeah, and do you recall they used to say that when your name finally made it to the first page, you were said to be on the **'DEATH LIST!?!'**"

Errata

By: David Dykstra, retired Deputy Director-Equipment Project Engineering, Capital Engineering, Metro-North Railroad (MNR)

I wish to offer two items of errata to Chuck's earlier volume, *Unit Trains and Other Railroad Stories*.

On page 94 is a story *Welds vs. Rivets*. David Dell writes on Canadian cars arriving with grab irons welded on and AAR rules requiring riveted attachment. Canadian and Mexican Railroads all interchange and all follow American Association of Railroads (AAR) rules that sets the standards for free interchange of equipment. If not, the rolling stock is limited to home lines or special agreements between participating roads. (Reference notes of non-standard care movements on pages 189-195, "Equipment Movements"). The AAR does not specify grab iron attachment; but the FRA does require rivet connection or threaded fasteners that have been rendered permanent by peening or otherwise damaging the threads to assure permanent attachment. I plan to write more on this in a later volume on the design of Metro-North's car design M-8.

On page 157 a picture of an HO Penn Central 40 foot boxcar appears. There is no story attached. I played with toy trains from an early age. When I went off to college, Purdue had a 20 x 30 foot HO model railroad and things got more serious. I was introduced to Kit Bashing (again more on the in writing about 12"/1' car equipment...FL-9AC). I desired to built a 60 foot double-door boxcar and found two 50 foot single door cars could be cut and reassembled into the longer car. Being cheap, there was no such thing as scrap...just pieces for which a use as yet to be found. In 1968, Penn Central determined to cease all passenger service west of Buffalo and Pittsburgh. This would have made it very difficult to travel from Indiana to my home in Buffalo. Suddenly there was a use for those two car ends...a social comment on Penn Central. Note there is a marking on the car, "Do Not Load or Unload this car" having left off the remainder of the instruction..."Unless all doors are open."

There were a surprising number of proper Dow Chemical cars also running on the layout for another social comment, in favor of Dow...then out of favor for making material for the Viet Nam War effort; but that is another story...

My grandson, Finn, learning how to run trains.

Rule 104

By: C. H. Geletzke, Jr.

By telling you this story, perhaps you will conclude that I am going a little too far!?!

My wife and I have seven grandchildren living in three different states. At the present time, I would say that only one has the interest or potential of becoming a "railfan."

333

Charles H. Geletzke, Jr.

During this past week my daughter and son-in-law had to travel to California; so my wife and I agreed to take their two kids...ages eight and "almost" five. The "almost" five year old, Finn, is the prospective railfan. At his parents' home he has his own wooden *Brio* train set, that when set-up easily runs through three separate rooms! Over the last several years I have taken him to *Strasburg*, *The Mad River & Nickel Plate Railroad Museum*, and at the *East Broad Top* where he was personally presented an EBT engineer's hat by Dave Domitrovich!

We recently moved from Michigan to Pennsylvania to be closer to all of our "kids," which so far has been a true blessing! And since we are in a new home much of our "stuff" (particularly my models and my wood working tools) is still packed in boxes in our basement. So, the other day I dug out the *Lionel* trains, which belonged to our twin boys and set-up a small oval of track with one switch and a 90-degree diamond. To say that my grandson and my granddaughter, Josie, have loved running trains is an understatement! It has truly been a wonderful learning exercise for both of them. Before I go on any further, let me state that both of them have had a problem in one area...when they run a train out of the "Spur Track," they frequently forget to line the switch back to its "normal" position...lined for the Mainline. Naturally, when a train then runs around the railroad and encounters that misaligned switch it derails! Let me state that they are learning and that "practice does indeed make perfect"...well almost!

While the children are here my wife and I have been reading to them before bed each night. Last evening I read *The Train to TIMBUCTOO*, by Margaret Wise Brown (A GOLDEN BOOK-Copyright 1951) to Finn for the second time this week. (Let me state that was a book which I too loved as a child!) We were lying side by side on the bed in one of our spare bedrooms and when I finished, I said to Finn, "You really did a great job running your railroad today!" (I had even arranged several simple switching scenarios for him to work out and master. This really seemed to peak his interest!)

At that, Finn turned me and said, "But Papa, I'm still having a hard time remembering to line that switch back!"

I then assured him once again that he was doing a good job and I said. "You know, occasionally, even on the BIG RAILROADS they sometimes have a hard time remembering to do that!?! So guess what? They wrote a RULE about that…it is called RULE 104!"

Finn gave me the strangest look; but I reached over and right there on the book shelf, just to the left of his bed, was a copy of *RIGHTS OF TRAINS*, by the late Harry W. Forman and revised by Peter Josserand.

Finn immediately responded, "That's really old!"

I explained that, "Yes. My copy was printed in 1951…72 years ago and the original book was written in 1904…119 years ago!"

Finn was impressed!

I then told the young man that the railroads, even today, have lots of rules and it is extremely important for us to be familiar with them and to always follow them!

Now I know what you are thinking…that this is way over the head of an "almost" five year old; but he began to ask more questions. With that I turned to RULE 104, HAND OPERATED SWITCHES, and began reading…"(1) Main-track switches must be lined and locked for main track when not in use…etc."

Granted, I did not go into a great deal of detail; but we did discuss how even the REAL RAILROADS can have problems and derailments when switches are not restored and the rules not followed.

I was truly impressed by the interest he expressed and the questions he asked. I could see the wheels turning in his mind.

Now I'm wondering what are we going to discuss tonight…perhaps "RULE 99!?!"

Finn working a "flagging" job at Strasburg on November 25, 2022. You professionals will note the fusee sticking out of his overall pocket!

Author Chuck Geletzke poses with *Lancaster Barnstormer's* mascot "Cylo" at *Clipper Magazine Stadium* in Lancaster, PA on June 6, 2023.

About the Author

Charles H. Geletzke, Jr. was raised in Royal Oak, Michigan and graduated from *Royal Oak Kimball High School* in 1967

337

Charles H. Geletzke, Jr.

and shortly began a railroad career, which would span 45-years. A Marketing major, Mr. Geletzke worked his way through *Central Michigan University* in Mt. Pleasant, Michigan as a roundhouse Fire builder (Laborer) and Brakeman for the *Grand Trunk Western Railroad* and during his Senior year as a Carman Helper and Switchman for the *Delray Connecting Railroad*. In 1971 he graduated with a Bachelor of Business Administration Degree. Mr. Geletzke additionally served in a *United States Marine Corps Reserve* Infantry Battalion and was later conscripted into the *U. S. Army's 226th Railway Shop Battalion*. Following graduation he worked for the *Delray Connecting*, the *Missouri Pacific Railroad, Grand Trunk Western* (again), the *Detroit & Toledo Shore Line Railroad*, and the *Canadian National Railroad*, from which he retired in 2011. During these years the author worked in both managerial and labor positions…mostly as a Locomotive Engineer. Chuck and his wife of almost 47-years, Leslie, have three married children and seven grandchildren. Retired now for almost 12-years, Chuck and Leslie have recently moved to Mount Joy, Pennsylvania, are active in their new church and he is still Vice President of the *Grand Trunk Western Railroad Historical Society*. Currently, Mr. Geletzke has become active at the *East Broad Top Railroad*, helping out with the *Friends of the East Broad Top*. Other interests include model railroading, woodworking, college football (Chuck is a *Navy* fan!), baseball (is a senior season ticket holder with the *Lancaster Barnstormer's*), jazz, and writing for various railroad and historical publications. Author Geletzke has previously written eight books including…***The Detroit & Toledo Shore Line Railroad-Expressway For Industry*** (co-authored with the late Wilbur E. Hague); ***When Deadhead Counted As Rest and Other Railroad Stories***; ***With the Slack That Will Do, and Other Railroad Stories***; ***So, You Think You'd Like to Railroad and Other Railroad Stories***; ***Don't Flush in the Station and Other Railroad Stories***; ***Inside Railroading and Other Railroad Stories***; ***Go Ahead and Backup and Other Railroad Stories***; and ***Unit Trains and Other Railroad Stories***. I still feel as if I have not even

338

"Soak It!!!"… and Other Railroad Stories scratched the surface writing the stories that I have yet to tell. Lord willing, I will continue to write as long as I am able. Thank you for your continued interest!

Made in the USA
Middletown, DE
29 October 2023

41496360R00189